THE
Expositor's
Bible
Commentary

with The New International Version

MARK

Walter W. Wessel

ZondervanPublishingHouse
Grand Rapids, Michigan

A Division of HarperCollinsPublishers

General Editor:

FRANK E. GAEBELEIN

Former Headmaster, Stony Brook School
Former Coeditor, *Christianity Today*

Associate Editors:

J. D. DOUGLAS

Editor, *The New International
Dictionary of the Christian Church*

RICHARD P. POLCYN

Mark
Copyright © 1995 by Walter W. Wessel

Requests for information should be addressed to:
Zondervan Publishing House
Grand Rapids, Michigan 49530

Library of Congress Cataloging-in-Publication Data

The expositor's Bible commentary : with the New International Version of the Holy Bible /
Frank E. Gaebelein, general editor of series.
    p.   cm.
    Includes bibliographical references and index.
    Contents: v. 1–2. Matthew / D. A. Carson — Mark / Walter W. Wessel — Luke / Walter L.
Liefeld — John / Merrill C. Tenney — Acts / Richard N. Longenecker — Romans / Everett
F. Harrison — 1 and 2 Corinthians / W. Harold Mare and Murray J. Harris — Galatians and
Ephesians / James Montgomery Boice and A. Skevington Wood
    ISBN: 0-310-49981-X (softcover)
    1. Bible N.T. — Commentaries. I. Gaebelein, Frank Ely, 1899–1983.
BS2341.2.E96 1995
220.7-dc 00
          94-47450
          CIP

Printed in the United States of America

95 96 97 98 99 00 / ❖ DH / 10 9 8 7 6 5 4 3 2

CONTENTS

PREFACE

The title of this work defines its purpose. Written primarily by expositors for expositors, it aims to provide preachers, teachers, and students of the Bible with a new and comprehensive commentary on the books of the Old and New Testaments. Its stance is that of a scholarly evangelicalism committed to the divine inspiration, complete trustworthiness, and full authority of the Bible. Its seventy-eight contributors come from the United States, Canada, England, Scotland, Australia, New Zealand, and Switzerland, and from various religious groups, including Anglican, Baptist, Brethren, Free, Independent, Methodist, Nazarene, Presbyterian, and Reformed churches. Most of them teach at colleges, universities, or theological seminaries.

No book has been more closely studied over a longer period of time than the Bible. From the Midrashic commentaries going back to the period of Ezra, through parts of the Dead Sea Scrolls and the Patristic literature, and on to the present, the Scriptures have been expounded. Indeed, there have been times when, as in the Reformation and on occasions since then, exposition has been at the cutting edge of Christian advance. Luther was a powerful exegete, and Calvin is still called "the prince of expositors."

Their successors have been many. And now, when the outburst of new translations and their unparalleled circulation have expanded the readership of the Bible, the need for exposition takes on fresh urgency.

Not that God's Word can ever become captive to its expositors. Among all other books, it stands first in its combination of perspicuity and profundity. Though a child can be made "wise for salvation" by believing its witness to Christ, the greatest mind cannot plumb the depths of its truth (2 Tim. 3:15; Rom. 11:33). As Gregory the Great said, "Holy Scripture is a stream of running water, where alike the elephant may swim, and the lamb walk." So, because of the inexhaustible nature of Scripture, the task of opening up its meaning is still a perennial obligation of biblical scholarship.

How that task is done inevitably reflects the outlook of those engaged in it. Every Bible scholar has presuppositions. To this neither the editors of these volumes nor the contributors to them are exceptions. They share a common commitment to the supernatural Christianity set forth in the inspired Word. Their purpose is not to supplant the many valuable commentaries that have preceded this work and from which both the editors and contributors have learned: It is rather to draw on the resources of contemporary evangelical scholarship in producing a new reference work for understanding the Scriptures.

A commentary that will continue to be useful through the years should handle contemporary trends in biblical studies in such a way as to avoid becoming outdated when critical fashions change. Biblical criticism is not in itself inadmissable, as some have mistakenly thought. When scholars investigate the authorship, date, literary characteristics, and purpose of a biblical document, they are practicing biblical criticism. So also when, in order to ascertain as nearly as possible the original form of the text, they deal with variant readings, scribal errors, emendations, and other phenomena in the manuscripts. To do these things is essential to responsible exegesis and exposition. And always there is the need to distinguish hypothesis from fact, conjecture from truth.

The chief principle of interpretation followed in this commentary is the grammatico-historical one—namely, that the primary aim of the exegete is to make clear the meaning of the text at the time and in the circumstances of its writing. This endeavor to understand what in the first instance the inspired writers actually said must not be confused with an inflexible literalism. Scripture makes lavish use of symbols and figures of speech; great portions of it are poetical. Yet when it speaks in this way, it speaks no less truly than it does in its historical and doctrinal portions. To understand its message requires attention to matters of grammar and syntax, word meanings, idioms, and literary forms—all in relation to the historical and cultural setting of the text.

The contributors to this work necessarily reflect varying convictions. In certain controversial matters the policy is that of clear statement of the contributors' own views followed by fair presentation of other ones. The treatment of eschatology, though it reflects differences of interpretation, is consistent with a general premillennial position. (Not all contributors, however, are premillennial.) But prophecy is more than prediction, and so this commentary gives due recognition to the major lode of godly social concern in the prophetic writings.

THE EXPOSITOR'S BIBLE COMMENTARY is presented as a scholarly work, though not primarily one of technical criticism. In its main portion, the Exposition, and in Volume 1 (General and Special Articles), all Semitic and Greek words are transliterated and the English equivalents given. As for the Notes, here Semitic and Greek characters are used but always with transliterations and English meanings, so that this portion of the commentary will be as accessible as possible to readers unacquainted with the original languages.

It is the conviction of the general editor, shared by his colleagues in the Zondervan editorial department, that in writing about the Bible, lucidity is not incompatible with scholarship. They are therefore endeavoring to make this a clear and understandable work.

The translation used in it is the New International Version (North American Edition). To the International Bible Society thanks are due for permission to use this most recent of the major Bible translations. It was chosen because of the clarity and beauty of its style and its faithfulness to the original texts.

To the associate editor, Richard P. Polcyn, and to the contributing editors— Dr. Walter C. Kaiser, Jr., Dr. Bruce K. Waltke, and Dr. Ralph H. Alexander for the Old Testament, and Dr. James Montgomery Boice and Dr. Merrill C. Tenney for the New Testament—the general editor expresses his gratitude for their unfailing cooperation and their generosity in advising him out of their expert scholarship. And to the many other contributors he is indebted for their invaluable part in this work. Finally, he owes a special debt of gratitude to Dr. Robert K. DeVries, publisher, The Zondervan Corporation, and Miss Elizabeth Brown, secretary, for their assistance and encouragement.

Whatever else it is—the greatest and most beautiful of books, the primary source of law and morality, the fountain of wisdom, and the infallible guide to life—the Bible is above all the inspired witness to Jesus Christ. May this work fulfill its function of expounding the Scriptures with grace and clarity, so that its users may find that both Old and New Testaments do indeed lead to our Lord Jesus Christ, who alone could say, "I have come that they may have life, and have it to the full" (John 10:10).

FRANK E. GAEBELEIN

ABBREVIATIONS

A. General Abbreviations

A	Codex Alexandrinus	Nestle	Nestle (ed.) *Novum Testamentum Graece*
Akkad.	Akkadian		
ℵ	Codex Sinaiticus	no.	number
Ap. Lit.	Apocalyptic Literature	NT	New Testament
Apoc.	Apocrypha	obs.	obsolete
Aq.	Aquila's Greek Translation of the Old Testament	OL	Old Latin
		OS	Old Syriac
Arab.	Arabic	OT	Old Testament
Aram.	Aramaic	p., pp.	page, pages
b	Babylonian Gemara	par.	paragraph
B	Codex Vaticanus	Pers.	Persian
C	Codex Ephraemi Syri	Pesh.	Peshitta
c.	*circa*, about	Phoen.	Phoenician
cf.	*confer*, compare	pl.	plural
ch., chs.	chapter, chapters	Pseudep.	Pseudepigrapha
cod., codd.	codex, codices	Q	Quelle ("Sayings" source in the Gospels)
D	Codex Bezae		
DSS	Dead Sea Scrolls (see E.)	qt.	quoted by
ed., edd.	edited, edition, editor; editions	q.v.	*quod vide*, which see
e.g.	*exempli gratia*, for example	R	Rabbah
Egyp.	Egyptian	rev.	revised, reviser, revision
et al.	*et alii*, and others	Rom.	Roman
EV	English Versions of the Bible	RVm	Revised Version margin
fem.	feminine	Samar.	Samaritan recension
ff.	following (verses, pages, etc.)	SCM	Student Christian Movement Press
fl.	flourished	Sem.	Semitic
ft.	foot, feet	sing.	singular
gen.	genitive	SPCK	Society for the Promotion of Christian Knowledge
Gr.	Greek		
Heb.	Hebrew	Sumer.	Sumerian
Hitt.	Hittite	s.v.	*sub verbo*, under the word
ibid.	*ibidem*, in the same place	Syr.	Syriac
id.	*idem*, the same	Symm.	Symmachus
i.e.	*id est*, that is	T	Talmud
impf.	imperfect	Targ.	Targum
infra.	below	Theod.	Theodotion
in loc.	*in loco*, in the place cited	TR	Textus Receptus
j	Jerusalem or Palestinian Gemara	tr.	translation, translator, translated
Lat.	Latin	UBS	Tha United Bible Societies' Greek Text
LL.	Late Latin		
LXX	Septuagint	Ugar.	Ugaritic
M	Mishnah	u.s.	*ut supra*, as above
masc.	masculine	v., vv.	verse, verses
mg.	margin	viz.	*videlicet*, namely
Mid	Midrash	vol.	volume
MS(S)	manuscript(s)	vs.	versus
MT	Masoretic text	Vul.	Vulgate
n.	note	WH	Westcott and Hort, *The New Testament in Greek*
n.d.	no date		

B. Abbreviations for Modern Translations and Paraphrases

AmT	Smith and Goodspeed, *The Complete Bible, An American Translation*	Mof	J. Moffatt, *A New Translation of the Bible*
ASV	American Standard Version, American Revised Version (1901)	NAB	The New American Bible
		NASB	New American Standard Bible
		NEB	The New English Bible
		NIV	The New International Version
Beck	Beck, *The New Testament in the Language of Today*	Ph	J. B. Phillips *The New Testament in Modern English*
BV	Berkeley Version (The Modern Language Bible)	RSV	Revised Standard Version
		RV	Revised Version — 1881–1885
JB	The Jerusalem Bible	TCNT	Twentieth Century New Testament
JPS	*Jewish Publication Society Version of the Old Testament*	TEV	Today's English Version
KJV	King James Version	Wey	*Weymouth's New Testament in Modern Speech*
Knox	R.G. Knox, *The Holy Bible: A Translation from the Latin Vulgate in the Light of the Hebrew and Greek Original*	Wms	C. B. Williams, *The New Testament: A Translation in the Language of the People*
LB	The Living Bible		

C. Abbreviations for Periodicals and Reference Works

AASOR	*Annual of the American Schools of Oriental Research*	BASOR	*Bulletin of the American Schools of Oriental Research*
AB	*Anchor Bible*	BC	Foakes-Jackson and Lake: *The Beginnings of Christianity*
AIs	de Vaux: *Ancient Israel*		
AJA	*American Journal of Archaeology*	BDB	Brown, Driver, and Briggs: *Hebrew-English Lexicon of the Old Testament*
AJSL	*American Journal of Semitic Languages and Literatures*	BDF	Blass, Debrunner, and Funk: *A Greek Grammar of the New Testament and Other Early Christian Literature*
AJT	*American Journal of Theology*		
Alf	Alford: *Greek Testament Commentary*		
ANEA	*Ancient Near Eastern Archaeology*	BDT	Harrison: *Baker's Dictionary of Theology*
		Beng.	Bengel's *Gnomon*
ANEP	Pritchard: *Ancient Near Eastern Pictures*	BETS	*Bulletin of the Evangelical Theological Society*
ANET	Pritchard· *Ancient Near Eastern Texts*	BH	*Biblia Hebraica*
		BHS	*Biblia Hebraica Stuttgartensia*
ANF	Roberts and Donaldson: *The Ante-Nicene Fathers*	BJRL	*Bulletin of the John Rylands Library*
A-S	Abbot-Smith: *Manual Greek Lexicon of the New Testament*	BS	*Bibliotheca Sacra*
		BT	*Babylonian Talmud*
AThR	*Anglican Theological Review*	BTh	*Biblical Theology*
BA	*Biblical Archaeologist*	BW	*Biblical World*
BAG	Bauer, Arndt, and Gingrich: *Greek-English Lexicon of the New Testament*	CAH	*Cambridge Ancient History*
		CanJTh	*Canadian Journal of Theology*
		CBQ	*Catholic Biblical Quarterly*
BAGD	Bauer, Arndt, Gingrich, and Danker: *Greek-English Lexicon of the New Testament* 2nd edition	CBSC	*Cambridge Bible for Schools and Colleges*
		CE	*Catholic Encyclopedia*
		CGT	*Cambridge Greek Testament*

CHS	Lange: *Commentary on the Holy Scriptures*	IDB	*The Interpreter's Dictionary of the Bible*
ChT	*Christianity Today*	IEJ	*Israel Exploration Journal*
DDB	*Davis' Dictionary of the Bible*	Int	*Interpretation*
Deiss BS	Deissmann: *Bible Studies*	INT	E. Harrison: *Introduction to the New Testament*
Deiss LAE	Deissmann: *Light From the Ancient East*	IOT	R. K. Harrison: *Introduction to the Old Testament*
DNTT	*Dictionary of New Testament Theology*	ISBE	*The International Standard Bible Encyclopedia*
EBC	*The Expositor's Bible Commentary*	ITQ	*Irish Theological Quarterly*
EBi	*Encyclopaedia Biblica*	JAAR	*Journal of American Academy of Religion*
EBr	*Encyclopaedia Britannica*		
EDB	*Encyclopedic Dictionary of the Bible*	JAOS	*Journal of American Oriental Society*
EGT	Nicoll: *Expositor's Greek Testament*	JBL	*Journal of Biblical Literature*
EQ	*Evangelical Quarterly*	JE	*Jewish Encyclopedia*
ET	*Evangelische Theologie*	JETS	*Journal of Evangelical Theological Society*
ExB	*The Expositor's Bible*		
Exp	*The Expositor*	JFB	Jamieson, Fausset, and Brown: *Commentary on the Old and New Testament*
ExpT	*The Expository Times*		
FLAP	Finegan: *Light From the Ancient Past*		
GKC	Gesenius, Kautzsch, Cowley, *Hebrew Grammar*, 2nd Eng. ed.	JNES	*Journal of Near Eastern Studies*
		Jos. Antiq.	Josephus: *The Antiquities of the Jews*
GR	*Gordon Review*	Jos. War	Josephus: *The Jewish War*
HBD	*Harper's Bible Dictionary*	JQR	*Jewish Quarterly Review*
HDAC	Hastings: *Dictionary of the Apostolic Church*	JR	*Journal of Religion*
		JSJ	*Journal for the Study of Judaism in the Persian, Hellenistic and Roman Periods*
HDB	Hastings: *Dictionary of the Bible*		
HDBrev.	Hastings: *Dictionary of the Bible*, one-vol. rev. by Grant and Rowley	JSOR	*Journal of the Society of Oriental Research*
HDCG	Hastings: *Dictionary of Christ and the Gospels*	JSS	*Journal of Semitic Studies*
		JT	*Jerusalem Talmud*
HERE	Hastings: *Encyclopedia of Religion and Ethics*	JTS	*Journal of Theological Studies*
		KAHL	Kenyon: *Archaeology in the Holy Land*
HGEOTP	Heidel: *The Gilgamesh Epic and Old Testament Parallels*	KB	Koehler-Baumgartner: *Lexicon in Veteris Testament Libros*
HJP	Schurer: *A History of the Jewish People in the Time of Christ*	KD	Keil and Delitzsch: *Commentary on the Old Testament*
		LSJ	Liddell, Scott, Jones: *Greek-English Lexicon*
HR	Hatch and Redpath: *Concordance to the Septuagint*	LTJM	Edersheim: *The Life and Times of Jesus the Messiah*
HTR	*Harvard Theological Review*	MM	Moulton and Milligan: *The Vocabulary of the Greek Testament*
HUCA	*Hebrew Union College Annual*		
IB	*The Interpreter's Bible*		
ICC	*International Critical Commentary*	MNT	Moffatt: *New Testament Commentary*

MST McClintock and Strong: *Cyclopedia of Biblical, Theological, and Ecclesiastical Literature*

NBC Davidson, Kevan, and Stibbs: *The New Bible Commentary*, 1st ed.

NBCrev. Guthrie and Motyer: *The New Bible Commentary*, rev. ed.

NBD J. D. Douglas: *The New Bible Dictionary*

NCB *New Century Bible*

NCE *New Catholic Encyclopedia*

NIC *New International Commentary*

NIDCC Douglas: *The New International Dictionary of the Christian Church*

NovTest *Novum Testamentum*

NSI Cooke: *Handbook of North Semitic Inscriptions*

NTS *New Testament Studies*

ODCC *The Oxford Dictionary of the Christian Church*, rev. ed.

Peake Black and Rowley: *Peake's Commentary on the Bible*

PEQ *Palestine Exploration Quarterly*

PNFl P. Schaff: *The Nicene and Post-Nicene Fathers* (1st series)

PNF2 P. Schaff and H. Wace: *The Nicene and Post-Nicene Fathers* (2nd series)

PTR *Princeton Theological Review*

RB *Revue Biblique*

RHG Robertson's *Grammar of the Greek New Testament in the Light of Historical Research*

RTWB Richardson: *A Theological Wordbook of the Bible*

SBK Strack and Billerbeck: *Kommentar zum Neuen Testament aus Talmud und Midrash*

SHERK *The New Schaff-Herzog Encyclopedia of Religious Knowledge*

SJT *Scottish Journal of Theology*

SOT Girdlestone: *Synonyms of Old Testament*

SOTI Archer: *A Survey of Old Testament Introduction*

ST *Studia Theologica*

TCERK Loetscher: *The Twentieth Century Encyclopedia of Religious Knowledge*

TDNT Kittel: *Theological Dictionary of the New Testament*

TDOT *Theological Dictionary of the Old Testament*

THAT *Theologisches Handbuch zum Alten Testament*

ThT *Theology Today*

TNTC *Tyndale New Testament Commentaries*

Trench Trench: *Synonyms of the New Testament*

TWOT *Theological Wordbook of the Old Testament*

UBD *Unger's Bible Dictionary*

UT Gordon: *Ugaritic Textbook*

VB Allmen: *Vocabulary of the Bible*

VetTest *Vetus Testamentum*

Vincent Vincent: *Word-Pictures in the New Testament*

WBC *Wycliffe Bible Commentary*

WBE *Wycliffe Bible Encyclopedia*

WC *Westminster Commentaries*

WesBC *Wesleyan Bible Commentaries*

WTJ *Westminster Theological Journal*

ZAW *Zeitschrift für die alttestamentliche Wissenschaft*

ZNW *Zeitschrift für die neutestamentliche Wissenschaft*

ZPBD *The Zondervan Pictorial Bible Dictionary*

ZPEB *The Zondervan Pictorial Encyclopedia of the Bible*

ZWT *Zeitschrift für wissenschaftliche Theologie*

D. Abbreviations for Books of the Bible, the Apocrypha, and the Pseudepigrapha

OLD TESTAMENT

Gen	2 Chron	Dan
Exod	Ezra	Hos
Lev	Neh	Joel
Num	Esth	Amos
Deut	Job	Obad
Josh	Ps(Pss)	Jonah
Judg	Prov	Mic
Ruth	Eccl	Nah
1 Sam	S of Songs	Hab
2 Sam	Isa	Zeph
1 Kings	Jer	Hag
2 Kings	Lam	Zech
1 Chron	Ezek	Mal

NEW TESTAMENT

Matt	1 Tim
Mark	2 Tim
Luke	Titus
John	Philem
Acts	Heb
Rom	James
1 Cor	1 Peter
2 Cor	2 Peter
Gal	1 John
Eph	2 John
Phil	3 John
Col	Jude
1 Thess	Rev
2 Thess	

APOCRYPHA

1 Esd	1 Esdras
2 Esd	2 Esdras
Tobit	Tobit
Jud	Judith
Add Esth	Additions to Esther
Wisd Sol	Wisdom of Solomon
Ecclus	Ecclesiasticus (Wisdom of Jesus the Son of Sirach)
Baruch	Baruch
Ep Jer	Epistle of Jeremy
S Th Ch	Song of the Three Child (or Young Men)
Sus	Susanna
Bel	Bel and the Dragon
Pr Man	Prayer of Manasseh
1 Macc	1 Maccabees
2 Macc	2 Maccabees

PSEUDEPIGRAPHA

As Moses	Assumption of Moses
2 Baruch	Syriac Apocalypse of Baruch
3 Baruch	Greek Apocalypse of Baruch
1 Enoch	Ethiopic Book of Enoch
2 Enoch	Slavonic Book of Enoch
3 Enoch	Hebrew Book of Enoch
4 Ezra	4 Ezra
JA	Joseph and Asenath
Jub	Book of Jubilees
L Aristeas	Letter of Aristeas
Life AE	Life of Adam and Eve
Liv Proph	Lives of the Prophets
MA Isa	Martyrdom and Ascension of Isaiah
3 Macc	3 Maccabees
4 Macc	4 Maccabees
Odes Sol	Odes of Solomon
P Jer	Paralipomena of Jeremiah
Pirke Aboth	Pirke Aboth
Ps 151	Psalm 151
Pss Sol	Psalms of Solomon
Sib Oracles	Sibylline Oracles
Story Ah	Story of Ahikar
T Abram	Testament of Abraham
T Adam	Testament of Adam
T Benjamin	Testament of Benjamin
T Dan	Testament of Dan
T Gad	Testament of Gad
T Job	Testament of Job
T Jos	Testament of Joseph
T Levi	Testament of Levi
T Naph	Testament of Naphtali
T 12 Pat	Testaments of the Twe Patriarchs
Zad Frag	Zadokite Fragments

E. Abbreviations of Names of Dead Sea Scrolls and Related Texts

CD	Cairo (Genizah text of the) Damascus (Document)	1QSa	Appendix A (Rule of the Congregation) to 1Qs
DSS	Dead Sea Scrolls	1QSb	Appendix B (Blessings) to 1QS
Hev	Nahal Hever texts	3Q15	Copper Scroll from
Mas	Masada Texts		Qumran Cave 3
Mird	Khirbet mird texts	4QExod ᵃ	Exodus Scroll, exemplar
Mur	Wadi Murabba'at texts		"a" from Qumran Cave 4
P	Pesher (commentary)	4QFlor	Florilegium (or Eschatological
Q	Qumran		Midrashim) from Qumran
1Q, 2Q, etc.	Numbered caves of Qumran, yielding written material; followed by abbreviation of biblical or apocryphal book.		Cave 4
		4Qmess ar	Aramaic "Messianic" text from Qumran Cave 4
		4QpNah	Pesher on portions of
QL	Qumran Literature		Nahum from Qumran Cave 4
1QapGen	Genesis Apocryphon of Qumran Cave 1	4QPrNab	Prayer of Nabonidus from Qumran Cave 4
1QH	*Hodayot* (Thanksgiving Hymns) from Qumran Cave 1	4QpPs37	Pesher on portions of Psalm 37 from Qumran Cave 4
1QIsa ᵃ·ᵇ	First or second copy of Isaiah from Qumran Cave 1	4QTest	Testimonia text from Qumran Cave 4
1QpHab	Pesher on Habakkuk from Qumran Cave 1	4QTLevi	Testament of Levi from Qumran Cave 4
1QM	*Milhamah* (War Scroll)	4QPhyl	Phylacteries from Qumran Cave 4
1QpMic	Pesher on portions of Micah from Qumran Cave 1	11QMelch	Melchizedek text from Qumran Cave 11
1QS	*Serek Hayyahad* (Rule of the Community, Manual of Discipline)	11QtgJob	Targum of Job from Qumran Cave 11

TRANSLITERATIONS

Hebrew

א	=	'	ד	=	$\underline{d}$	י	=	y	ס	=	s	ר	=	r
ב	=	b	ה	=	h	כ	=	k	ע	=	'	שׂ	=	ś
ב	=	$\underline{b}$	ו	=	w	ך כ	=	$\underline{k}$	פ	=	p	שׁ	=	š
ג	=	g	ז	=	z	ל	=	l	ף פ	=	$\underline{p}$	ת	=	t
ג	=	$\underline{g}$	ח	=	ḥ	ם מ	=	m	צ ץ	=	ṣ	ת	=	$\underline{t}$
ד	=	d	ט	=	ṭ	ן נ	=	n	ק	=	q			

(ה) ָ	=	â (h)	ָ	=	ā	ַ	=	a	ֵ֫	=	^{a}
ֵ	=	ê	ֵ	=	ē	ֶ	=	e	ֵ֫	=	^{e}
ִי	=	î	ֹ	=	ō	ִ	=	i	ְ	=	^{e} (if vocal)
ֹ	=	ô				ָ	=	o	ָ֫	=	^{o}
ֹ	=	û				ֻ	=	u			

Aramaic

' b g d h w z ḥ ṭ y k l m n s ' p ṣ q r ś š t

Arabic

' b t ṯ ǧ ḥ ḫ d ḏ r z s š ṣ ḍ ṭ ẓ ' ġ f q k l m n h w y

Ugaritic

' b g d ḏ h w z ḥ ḫ ṭ ẓ y k l m n s ṣ ' ġ p ṣ q r š t ṯ

Greek

α	—	a	π	—	p	ai — ai
β	—	b	ρ	—	r	aὐ — au
γ	—	g	σ,ς	—	s	ει — ei
δ	—	d	τ	—	t	εὐ — eu
ε	—	e	υ	—	y	ηὐ — ēu
ζ	—	z	φ	—	ph	οι — oi
η	—	ē	χ	—	ch	οὐ — ou
θ	—	th	ψ	—	ps	υι — hui
ι	—	i	ω	—	ō	
κ	—	k				ῥ — rh
λ	—	l	γγ	—	ng	ʽ — h
μ	—	m	γκ	—	nk	
ν	—	n	γξ	—	nx	ᾳ — ā
ξ	—	x	γχ	—	nch	ῃ — ē
ο	—	o				ῳ — ō

MARK

Walter W. Wessel

MARK

Introduction

The Gospel of Mark is a succinct, unadorned yet vivid account of the ministry, suffering, death, and resurrection of Jesus. Mark presents the narrative in an appealing way, for he tells the Good News about Jesus Christ so simply that a child can understand it. Nevertheless his Gospel, as Peter said of Paul's letters, also contains "some things that are hard to understand" (2 Peter 3:16). Like a pool of pure water, it is far deeper than it looks. Therefore one ought to approach the study of this book humbly and with due recognition of the need for wisdom from almighty God and enlightenment from the Holy Spirit.

1. The Place of Mark's Gospel in Biblical Studies

Today the Gospel of Mark occupies a prominent place in biblical studies. It was not always so. Even though early tradition associated this Gospel with the apostle Peter, it soon was relegated to a position inferior to that of the other Gospels. In MSS of the Gospels, Mark never occupies the first position (with the one exception of Codex Bobiensis), and sometimes it occupies the last (e.g., codices Bezae and Washington). There are few quotations from Mark in the writings of either the apostolic fathers or the second-century Apologists. Augustine thought it was an abridgement of Matthew's Gospel, despite the fact that—though Matthew is longer —in almost every case where there are parallels, Mark's treatment is more extensive. The first commentary on Mark we have any record of is the one by Victor of Antioch in the fifth century. He sought in vain to find other commentaries on it and finally had to resort to gleaning incidental remarks on the text of Mark he found in commentaries on the other Gospels. From the time of Victor till the rise of modern biblical criticism, little attention was paid to Mark's Gospel. It is not difficult to explain this. Mark was not written by an apostle (as were Matthew and John); its language was rough and ungrammatical; and it was generally believed to be an abridgement of Matthew. So for centuries Mark remained in the shadows.

In the nineteenth century a dramatic change came. When as a result of modern biblical studies scholars concluded that Mark was the first Gospel to be written and that both Matthew and Luke used Mark in some form as a major source for writing their Gospels, interest in Mark's Gospel skyrocketed. The theory of "the priority of Mark" became one of the "sure results" of nineteenth-century biblical scholarship. This theory is usually credited to H.J. Holtzmann's *Die synoptischen Evangelien* (Leipzig: Wilhelm Engelmanns, 1863). Much work on the synoptic problem pointing in the direction of the priority of Mark had been done in Germany before Holtzmann's time, especially by Koppe, Lachman, Lessing, Reimarus, and Weisse; but it was Holtzmann who put it all together and popularized the theory.

The immediate response to Holtzmann's work brought Mark's Gospel to a place of prominence, especially in the Life-of-Jesus movement of the nineteenth century. Mark was seen as the original Gospel, containing the uninterpreted historical facts about Jesus of Nazareth. Whereas Matthew and Luke represented expansions and interpretations of the story of Jesus, Mark was considered to be pure gospel. And since this Gospel, with its emphasis on the humanity of Jesus lent itself in such a remarkable way to the preconceived christological notions of the nineteenth-century liberal theologians, they warmly embraced it. Martin (*Mark*, p. 37) observes that "with the Life-of-Jesus movement Mark's gospel came into its own, after centuries of neglect. Studies in literary criticism, gospel order and theological implicates all contrived to push this gospel into a prominent place."

The critical study of Mark's Gospel was in full swing. Martin Kähler (*The So-called Historical Jesus and the Historic, Biblical Christ* [Philadelphia: Fortress, 1964; German ed., 1896]) raised serious doubts about the Life-of-Jesus movement's understanding of Mark's Gospel by pointing out the kerygmatic nature of the Markan material (i.e., it contains essentially preaching rather than historical materials). Even more devastating was W. Wrede's *The Messianic Secret* (Greenwood, S.C.: Attic, 1971; German ed., 1901). Mark, Wrede argued, is far from being a simple, historical account of the life of Jesus. The truth is, the author had a theological axe to grind. Before the Resurrection, belief in Jesus as the Messiah never occurred to anyone. When, however, that belief did arise, there was an attempt to read it back into the accounts of Jesus. The messianic secret in Mark is such an attempt. Wrede's theory was so radical that it did not receive widespread acceptance. Nonetheless it succeeded in undermining further the assumption that Mark was a straightforward historical account of the life of Jesus.

The next stage in the history of Mark's Gospel in the church is form criticism—a school of Gospel criticism that dominated Markan studies from about 1919 to 1954. Its chief architects were the German scholars R. Bultmann, M. Dibelius, and K.L. Schmidt. The main assumption of form criticism is that the units of Gospel tradition circulated orally before they were written down and that in the oral period these units were shaped, even created, by the *Sitz im Leben* (life setting) of the early Christian community. This tradition, already formed and shaped, was collected and pieced together into our Gospels. Thus the Gospel writers were essentially scissors-and-paste men, collectors, vehicles of tradition, editors. The Gospels themselves are more the products of the community than of the individual authors they are ascribed to. Furthermore, they record the history of the church more than the history of Jesus.

This approach to the Gospels completely ruled out the possibility of an account of Jesus in any truly historical sense. Schmidt insisted that there were only separate units of tradition artificially put together, usually on a topical rather than a chronological basis; and since these units reflect more the life of the church than that of Jesus, they have little historical value.

Form criticism also undercut the tradition that Mark is based on the eyewitness reminiscences of Peter. It held that the Gospel is not to be regarded as a factual apostolic account of Jesus' life but is rather a community product, evoked and shaped by the vicissitudes of early Christianity.

With the emergence of redaction criticism, a more positive and constructive approach to the Gospels began. This new direction for Markan studies was initiated by Willi Marxsen. Form criticism, as we have seen, had not assigned any significant role to the Gospel writers. They were mere collectors, scissors-and-paste men. But with the coming of redaction criticism, attention turned to the editorial role of the Gospel writers. The chief concern was how these men handled the tradition, both oral and written, that came into their hands. Form criticism dealt with the individual units of tradition. Redaction criticism, however, focuses on each Gospel as a whole and on the distinctive manner in which each Evangelist wrote his Gospel. It is particularly interested in the Evangelists as theologians, i.e., as arrangers and shapers of the tradition in order to fulfill a particular theological purpose or set of purposes. Thus this approach recognizes a third life setting in the production of the Gospels. Not only is there (1) the life setting of Jesus and (2) that of the early church, but there is also (3) that of the Evangelist himself. Redaction criticism deals especially with investigating this third *Sitz im Leben*.

In Marxsen's hands redaction criticism does less than justice to the historicity of the Gospel of Mark. This, however, results more from his faulty presuppositions about the nature of the tradition than from his interpretive method. The insights of redaction criticism offer creative interpretive possibilities within a context of the historical reliability of Mark's Gospel. This hermeneutical approach is reflected in this commentary. (On redaction criticism, cf. also EBC 1:448–49.)

2. Authorship

a. Early Tradition

Although the Gospel of Mark is anonymous, there is a strong and clear early tradition that Mark was its author and that he was closely associated with the apostle Peter, from whom he obtained his information about Jesus. The earliest reference is found in the church historian Eusebius, who quoted from a lost work (*Exegesis of the Lord's Oracles*) written by Papias, bishop of Hierapolis, about A.D. 140. Papias, in turn, quotes the Elder, probably the elder John, referred to elsewhere by Eusebius. The quotation in Eusebius follows:

> The Elder said this also: Mark, who became Peter's interpreter, wrote accurately, though not in order, all that he remembered of the things said or done by the Lord. For he had neither heard the Lord nor been one of his followers, but afterwards, as I said, he had followed Peter, who used to compose his discourses with a view to the needs of his hearers, but not as though he were drawing up a connected account of the Lord's sayings. So Mark made no mistake in thus recording some things just as he remembered them. For he was careful of this one thing, to omit none of the things he had heard and to make no untrue statements therein. (*Ecclesiastical History* 3.39.15)

5

This tradition suggests several important points about Mark's Gospel: (1) behind Mark is the eyewitness account and apostolic authority of Peter; (2) Mark did not write his account about Jesus in chronological sequence; (3) nevertheless Mark was careful to record accurately what Peter said.

The Papias tradition, with its insistence on the apostolic, eyewitness source of Mark's Gospel, runs counter to the form-critical understanding of the tradition. Yet to accept Mark's dependence on Peter does not rule out Mark's role as the redactor of the received tradition. There may even be a hint of this possibility in Papias's reference to Mark's nonsequential arrangement of the tradition. If the tradition he received from Peter was in the form of disconnected homilies, Mark had much work to do in transforming Peter's preaching into a Gospel. This would allow him the freedom to impress on the received tradition his own theological concerns with a view to the special needs of the community he addressed his Gospel to. There do not seem to be any compelling reasons for rejecting the Papias tradition—even though, as Martin (*Mark*, pp. 80–83) has recently shown, Papias's immediate concern was to establish the apostolic authority of Mark in the face of Marcion's championing of the Gospel of Luke.

Another early tradition, the Anti-Marcionite Prologue to Mark (A.D. 160–80), mentions Mark as a Gospel writer and connects him with Peter. The passage, which is fragmentary, reads: ". . . Mark declared, who is called 'stump-fingered' because he had short fingers in comparison with the size of the rest of his body. He was Peter's interpreter. After the death of Peter himself he wrote down this same gospel in the regions of Italy." The two items of additional information found here are (1) Mark wrote his Gospel after the death of Peter and (2) he wrote it in Italy.

Irenaeus (c. A.D. 180) adds his testimony in agreement with the Anti-Marcionite Prologue: "And after their [Peter's and Paul's] death, Mark, the disciple and interpreter of Peter, himself also handed down to us in writing the things preached by Peter" (*Contra Haereses* 3.1.2).

The first line of the Muratorian Canon (c. A.D. 200) that has been preserved reads: "at which he was present so he wrote them down." The immediate context of the line makes it clear that "he" refers to Mark and "which" refers to the preaching of Peter.

The importance of the tradition cited above is increased by its geographical spread. At least three different church centers are represented: Hierapolis (Papias), Rome (Anti-Marcionite Prologue and the Muratorian Fragment), and Lyons (Irenaeus) (Lane, p. 10). The tradition is repeated later by Tertullian of North Africa and Clement of Alexandria.

b. *John Mark in the Biblical Tradition*

It is generally, though by no means unanimously, agreed that the Mark who is associated with Peter in the early tradition and identified as the author of the Gospel is also the John Mark of the NT. He is first mentioned in connection with his mother, who lived in the house in Jerusalem Peter went to on his release from prison (Acts 12:12). Mark accompanied Paul and Barnabas when they returned to Antioch from Jerusalem after the famine visit (Acts 12:25). Mark next appears as a "helper" (*hypēretēs*) to Paul and Barnabas on their first missionary journey (Acts 13:5). What Mark's function was is not clear; but whatever its nature, it brought him into close relationship with Paul and Barnabas.

Unfortunately Mark did not last long as a missionary helper. At Perga, in Pamphylia, he deserted to return to Jerusalem (Acts 13:13). Paul must have felt strongly about Mark's behavior on this occasion, because when Barnabas proposed taking Mark on the second journey, Paul flatly refused, a refusal that caused Barnabas to separate from Paul (Acts 15:36–39). Barnabas took Mark, who was his cousin, and sailed for Cyprus. No further mention is made of either of them in the Book of Acts.

In the Epistles Mark is seen with Paul at Rome at the time of the writing of Colossians. Paul sends Mark's greetings and adds: "You have received instructions about him; if he comes to you, welcome him" (Col 4:10; cf. Philem 24, written at the same time). Apparently Mark was at this point just beginning to win his way back into Paul's confidence. By the end of Paul's life, Mark was back in full favor. From Rome Paul wrote to Timothy: "Get Mark and bring him with you, because he is helpful to me in my ministry" (2 Tim 4:11). Peter also witnesses to Mark's presence in Rome about this time (1 Peter 5:13).

In summary we may say that though strictly speaking Mark's Gospel is anonymous, the early tradition of the church identifies the author with Mark, who was closely associated with the apostle Peter and from whom he received the tradition of the things said and done by our Lord. This tradition did not come to Mark as a finished, sequential account of the life of Jesus but in the form of the preaching of Peter, preaching that had been directed to the needs of the early Christian community. It is this material, arranged and shaped by Mark, that forms the nucleus of this Gospel.

The biblical material mentions a John Mark, cousin of Barnabas and associate of Paul, especially in the later stages of Paul's life. It is this Mark we identify as the author of the Gospel.

In addition to the early tradition, two other considerations point to the Markan authorship.

1. It seems unlikely that the church would have deliberately assigned the authorship of a Gospel to a person of secondary importance like Mark, who was neither an apostle nor otherwise prominent in the early church, unless there were strong historical reasons for doing this.

2. It may be, as Rawlinson (p. xxxi) points out, that "the interest in Mark displayed by Luke in the Acts . . . may be due not exclusively to the fact that he was the cause of the breach between Barnabas and Paul, but to the further fact also that Luke knew him to have been the author of a Gospel of which he had himself made use in the composition of his own."

The tradition of the Markan authorship, though called in question from time to time, remains secure.

3. Date

It is not possible to date Mark's Gospel with precision. The external evidence is divided. Both Irenaeus and the Anti-Marcionite Prologue say that Mark's Gospel was written after the death of Peter. (Irenaeus says that Paul also was dead at the time of its writing.) Against this is the claim of the Alexandrians that Mark was written while Peter was still alive. Irenaeus and the Anti-Marcionite Prologue are the more credible witnesses, though Irenaeus's testimony is not above question because of his erroneous statement that the Gospel of Matthew was written when Peter and Paul were still preaching.

The external evidence for the date of Mark suggests a *terminus a quo* of A.D. 64, the date of the martyrdom of Peter, or, if Irenaeus is right, A.D. 67, the most likely date of the martyrdom of Paul.

The internal evidence seems to support a date for the Gospel after Peter's death. Mark is very frank in pointing out the failures of Peter—a frankness more easily understood if Peter had already been martyred and had achieved a leading place in the affection of the early church. No recitation of his past failures could then threaten his high position. It could, however, be used to encourage and strengthen a suffering church, itself facing martyrdom.

The most likely *terminus ad quem* for the dating of Mark is the destruction of Jerusalem in A.D. 70, since the Gospel makes no reference to that catastrophe. In fact, Mark says nothing at all of the Jewish War (A.D. 66–70), which was climaxed by the destruction of the Holy City. This has led some scholars to suggest a *terminus ad quem* as early as 67, a date before the hostilities began in earnest. Also, the use of Mark by Matthew and Luke make a dating later than 70 unlikely.

The recent suggestion by the papyrologist Jose O'Callaghan that certain papyrus fragments found in Cave 7 at Qumran are bits of a copy of the Gospel of Mark and date from the first half of the first century A.D. has been largely rejected by NT scholars (cf. EBC 1:420–21, n. 1). The evidence O'Callaghan presents is far too fragmentary to be reliable.

Although we cannot be certain of it, the best estimate for dating the Gospel is the last half of the decade A.D. 60–70. This date embraces the period immediately following the great fire of A.D. 64, when intense persecution began to be directed against Christians in Rome. There are good reasons to believe that the Gospel of Mark was written to meet this crisis in the Roman church (see Section 5: Life Setting).

4. Origin and Destination

Although again certainty escapes us, we may arrive at reasonably reliable answers to the questions of the place of origin and the destination of the Gospel.

a. Origin

Early church tradition locates the writing of the Gospel either "in the regions of Italy" (Anti-Marcionite Prologue) or in Rome (Irenaeus, Clement of Alexandria). These church fathers also closely associate Mark's writing of the Gospel with the apostle Peter. The above evidence is consistent with (1) the historical likelihood that Peter was in Rome toward the end of his life and probably was martyred there and (2) the biblical evidence that Mark too was in Rome about the same time and was closely associated with Peter (cf. 2 Tim 4:11 and 1 Peter 5:13, where the word "Babylon" is probably a cryptogram for Rome). There is the further evidence that quotations from Mark's Gospel first appear in 1 Clement 15:2 and Hermas (*Similitudes* 5:2). Both these writings are associated with Rome.

The only contrary witness in the early tradition is Chrysostom, who locates Mark's writing in Egypt (*Homilies in Matt. i*); but he has probably misunderstood the statement of Eusebius (*Ecclesiastial History* 2.16.1): "They say that Mark set out for Egypt and was first to preach there the gospel which he composed" (cf. Johnson, p. 15).

Recent attempts to locate the writing of the Gospel in Antioch (Bartlett) or Galilee (Marxsen) have not met with much success. The arguments in favor of Rome are too strong.

b. Destination

Here too all indicators point to Roman or at least to Gentile readers. Mark explains Jewish customs that would be unfamiliar to Gentile readers (7:2–4; 15:42); he translates Aramaic words (3:17; 5:41; 7:11, 34; 15:22); he uses Latinisms and Latin loan words, a practice that in itself is no evidence of Gentile readership, but the large number of them (especially in comparison with Matthew and Luke) seems to suggest such readership; he reveals a special interest in persecution and martyrdom (8:34–38; 13:9–13), subjects particularly relevant to Roman Christians; and, finally, the immediate acceptance and widespread influence of his Gospel (Matthew and Luke built their Gospels on it) suggests a powerful church behind it. No church better fits the description than Rome.

5. Life Setting

Mark's Gospel is traditionally associated with Rome. It is in the Christian community there that we must look for its occasion and purpose. There are two suggestions as to the life setting of the Gospel.

a. In the persecutions of the Roman church A.D. 65–67

In A.D. 64 a devastating fire broke out in Rome. More than half the city was destroyed; and strong rumors persisted, despite all attempts to quash them, that the emperor Nero had himself deliberately set it. Tacitus, the Roman historian, describes the situation that followed:

> But neither human help, nor imperial munificence, nor all the modes of placating Heaven, could stifle scandal or dispel the belief that the fire had taken place by order. Therefore, to scotch the rumour, Nero substituted as culprits, and punished with the utmost refinements of cruelty, a class of men, loathed for their vices, whom the crowd styled Christians. Christus, the founder of the name, had undergone the death penalty in the reign of Tiberius, by sentence of the procurator Pontius Pilatus, and the pernicious superstition was checked for a moment, only to break out once more, not merely in Judaea, the home of the disease, but in the capital itself, where all things horrible or shameful in the world collect and find a vogue. First, then, the confessed members of the sect were arrested; next, on their disclosures, vast numbers were convicted, not so much on the count of arson as for hatred of the human race. And derision accompanied their end: they were covered with wild beasts' skins and torn to death by dogs; or they were fastened on crosses, and when daylight failed were burned to serve as lamps by night. Nero had offered his Gardens for the spectacle, and gave an exhibition in his Circus, mixing with the crowd in the habit of a charioteer, or mounted on his car. Hence, in spite of a guilt which had earned the most exemplary punishment,

there rose a sentiment of pity, due to the impression that they were being sacrificed not for the welfare of the state but to the ferocity of a single man. (*Annals* 15.44)

If the Gospel of Mark was written sometime during the period A.D. 65–67, this passage from Tacitus sheds much light on its life setting. The Roman church was experiencing the fires of persecution. Even martyrdom was not unknown among its members. Mark addresses himself to this situation. His purpose in writing was "not historical or biographical, but it was intensely practical. He was writing a book for the guidance and support of his fellow Christians in a situation of intense crisis. The martyrdoms had fallen off, but there was no assurance—with Nero on the throne— when they might begin again; the last days could not be far off (Ch 13), and every Christian's lamp must be trimmed, every Christian's loins girded for the struggle" (Grant, pp. 633–34).

The way Mark prepares his Christian readers for suffering is by placing before them the passion experience of Jesus. Jesus' way was a *via dolorosa*. The way of discipleship for Christians is the same way—the way of the Cross. About one-third of Mark's Gospel is devoted to the death of Jesus. And not only in the passion of Jesus is the theme of suffering found. Many explicit and veiled references occur elsewhere in the life of Jesus in Mark: in the temptation experience—he was in the wilderness with wild beasts (1:12–13); in the misunderstanding of his family (3:21, 31–35) and people generally (3:22, 30); in his statements about the cost of discipleship (8:34–38); and in his references to persecutions (10:30, 33–34, 45; 13:8, 11–13).

In addition, as Martin (following W. Popkes) has recently pointed out, it may be that *meta to paradothēnai ton Iōannēn* in 1:14 should be translated "after John was delivered over to death," rather than "after John was delivered over to prison." If this is true, then Mark's interest in John is more theological than historical. He wants to show that "the fate of John and the fate of Jesus run parallel; and both end by their being delivered up by God to death" (*Mark*, p. 67). On this understanding the implication for the Roman church is clear. Faithfulness and obedience as a follower of Jesus Christ will inevitably lead to suffering and perhaps even death.

b. *In the emergence of heretical theological teachings*

Most of the recent studies of Mark's Gospel have focused on its theology and particularly its christology (Luz, Schulz, Schweizer, Weeden). The most suggestive study to date is Martin's *Mark: Evangelist and Theologian*. The occasion for the writing of Mark's Gospel is traced to the "situation which arose after Paul's death or, at least, in areas where the influence of Paul's kerygmatic theology had sufficiently been diluted as to suggest a loss of grip on the historical events underlying his kerygma" (p. 161). Mark has caught the essence of Paul's thought and has stated it in language to which Paul had no access (the tradition about Jesus). Mark does this to compensate for a christology that exalted the divine-man status of Jesus at the expense of his true humanity. Thus in Mark we find the emphasis on Jesus' true humanity, underscored by his sufferings.

This setting for the Gospel has much to commend it. It recognizes the theological or, better, christological concerns of the author as well as his more directly pastoral concerns. Mark is no ivory-tower theologian. "The nature of the Christian life, as he understands it, carries the same pattern as his christology. The disciple is bidden to take up his cross and then follow the Lord who entered his glory by way of suffering and outward defeat" (ibid).

Perhaps the convergence of increased persecutions and false christological ideas in the Roman church constituted the life setting that gave rise to the writing of this first Gospel about Jesus Christ, the Son of God.

6. Literary Form

The nature of the literary form of Mark's writing has stimulated much discussion among NT scholars in recent years. Mark starts out with the statement "The beginning of the gospel about Jesus Christ." But what *is* a Gospel?

Perhaps it is best to state first what a Gospel is not. It is not a biography. A biography is an organized historical account of a person, usually beginning with a description of his background and family and continuing through each significant event or period of his life (birth, childhood, education, marriage, career, etc.). But Mark has no genealogy, no birth narrative, and says nothing of Jesus' boyhood or adolescence. Mark starts right out, after quoting from the OT, with Jesus as a full-grown man.

If the Gospel of Mark is not a biography of Jesus, what literary classification does it fall into? The word he uses is "gospel"—a word Mark himself seems to have created to describe the literary form of his work. The old Greek words used for biographies (*bioi* ["lives"], *praxeis* ["acts"], *apomnemoneumata* ["memoirs"]) would not do because Mark's work is not simply a historical account. It is rather "preaching materials, designed to tell the story of God's saving action in the life, ministry, death and resurrection of Jesus of Nazareth" (Martin, *Mark*, p. 21). Mark calls his work a Gospel because it contains the preached gospel.

This understanding of Mark's Gospel must not be taken as in any way depreciating the historical nature of the material it contains. The preaching that the Gospel enshrines arose out of the historical events of the career of Jesus. Without that history, the Good News that constitutes the gospel does not exist. Schweizer (p. 24), after stressing the kerygmatic nature of Mark's Gospel, remarks, "And yet it is really a history book, since Mark knows that these essentials [of the preached Good News] will not be found anywhere except in the record of the events of these years [of the ministry of Jesus]."

This means that though the material found in Mark's Gospel is rooted in what happened in Palestine during the first century of our era, it also bears the stamp of the man God chose to put it into its final form. Mark does not write as a disinterested historian. He writes as a preacher conveying God's good news of salvation by emphasizing Jesus' saving ministry (Mark devotes about one-third of his Gospel to Jesus' passion). Mark also writes as a theologian, arranging and interpreting the tradition to meet the needs of his hearers. (Mark has an intensely practical and theological purpose. See Section 5 of Introduction.)

7. Language and Style

The vocabulary of Mark's Gospel is rather limited. He uses 1,270 different words, of which 80 are peculiar to him among the NT writers. Luke's Gospel, by contrast, contains 250 words not found elsewhere in the NT.

Mark is fond of transliterating Latin words (at least ten of them) into Greek, and occasionally his Greek shows an underlying Latin construction or expression (cf. *symboulion edidoun* [3:6], *rhapismasin . . . elabon* [14:65], and *tini to hikanon poiē-sai* [15:15]).

A more important influence on Mark's language is Aramaic. Some of the more obvious evidences of this are the use of parataxis in preference to subordinating clauses, the use of *polla* ("many") as an adverb, the introduction of direct speech with the participle *legōn* ("saying"), the use of the *ērxato* ("began") as a redundant verb, and the use of the genitival pronoun. This strong Aramaic influence accounts in large measure for the rough, ungrammatical Greek often found in Mark's Gospel. Rawlinson (p. xxxi) likens Mark's Greek to that spoken by the lower classes at Rome, especially those who might have come from Palestine or Syria and who spoke Aramaic as their mother tongue.

Although Mark's facility with the Greek language is clearly inferior to that of Luke and other NT writers, he manages to achieve a remarkably forceful, fresh, and vigorous style. He uses the historical present (present tense used to describe a past event) over 150 times and the adverb *euthys* ("immediately") occurs 41 times. Thus he gives his readers the impression of listening to an on-the-spot report. Intimate details, such as one would expect from an eyewitness, abound: e.g., the reaction of the crowds (1:27; 2:12); the emotional responses of Jesus (1:41, 43; 3:5; 7:34); the reactions of the disciples (9:5–6, 10; 10:24, 32).

Another important feature of Mark's style is his vigorous interaction with his readers (cf. Lane, pp. 26ff.). He accomplishes this by (1) directly addressing them (cf. 2:10, where the words "But that you may know that the Son of Man has author-ity on earth to forgive sins" are probably a parenthetical statement by Mark ad-dressed to his Roman readers—see commentary—and 7:19: "In saying this, Jesus declared all foods clean"); (2) addressing his readers through the words of Jesus (cf. 13:37: "What I say to you, I say to everyone: 'Watch!' "); (3) rhetorical questions addressed to them (cf. the question that occurs at the end of the story of the stilling of the waves, asked by the disciples but addressed to Mark's readers: "Who is his? Even the wind and the waves obey him" [4:41]). Mark wants his readers to be participants, not mere observers. He wants them to respond to what he tells them about Jesus by saying of him, "He is the Christ, the Son of God."

8. Bibliography

Books

Alexander, J.A. *The Gospel According to Mark*. New York: Scribner, 1858.
Anderson, Hugh. *The Gospel of Mark*. NCB. Greenwood, S.C.: Attic, 1976.
Beasley-Murray, G.R. *Jesus and the Future*. London: Macmillan, 1954.
———. *A Commentary on Mark Thirteen*. London: Macmillan, 1957.
Bratcher, R.G., and Nida, E.A. *Translator's Handbook on Mark*. Leiden: E.J. Brill, 1961.
Calvin, John. *Commentary on a Harmony of the Evangelists*. 3 vols. Grand Rapids: Baker, 1979.
Carrington, P. *The Primitive Christian Calendar*. Cambridge: Cambridge University Press, 1952.
Cole, A. *The Gospel According to Mark*. TNTC. Grand Rapids: Eerdmans, 1961.

Cranfield, C.E.B. *The Gospel According to Saint Mark*. Cambridge: Cambridge University Press, 1959.

Earle, Ralph. *The Gospel According to Mark*. The Evangelical Commentary on the Bible. Grand Rapids: Zondervan, 1957.

Farmer, W.R. *The Synoptic Problem*. New York: Macmillan, 1964.

———. *The Last Twelve Verses of Mark*. Cambridge: Cambridge University Press, 1974.

Gould, E.P. *The Gospel According to Saint Mark*. ICC. Edinburgh: T. & T. Clark, 1932.

Grant, F.C. *The Gospel According to St. Mark*. Vol. 7. IB. New York: Abingdon, 1951.

Guy, Harold A. *The Origin of the Gospel of Mark*. London: Hodder & Stoughton, 1954.

Hunter, A.M. *The Gospel According to Saint Mark*. Torch Bible Commentary. London: SCM, 1967.

Johnson, S.E. *The Gospel According to St. Mark*. Harper's New Testament Commentary. New York: Harper and Brothers, 1960.

Klostermann, E. *Das Markusevangelium*. Handbuch zum Neuen Testament. Tübingen: Mohr, 1950.

Lagrange, M.J. *Évangile selon Saint Marc*. Études Bibliques. Paris: Librairie Le Coffre, 1947.

Lane, William L. *The Gospel According to Mark*. NIC. Grand Rapids: Eerdmans, 1974.

Lightfoot, R.H. *The Gospel Message of St. Mark*. Oxford: Clarendon, 1950.

Lohmeyer, E. *Das Evangelium des Markus*. Kritisch-Exegetischer Kommentar über das Neue Testament. Göttingen: Vandenhoeck und Ruprecht, 1967.

Martin, R.P. *Mark: Evangelist and Theologian*. Grand Rapids: Zondervan, 1972.

Marxsen, W. *Mark the Evangelist*. Nashville: Abingdon, 1969.

Mauser, Ulrich W. *Christ in the Wilderness*. London: SCM, 1963.

Moore, A.L. *The Parousia in the New Testament*. Leiden: Brill, 1966.

Morison, James. *A Practical Commentary on the Gospel According to St. Mark*. London: Hodder & Stoughton, 1889.

Moule, C.F.D. *The Gospel According to Mark*. The Cambridge Bible Commentary. Cambridge: Cambridge University Press, 1965.

Nineham, D.E. *Saint Mark*. Pelican Gospel Commentary. Baltimore: Penguin, 1963.

Plummer, A. *The Gospel According to St. Mark*. CGT. Cambridge: Cambridge University Press, 1914.

Rawlinson, A.E.J. *The Gospel According to St. Mark*. WC. London: Methuen, 1949.

Robinson, J.M. *The Problem of History in Mark*. London: SCM, 1957.

Ropes, J.H. *The Synoptic Gospels*. Harvard: Harvard University Press, 1934.

Schlatter, A. *Die Evangelien nach Markus und Lukas*. Stuttgart: Calwer Verlag, 1947.

Schweizer, Eduard. *The Good News According to Mark*. ET. London: SPCK, 1971.

Stonehouse, Ned B. *The Witness of Matthew and Mark to Christ*. Philadelphia: Presbyterian Guardian, 1944.

Swete, H.B. *The Gospel According to St. Mark*. Macmillan New Testament Commentaries. London: Macmillan, 1927.

Taylor, Vincent. *The Gospel According to St. Mark*. London: Macmillan, 1952.

Articles

Cranfield, C.E.B. "St. Mark 13." *Scottish Journal of Theology* 6 (1953): 189–96, 287–303; 7 (1954): 284–303.

———. "Gospel of Mark." *The Interpreter's Dictionary of the Bible*. Vol. 3. Edited by George Buttrick. New York: Abingdon, 1962.

Dunn, J.D.G. "The Messianic Secret in Mark." *Tyndale Bulletin* 21 (1970): 92–117.

Grayston, K. "The Study of Mark XIII." *Bulletin of the John Rylands Library* 56 (1974): 371–87.

Longenecker, R.N. "The Messianic Secret in the Light of Recent Discoveries." *Evangelical Quarterly* 41 (1969): 207–15.

Marshall, I.H. "Son of God or Servant of Jahweh? A Reconsideration of Mark 1:11." NTS 15 (1965): 326–36.

Martin, R.P. "A Gospel in Search for a Life-Setting." *Expository Times* 80 (1969): 361–64.

Moule, C.F.D. "Mark 4:1–20 Yet Once More." *Neotestamentica et Semitica*. Studies in Honour of Matthew Black. Edited by E. Earle Ellis and Max Wilcox. Edinburgh: T. & T. Clark (1969), pp. 95–113.

Wenham, David. "Recent Study of Mark 13." *Theological Students' Fellowship Bulletin* 71 (1975): 6–15.

9. Outline

    I. Prologue (1:1–13)
      A. Preparing the Way (1:1–8)
      B. The Baptism of Jesus (1:9–11)
      C. The Temptation of Jesus (1:12–13)
   II. The Early Galilean Ministry (1:14–3:6)
      A. Calling the First Disciples (1:14–20)
      B. Driving Out an Evil Spirit (1:21–28)
      C. Healing Peter's Mother-in-law (1:29–31)
      D. Healing Many People (1:32–34)
      E. Leaving Capernaum (1:35–39)
      F. Healing a Leper (1:40–45)
      G. Conflict With the Religious Leaders (2:1–3:6)
         1. Healing a paralytic (2:1–12)
         2. Eating with sinners (2:13–17)
         3. A question about fasting (2:18–22)
         4. The Lord of the Sabbath (2:23–3:6)
            a. Picking grain on the Sabbath (2:23–28)
            b. Healing on the Sabbath (3:1–6)
  III. The Later Galilean Ministry (3:7–6:13)
      A. Withdrawal to the Lake (3:7–12)
      B. Selection of the Twelve (3:13–19)
      C. Jesus, His Family, and the Beelzebub Controversy (3:20–35)
         1. Charged with insanity (3:20–21)
         2. Charged with demon possession (3:22–30)
         3. Jesus' true family (3:31–35)
      D. Parables About the Kingdom of God (4:1–34)
         1. Parable of the sower (4:1–9)
         2. Secret of the kingdom of God (4:10–12)
         3. Interpretation of the parable of the sower (4:13–20)
         4. Parables of the lamp and the measure (4:21–25)
         5. Parable of the secretly growing seed (4:26–29)
         6. Parable of the mustard seed (4:30–32)
         7. Summary statement on parables (4:33–34)
      E. Triumph Over Hostile Powers (4:35–5:43)
         1. Calming the storm (4:35–41)
         2. Healing the demon-possessed man (5:1–20)
         3. Jairus's plea in behalf of his daughter (5:21–24)
         4. Healing a woman with a hemorrhage (5:25–34)
         5. Raising Jairus's daughter (5:35–43)
      F. Rejection at Nazareth (6:1–6a)
      G. Sending Out the Twelve (6:6b–13)
  IV. Withdrawal From Galilee (6:14–8:30)
      A. Popular Views of Jesus' Identity (6:14–16)
      B. Death of John the Baptist (6:17–29)
      C. Feeding the Five Thousand (6:30–44)
      D. Walking on the Water (6:45–52)

Text and Exposition

I. Prologue (1:1–13)

A. *Preparing the Way*

1:1–8

> [1]The beginning of the gospel about Jesus Christ, the Son of God. [2]It is written in Isaiah the prophet:
>
> > "I will send my messenger ahead of you,
> > who will prepare your way"—
> > [3]"a voice of one calling in the desert,
> > 'Prepare the way for the Lord,
> > make straight paths for him.' "
>
> [4]And so John came, baptizing in the desert region and preaching a baptism of repentance for the forgiveness of sins. [5]The whole Judean countryside and all the people of Jerusalem went out to him. Confessing their sins, they were baptized by him in the Jordan River. [6]John wore clothing made of camel's hair, with a leather belt around his waist, and he ate locusts and wild honey. [7]And this was his message: "After me will come one more powerful than I, the thongs of whose sandals I am not worthy to stoop down and untie. [8]I baptize you with water, but he will baptize you with the Holy Spirit."

1 The first verse seems to be a title. Whether it is intended to refer to the entire Gospel or only to the ministry of John the Baptist is not clear. Since in Acts 1:22 the starting point of the Good News is stated to be "from John's baptism" (cf. also Acts 10:37; 13:24; Matt 11:12; Luke 16:16; John 1:6), Mark may have this in mind here. Another possibility, however, is that by the use of the word *archē* ("beginning") Mark is imitating the opening verse of the LXX (*en archē*, "in the beginning," Gen 1:1) and wants his readers to realize that his book is a new beginning in which God reveals the Good News of Jesus Christ. Taken in this way, the first verse is not only a title for the entire book but a claim to its divine origin.

The word "gospel" comes from the old English "god-spel" ("good news") and translates accurately the Greek *euangelion*. The Greek word originally meant the reward for bringing good news but later came to mean the Good News itself. In the NT the Good News is that God has provided salvation for all men through the life, death, and resurrection of Jesus Christ. For Mark to convey this Good News, he has created a new literary genre—"gospel." His use of this term strongly indicates the nature of the material as being kerygmatic. "Mark's book has come to be called *a* Gospel because it contains *the* Gospel—the announcement of the Christian good news" (Moule, *Gospel of Mark*, p. 8).

In the rendering "about Jesus Christ," the NIV translators have opted for the objective genitive. If a choice has to be made (and translators must make choices), this is probably to be preferred to the subjective genitive—"by Jesus Christ." Mark's intent seems to be to proclaim the gospel, already known and experienced by the Roman believers, by rooting it in the events of Jesus' life. There are indications that they had lost hold of these historical roots. Thus it is the gospel "about Jesus Christ."

"Jesus" is the Greek form of the Hebrew "Joshua," which means "Yahweh is salvation" or "salvation of Yahweh." It is the name revealed by the angel to Joseph before Jesus was born, and it was given as descriptive of our Lord's mission—"and you are to give him the name Jesus, because he will save his people from their sins" (Matt 1:21). "Christ" is the Greek word for "anointed," behind which is the Hebrew *māšiaḥ*, from which the English word "messiah" is derived (cf. 8:29 for a full discussion of the word).

Some MSS omit the last phrase of v.1, "the Son of God." There are good reasons, however, for including it: (1) the evidence from the MSS is very strong (see Notes at the end of this section); (2) it is easy to account for its omission by homoioteleuton (i.e., by the scribe accidentally omitting the two words *huiou theou*, "Son of God") because the two previous words (*Iēsou Christou*) have the same endings; (3) Son of God is an important theme in Mark's Gospel (cf. 1:11; 3:11; 5:7; 9:7; 12:6; 13:32; 14:36, 61; 15:39).

2–3 Mark cites the OT to show that any true understanding of the ministry of Jesus must be firmly grounded there. The verb translated "is written" (v.2) is in the perfect tense. It denotes completed action in the past with continuing results. "It was written and still is" is the sense. The frequency with which this tense of the verb is used by the writers of the NT to introduce OT quotations underscores their strong belief in the unchanging authority of the Scriptures.

In the KJV "in the prophets" is read for "in Isaiah the prophet." The attestation for KJV's reading is very weak. It doubtless arose because the quotations that follow are not only from Isaiah but include one from Malachi as well. The first part of the quotation in v.2 agrees verbatim with the LXX of Exodus 23:20a. The second part is from the Hebrew of Malachi 3:1 but differs from both the Hebrew and LXX in reading "your way" instead of "the way before me." By this change in persons, allowance was made for a messianic interpretation of this passage. These two texts were similarly combined by the rabbis (cf. Exodus R 23:20), who apparently identified Elijah (Mal 3:1) with the messenger of Exodus 23:20.

The quotation in v.3 is taken from the LXX text of Isaiah 40:3, the only difference being the substitution by Mark (or perhaps he found the text already altered) of "of him" for "of our God." This applies the statement to Jesus, since the antecedent is "Lord," a title the early church used for him.

Mark brings together these OT texts in a striking way. He probably found the Exodus text already combined with Malachi 3:1. It is God's promise of a messenger "to guard you on the way and to bring you to the place I have prepared" (Exod 23:20), i.e., through the wilderness to the Promised Land. Mark adds a third text to this matrix, Isaiah 40:3, which looks forward to the coming of another messenger "in the desert" who will go before the people of God in a second Exodus to prepare for the revelation of God's salvation in Christ.

4 Unlike Matthew and Luke, Mark has no nativity narrative. It is possible that the traditions concerning the birth and infancy of Jesus were unknown to him. More likely they were of no use for Mark's purpose. He has no interest in writing a biography, as such, of Jesus. His concerns are kerygmatic and theological, i.e., he wants to highlight the saving facts and their theological meaning for the Roman church. Thus he immediately begins with the ministry of John the Baptist as the forerunner of the Messiah. This is precisely where Peter begins in his proclamation of the gospel in Acts 10:37: "You know what has happened throughout Judea, beginning in Galilee after the baptism that John preached."

John appears suddenly, "baptizing in the desert region." Although the word *erēmos* ("desert," "wilderness") does not necessarily refer to dry, arid land but means essentially uninhabited territory—open, wild territory—in contrast to the cultivated and inhabited areas of the country, the specific reference here is to the arid regions west of the Dead Sea. (Matthew 3:1 locates John's ministry in the Judean desert.) This general area was the abode of the Qumran sect. It is likely that John came in contact with these people. He certainly must have known of them. What influences they exerted on him are not known. Perhaps his ascetic life and stern discipline were derived from them. However, neither his baptismal practices nor his great emphasis on ethical conduct and eschatological judgment seems to have come from them.

John was "preaching a baptism of repentance for the forgiveness of sins." "Of repentance" is a genitive of quality. It was a repentance-baptism John was preaching, i.e., the baptism indicated that repentance had already occurred or was being accompanied by it. *Metanoia* ("repentance") means etymologically "a change of mind"; but as Taylor (p. 154) says, "In the NT it is used in a deeper sense, indicating a deliberate turning." The end result (*eis*, "for") is the forgiveness of sins. God's direct response to true repentance is forgiveness.

5 John's preaching caused great excitement. Mark says, "The whole Judean countryside and all the people of Jerusalem went out to him." The verb "went out" (*exeporeueto*) is in the imperfect tense and suggests that they "kept going out" to him. Although there is an element of hyperbole in Mark's report, it nevertheless implies that John's preaching aroused much interest and created a great stir. Jerusalem is at least twenty miles from the Jordan River and about four thousand feet above it. It was hard going down the rugged Judean hills to the Jordan and even harder coming back up. No exclusively ethical preacher, as Josephus would have us believe John was (Antiq. XVIII, 117 [v.2]), could have attracted that kind of interest. John preached the coming of the Messiah. This raised popular excitement to a fever pitch. Although great numbers came seeking baptism, John baptized no one who did not make an open confession of sin.

6 John is described as a typical "holy man" of the Near East. His clothing was woven of camel's hair and held in place by "a leather belt around his waist" (cf. 2 Kings 1:8, where Elijah is similarly described). His food consisted of locusts (cf. Lev 11:21–22, where they are listed among clean foods) and wild honey. The wild honey is bees' honey and not, as has sometimes been suggested, carob pods or sap from various trees in the area.

7–8 In Mark's account John's message is very brief. Mark includes nothing of John's pointed ethical admonitions to the Pharisees and Sadducees (Matt 3:7–10), to the crowds (Luke 3:10–11), or to the tax collectors and soldiers (Luke 3:12–14). Instead he focuses on the coming of the Mighty One who will baptize with the Holy Spirit (v.7). So great is this Mighty One that John does not consider himself worthy even to untie his sandals for him.

John now contrasts his baptism with that of the Coming One (v.8). John's baptism is water baptism; that of the Coming One is Holy Spirit baptism. Again the emphasis is on the superiority (this time in terms of ministry) of the Coming One to John. Moule's comment is to the point: "The Baptist evidently meant that the great coming One would not merely cleanse with water but would bring to bear, like a deluge, the purging, purifying, judging presence of God himself" (*Gospel of Mark,* p. 10). This is what happened in a dramatic way at Pentecost (Acts 2) in fulfillment of Christ's promise (Acts 1:5).

Notes

1 For a complete discussion of the many interpretations of ἀρχή (*archē,* "beginning"), see Cranfield, *Gospel of Mark,* pp. 34–35.

The reading that includes υἱοῦ θεοῦ (*huiou theou,* "Son of God") is found in the great majority of MSS. It is however missing from Sinaiticus (א). What raises a question is the split between Vaticanus (B) and Sinaiticus. Otherwise there is little doubt that the phrase "Son of God" is original. Taylor (p. 120) remarks, "Beyond question this title represents the most fundamental element in Mark's Christology." It occurs at the beginning (1:1) and the end (15:39) in this Gospel.

3 The urgency of the action is stressed by the use of the aorist imperative ἑτοιμάσατε (*hetoimasate,* "Prepare now!"). In the OT passage cited (Isa 40:3), κύριος (*kyrios,* "Lord") refers, of course, to Yahweh. Here it refers to the Lord Jesus.

4 Grant (p. 649) thinks that βάπτισμα μετανοίας (*baptisma metanoias*) is "a Semitism, meaning 'a baptism which symbolized or expressed repentance.'"

B. *The Baptism of Jesus*

1:9–11

> 9At that time Jesus came from Nazareth in Galilee and was baptized by John in the Jordan. 10As Jesus was coming up out of the water, he saw heaven being torn open and the Spirit descending on him like a dove. 11And a voice came from heaven: "You are my Son, whom I love; with you I am well pleased."

Jesus probably began his public ministry about A.D. 27, when he was approximately thirty years old. His childhood and youth, about which we know almost nothing, were spent in the village of Nazareth in Galilee. Two events, however, immediately preceded the beginning of his ministry: his baptism by John and his temptation by the Devil.

9 "At that time" is a free translation of *en ekeinais tais hēmerais* ("in those days") and represents one of the frequent "seams" or connecting links in Mark's Gospel. These "seams" are Mark's way of putting together the stories about Jesus and often are helpful in probing into Mark's theological concerns.

The baptism of Jesus by John must have been a problem to the early church. Why did Jesus submit himself to a baptism of repentance for the forgiveness of sins? In Matthew's account John was reluctant to baptize Jesus: "I need to be baptized by you, and do you come to me?" (Matt 3:14). Jesus replied, "It is proper for us to do this to fulfill all righteousness" (v.15). "All righteousness" is a reference to God's plan and purpose for Jesus. Part of that plan was the complete identification of Jesus at the very outset of his ministry with man and his sin. This he did by submitting to

21

baptism. He had no sins of his own to confess. Rather he was proclaiming his identity with human nature, weakness, and sin (cf. 2 Cor 5:21).

10 NIV does not translate the adverb *euthys* ("immediately") in this verse. The frequent use of this adverb is characteristic of Mark (it occurs forty-one times) and gives his Gospel a certain air of breathlessness.

Mark seems to suggest that only Jesus saw "heaven being torn open and the Spirit descending," though he may have been so focusing on Jesus' experience that he says nothing of John's. Mark's use of the verb *schizō* ("tear," "rend") to describe what happened to the heavens shows his graphic style of writing. Matthew and Luke use the ordinary word *anoigō* ("open"). The tearing open of the heavens is probably to be understood as signifying a cosmic event (cf. T Levi 18:5–12: "The heavens shall be opened . . . the Father's voice . . . sin shall come to an end . . . and Beliar shall be bound by him." The language echoes Isaiah 64:1: "Oh, that you would rend the heavens and come down, that the mountains would tremble before you"). Whatever else the descent of the Spirit on Jesus meant, it clearly indicated his anointing for ministry. Jesus himself claimed this anointing in the synagogue at Nazareth when he said, "The Spirit of the Lord is on me" (Luke 4:18).

11 The rabbis taught that when God speaks in heaven, "the daughter of his voice" (*bat̲ gôl*), i.e., "an echo," is heard on earth. In what God says there is a fusing of the concept of the messianic King of the coronation Psalm (2:7) and that of the Lord's Servant of Isaiah (42:1). The main emphasis, however, is on the unique sonship of Jesus. Mark confesses Jesus as Son of God at the very outset of his Gospel (1:1). Here God confesses Jesus as his Son. "The Gospel is not a mystery story in which the identity of the main character has to be guessed; from the outset it is made clear who this is—the Son of God" (E. Best, *The Temptation and the Passion* [Cambridge: Cambridge University Press, 1965], p. 168).

The Father also witnesses to his approval of his Son. He knows the mission that has been given to the Son. At the very beginning of Jesus' fulfillment of that mission, God states his confidence in him. Lane (p. 58) points out that "the first clause of the declaration (with the verb in the present tense of the indicative mood) expresses an eternal and essential relationship. The second clause (the verb is in the aorist indicative) implies a past choice for the performance of a particular function in history."

Notes

11 "Whom I love" is a translation of ὁ ἀγαπητός (*ho agapētos*). Since seven out of fifteen times in the LXX *agapētos* translates יָחִיד (*yāḥîd*, "only one"), some commentators translate it "only" here (I.H. Marshall, "Son of God or Servant of Jahweh? A Reconsideration of Mark 1:11," NTS 15 [1965]: 326–36).

The verb εὐδόκησα (*eudokēsa*, "I am well pleased") may be taken as a timeless aorist or perhaps as representing the Hebrew stative perfect. The meaning then would be that God is always pleased with the Son.

C. *The Temptation of Jesus*

1:12–13

> ¹²At once the Spirit sent him out into the desert, ¹³and he was in the desert forty days, being tempted by Satan. He was with the wild animals, and angels attended him.

12 Mark emphasizes the close connection between the Baptism and the Temptation by the use of his characteristic word *euthys* ("at once"). The humbling of Jesus by his identification with man's failure and sin at the Baptism is continued by his subjection to the onslaughts of Satan. The same Holy Spirit who came on Jesus at the baptism drives him out into the desert.

13 Mark's account of the Temptation is very brief. He devotes only two verses to it whereas Matthew has eleven and Luke thirteen. No specific temptations are described and no victory over Satan is recorded. By this Mark wants to emphasize that Jesus' entire ministry was one continuous encounter with the Devil and not limited to a few temptations in the desert during a period of forty days. Indeed, in his Gospel he vividly describes this continuing conflict.

The forty days have symbolic significance and recall the experiences of Moses (Exod 24:18) and Elijah (1 Kings 19:8, 15) in the desert. Only Mark mentions the wild beasts—a touch that heightens the fierceness of Jesus' entire temptation experience.

Notes

---

12 The verb used to describe the Spirit's action is ἐκβάλλω (*ekballō*). Since Mark most often uses *ekballō* of the expulsion of demons (eleven times) and in this passage combines it with the vigorous word εὐθύς (*euthys*, "at once"), it ought to be translated by something stronger than NIV's "sent out"—e.g., "forced out" or "drove out." "Force is certainly involved. There is no need, however, of inferring resistance or unwillingness on the part of Jesus" (Bratcher and Nida, p. 32).

II. The Early Galilean Ministry (1:14–3:6)

A. *Calling the First Disciples*

1:14–20

> ¹⁴After John was put in prison, Jesus went into Galilee, proclaiming the good news of God. ¹⁵"The time has come," he said. "The kingdom of God is near. Repent and believe the good news!"
> ¹⁶As Jesus walked beside the Sea of Galilee, he saw Simon and his brother Andrew casting a net into the lake, for they were fishermen. ¹⁷"Come, follow me," Jesus said, "and I will make you fishers of men." ¹⁸At once they left their nets and followed him.

¹⁹When he had gone a little farther, he saw James son of Zebedee and his brother John in a boat, preparing their nets. ²⁰Without delay he called them, and they left their father Zebedee in the boat with the hired men and followed him.

The purpose of this section (1:14–3:6) is to describe the opening stage of the Galilean ministry. The introductory statement (1:14–15) is followed by the account of the calling of the first disciples (vv. 16–20), Jesus' ministry in and around Capernaum (vv. 21–34), and a series of conflict stories (2:1–3:6) that reach their climax in a plot to put Jesus to death. The call of Levi the tax collector (2:13–14) introduces one of the conflict stories.

14–15 The opening of Jesus' public ministry is related to that of John the Baptist. Not until "after John was put in prison" (v. 14) did Jesus begin his ministry. Mark apparently wants to show that John, the forerunner, completed his God-appointed task; and only after that had occurred did Jesus enter his ministry.

Although he gives neither the exact place nor the precise time of the beginning of Jesus' ministry (he shows little interest in such details), Mark says that the content of Jesus' preaching is "the good news of God." God is both its source (subjective genitive) and object (objective genitive); it is from God and about God. The gospel is good news, the very best news ever to come to the hearing of mankind, because it contains the message of forgiveness, restoration, and new life in Christ Jesus (cf. 2 Cor 5:17).

Jesus witnesses to God's action for man's salvation by saying, "The time has come" (v. 15). Time here is not simply chronological time (*chronos*) but the decisive time (*kairos*) for God's action. With the coming of Jesus, God was doing something special. "He marks the fulfillment of the special salvation-time which is distinguished from all other time" (Schweizer, p. 45).

The concept of the kingdom of God is basic to the teaching of Jesus. Although the term "kingdom of God" does not occur in either the OT or the Apocrypha, the idea is abundantly present in both. The OT is full of such statements as "The LORD will reign for ever and ever" (Exod 15:18); "The LORD is enthroned as King forever" (Ps 29:10); "I am the LORD, your Holy One, Israel's Creator, your King" (Isa 43:15).

An examination of such passages reveals that the Lord's kingship is both a present reality (God is exercising his authority now) and a future hope (God will reign in the eschaton—the End—when he finally puts down all opposition to his reign).

The same tension between the kingdom of God as both present and future exists in the teaching of Jesus. At the outset of his Galilean ministry Jesus proclaimed, "The kingdom of God is near" (Mark 1:15). Later, after driving out the demons from a possessed man and being accused of being in league with Beelzebub, Jesus replied, "But if I drive out demons by the Spirit of God, then the kingdom of God has come upon you" (Matt 12:28; cf. Luke 11:20). In Jesus' actions God's rule has invaded this world. It is present with men. But in other sayings the kingdom is spoken of as still future; e.g., "I say to you that many will come from the east and the west, and will take their places at the feast with Abraham, Isaac and Jacob in the kingdom of heaven" (Matt 8:11; cf. Matt 20:21).

The solution to the dilemma of both a present and a future kingdom is not to be found in rejecting one or the other (e.g., realized eschatology rejects a future kingdom and consistent eschatology a present one). Bruce Metzger pointedly says: "The kingdom of God in its essence is the reign of God, the personal relationship between the sovereign God and the individual. Thus there is no point in asking whether the kingdom is present or future, just as there is no point in asking whether the fatherhood of God is present or future. It is both" (*The New Testament* [New York: Abingdon, 1965], p. 148).

In Mark 1:15 the approach of the kingdom is emphasized. It has drawn near *spatially* (in Jesus' person) and *temporally* (since it ushers in the events of the End). "In the person of Jesus men are confronted by the Kingdom of God in its nearness" (Lane, p. 65). The only appropriate response is repentance and faith. There is an urgency about the nearness of God's kingdom. Since it ushers in the End, it speaks of judgment. Jesus thus proclaims God's kingdom so that men will repent and believe.

16 Jesus has begun to preach his message. Now he must gather around him men whom he can teach so that they may become sharers in that message. He calls them in the midst of everyday life where they really live. God's reign does not operate in a void. It assumes a people—a people subject to that rule. It involves the formation of a community.

Jesus found Simon and his brother Andrew along the shore of the Sea of Galilee. This beautiful body of water, 682 feet below sea level, fourteen miles long and six miles wide, is an inland lake (Luke calls it the Lake of Gennesaret [5:1]; another designation was Sea of Tiberias). Much of Jesus' ministry took place near this lake. In NT times there were numerous towns along its shores, especially the northern and western ones. Since its waters abounded with fish, the local fishing industry flourished. Simon and Andrew were casting a net into the sea when Jesus called them.

17–18 Mark says nothing of a previous encounter of these two disciples with Jesus (cf. John 1:35–42). Even if he was aware of such a tradition, it is doubtful whether he would have used it. Mark wants to show the urgency of the situation, consistent with the eschatological significance of Jesus' mission. Jesus called Simon and Andrew to the urgent task of rescuing men from the impending judgment (v.17; cf. the use of fishing in the context of judgment in the OT: e.g., Jer 16:16; Ezek 29:4–5; 38:4; Amos 4:2) that the coming of the kingdom in the person and work of Jesus presages. The urgency demands an immediate response. "At once" the two fishermen left their nets and followed him (v.18).

19–20 The same call is now extended to James and John, sons of Zebedee (v.19). They too respond without any hesitation (v.20). In their case something of the price of discipleship is indicated by the breaking of family ties—the leaving of their father's business. The mention of the hired men may imply that Zebedee was a man of wealth. It may also be included to indicate that by leaving their father to follow Jesus, James and John were not leaving him entirely alone to run his fishing business. However, the main emphasis in this call, as in that of Simon and Andrew, is on the immediate response to it.

Notes

14 The words translated "was put in prison" represent the single Greek word παραδοθῆναι (*paradothēnai*, "to be delivered over"). NIV assumes the delivering over was to prison. It is possible, however, especially if Mark is more interested in theology than historical sequence (Mark reserves the details of John's death till ch. 6), that the delivering over is to death. By this means Marks wants to heighten the similarity between John's and Jesus' ministry. They both end in death. Thus the shadow of the Cross falls over the ministry of Jesus at its very outset.

15 The verb πιστεύετε (*pisteuete*, "believe") is followed by the preposition ἐν (*en*, "in")—the only occurrence in the NT. Scholars have debated whether it means "believe in [the sphere of] the gospel" (whatever that means!) or simply "believe the gospel" (the "in" being an example of "translation Greek," i.e., the Greek carries over the Hebrew idiom). Marxsen (p. 135) finds no problem with the translation "believe in" because to believe in the gospel is to believe in Jesus Christ who is present in the gospel.

18 Ἀκολουθεῖν (*akolouthein*, "to follow") is frequently used in the Gospels "to describe attachment to the person of Jesus, personal surrender to His summons, and acceptance of his leadership" (Taylor, p. 169). For an excellent statement of the concept of discipleship in Mark's Gospel, see Schweizer, p. 49.

B. *Driving Out an Evil Spirit*

1:21–28

21They went to Capernaum, and when the Sabbath came, Jesus went into the synagogue and began to teach. 22The people were amazed at his teaching, because he taught them as one who had authority, not as the teachers of the law. 23Just then a man in their synagogue who was possessed by an evil spirit cried out, 24"What do you want with us, Jesus of Nazareth? Have you come to destroy us? I know who you are—the Holy One of God!"

25"Be quiet!" said Jesus sternly. "Come out of him!" 26The evil spirit shook the man violently and came out of him with a shriek.

27The people were all so amazed that they asked each other, "What is this? A new teaching—and with authority! He even gives orders to evil spirits and they obey him." 28News about him spread quickly over the whole region of Galilee.

21 In vv.21–34 Mark records what seems to have occurred on one memorable Sabbath day. The first incident occurred in the synagogue in Capernaum. The word "synagogue" can refer either to the local congregation or to the building in which the congregation met. The synagogue originated in the Exile as the result of Jews meeting together for prayer and the study of the Torah. In NT times synagogues were found all over the Hellenistic world wherever there were sufficient numbers of Jews to maintain one. The synagogue became Judaism's most enduring institution.

Capernaum was the home of Peter and became a kind of base of operations for Jesus' Galilean ministry. Jesus, like Paul (cf. Acts 13:15), used the "freedom of the synagogue"—a Jewish custom that permitted recognized visiting teachers to preach (based on the reading from the Law or Prophets) in the synagogue by invitation of its leaders—to bring the Good News to his countrymen. Tell Hum, located on the northwest corner of the Sea of Galilee, almost certainly marks the site of Capernaum.

22 We are not told what Jesus said in the synagogue on this occasion, only what the reaction of the congregation was. They were "amazed." The verb used is *exeplēs-sonto* (cf. 6:2; 7:37; 10:26; 11:18), a compound from *plēssō* ("strike," "smite"); it has a very strong meaning. People were astonished at Jesus' teaching "because he taught them as one who had authority." Jesus did not have to quote the authorities ("Rabbi so-and-so says such-and-such"). His authority came straight from God.

NIV regularly translates *grammateis* as "teachers of the law." Most readers of the Bible know them as "scribes." They were the scholars of the day, professionally trained in the interpretation and application of the law. Jesus often came into direct conflict with them.

23 Suddenly the synagogue service was disrupted by the cry of a man "possessed by an evil spirit." Jesus thus early in his ministry came into conflict with Satan. This is significant, for Jesus came to destroy the power of the Devil (1 John 3:8). Although the belief that sickness or deviant behavior can be attributed to demon possession has usually been relegated by modern man to superstition or obscurantism, recent developments in the study of the occult and demonism have tended to leave the question open. (Popular books like C.S. Lewis's *Screwtape Letters* [1946; reprint ed., Old Tappan, N.J.: Revell, 1976] and films such as "The Exorcist" have contributed to this openness.) Reports of demon possession now come not only from distant and remote mission fields but from the most sophisticated of our urban centers. The NT accounts of demonism do not seem so bizarre after all.

24 Although v.23 states that the man cried out, it was really the demon who had the man under his control who shouted. (Notice that Jesus speaks to the demon in v.25.) The "us" in the question "What do you want with us?" shows that the demon in the man speaks for his fellow demons also. They clearly seem to recognize Jesus. This is evident not only because they call him "Jesus of Nazareth" but because they recognize his mission. The question "Have you come to destroy us?" could just as well be a statement of fact (punctuation marks were added later to the MSS): "You have come to destroy us." The demons recognize—far more clearly than the synagogue congregation—the role of judgment in the ministry of Jesus.

The utterance of the name of Jesus and his title "the Holy One of God" may have been an attempt by the demon to get control over Jesus, since "it was widely believed at that time that if you knew a person's true identity and could utter his name, you could gain a magic power over him" (Nineham, p. 75).

25–26 Jesus needed no magical formulas to exorcise the demon. After ordering him, "Be quiet!" (v.25), Jesus simply spoke his word of power and the evil spirit convulsed the man "and came out of him with a shriek" (v.26).

27–28 Mark again reports the reaction of the people (v.27). Their amazement, which also reveals some alarm, prompted them to ask one another, "What is this?" The answer stresses both the newness of Jesus' teaching and its authority. They had had no previous experience with this kind of teaching. Jesus' authority was inherent within himself and therefore did not have to appeal to spells or incantations to exorcise the demon. One command accomplished it. The inevitable result was that Jesus' fame was spread "over the whole region of Galilee" (v.28), which, in view of

Luke's "throughout the surrounding area" (Luke 4:37), means "all that part of Galilee that surrounds Capernaum."

C. Healing Peter's Mother-in-law

1:29–31

> ²⁹As soon as they left the synagogue, they went with James and John to the home of Simon and Andrew. ³⁰Simon's mother-in-law was in bed with a fever, and they told Jesus about her. ³¹So he went to her, took her hand and helped her up. The fever left her and she began to wait on them.

29–31 The eyewitness details of this story suggest its Petrine origin. After all, Peter had a special interest in what occurred. The incident took place after Jesus left the synagogue (v.29) and went to the house of Simon and Andrew (probably near by; only Mark's account mentions Andrew). We are not told what caused Peter's mother-in-law's fever (v.30). It had, however, put her in bed; and Jesus was told about her. The healing is described simply, yet with interesting detail: "He went to her, took her hand and helped her up" (v.31). The cure was instantaneous and complete, for she got out of bed and began to serve the needs of her guests, which probably means she prepared food for them.

D. Healing Many People

1:32–34

> ³²That evening after sunset the people brought to Jesus all the sick and demon-possessed. ³³The whole town gathered at the door, ³⁴and Jesus healed many who had various diseases. He also drove out many demons, but he would not let the demons speak because they knew who he was.

32–34 "That evening after sunset" (v.32) would be, according to Jewish reckoning, the following day, since the Sabbath ends at sundown. The Sabbath having ended, people could now bring, without breaking the law, their sick and demon-possessed to him. Apparently Mark wants to emphasize that the exorcism of v.26 and the healing of v.31 were not isolated cases. Jesus' healing power was extended to large numbers: "All the sick and demon-possessed" were brought, and "Jesus healed many" and "drove out many demons." Mark does not describe the healings and exorcisms individually but shows by the use of "all" and "many" the mighty power of Jesus.

Again Jesus muzzles the demons, "because they knew who he was" (v.34). Luke is more specific: "because they knew he was the Christ" (Luke 4:41). This reluctance by Jesus to have the demons reveal him as the Messiah is best explained by Jesus' desire to show by word and deed what kind of Messiah he was (viz., one quite different from the popular conception of the Messiah) before he declared himself.

E. Leaving Capernaum

1:35–39

> ³⁵Very early in the morning, while it was still dark, Jesus got up, left the house and went off to a solitary place, where he prayed. ³⁶Simon and his companions

went to look for him, [37]and when they found him, they exclaimed: "Everyone is looking for you!"

[38]Jesus replied, "Let us go somewhere else—to the nearby villages—so I can preach there also. That is why I have come." [39]So he traveled throughout Galilee, preaching in their synagogues and driving out demons.

35 Although Mark makes no specific connection between v.35 and the preceding paragraph, he seems to be giving a sequence of events. Jesus, after a busy evening of healings and exorcisms, got up early the next morning and sought a quiet place to pray. In the other two places in Mark's Gospel where Jesus prays, he is faced with a crisis (6:46; 14:32–41). Here too there is a crisis, though not so definite a one as the other two. The crisis is the shallow and superficial response of the people to Jesus. They are only interested in what he can do to heal their physical afflictions. So Jesus seeks the strength that only communion and fellowship with the Father can provide.

36–37 The disciples (here [v.36] called "Simon and his companions"—not *mathētai*, perhaps because they are not acting like disciples) do not understand Jesus or his need for communion with the Father. So they go to look for him (Mark uses the verb *katadiōkein*, which literally means "to track down" or "hunt" and usually has a hostile sense). Apparently they think Jesus will be pleased to know that everyone was looking for him (v.37). They do not understand that this popular and shallow reception of him was the very reason he withdrew to pray.

38–39 Jesus' reply shows that he feared his healings and exorcisms were hindrances to understanding who he really was. The people of Capernaum were interested in him as a popular miracle-worker only. So Jesus suggests that they move on to other villages that he might "preach there also" (v.38). His coming into the world was more to proclaim God's Good News and all that was involved in discipleship and suffering than to be a popular miracle-worker. Healings and exorcisms had their place (v.39), but they were not to usurp the primary purpose for which Jesus had come. If Mark wrote his Gospel to refute a christological heresy that placed too much emphasis on Jesus as a miracle-worker, the relevance of these verses is clear.

F. Healing a Leper

1:40–45

[40]A man with leprosy came to him and begged him on his knees, "If you are willing, you can make me clean."

[41]Filled with compassion, Jesus reached out his hand and touched the man. "I am willing," he said. "Be clean!" [42]Immediately the leprosy left him and he was cured.

[43]Jesus sent him away at once with a strong warning: [44]"See that you don't tell this to anyone. But go, show yourself to the priest and offer the sacrifices that Moses commanded for your cleansing, as a testimony to them." [45]Instead he went out and began to talk freely, spreading the news. As a result, Jesus could no longer enter a town openly but stayed outside in lonely places. Yet the people still came to him from everywhere.

40 This pericope (vv.40–45) is connected with what precedes only by a *kai* ("and") and is followed by a story that is also introduced with a *kai*. The pericope apparently serves as a connecting link between 1:21–29 and 2:1–3:6—two clearly identifiable units in Mark's Gospel.

The word "leprosy" was used in biblical times to designate a wide variety of serious skin diseases. It was not limited to what we know as leprosy, or, to use the preferable medical term, Hansen's disease. Whatever variety of skin disorder the man had, it caused him much suffering. This suffering was social as well as physical. The law required that "the person with such an infectious disease must wear torn clothes, let his hair be unkempt, cover the lower part of his face and cry out, 'Unclean! Unclean!' As long as he has the infection he remains unclean. He must live alone; he must live outside the camp" (Lev 13:45–46). Instead of keeping his distance from Jesus, as the law demanded, the leper came directly to him and fell down on his knees to make his plea. He had no doubt that Jesus could heal him. He only wondered whether Jesus was willing. It is sometimes easier to believe in God's power than in his mercy.

41–42 On the assumption that the correct reading of v.41 is "being angered" and not "filled with compassion" (cf. Notes), the question arises why? Many answers have been suggested (cf. Cranfield, *Gospel of Mark*, p. 92). The best is that Jesus was angered in the presence of a foul disease that could only be the work of the Devil. Jesus' anger was focused neither on the man nor on the disease but on Satan whose work he came to destroy. Understood in this way, the incident becomes another example of the fierce conflict between Christ and Satan that plays such an important part in this Gospel.

Jesus also expressed compassion. He reached out and touched the unclean leper, an act that, according to the Mosaic Law, incurred defilement. Calvin (1:374) says: "By his word alone he might have healed the *leper;* but he applied, at the same time, the touch of his hand, to express the feeling of compassion. Nor ought this to excite our wonder, since he chose to take upon him our flesh, that he might cleanse us from our sins."

Jesus' touching of the leper not only resulted in his being cured (v.42) but also revealed Jesus' attitude toward the ceremonial law. He boldly placed love and compassion over ritual and regulation.

43 Both verbs in this verse seem to confirm the reading *orgistheis* ("being angry") in v.41. "Sent him away" is from *ekballō* (cf. note on 1:12), which often is used of driving out demons; and *embrimaomai* ("with a strong warning") is a word that originally meant "to snort like a horse." An element of anger or indignation is contained in Jesus' warning. Why? The best answer is that Jesus knew that the man would disobey him. The result was that Jesus could "no longer enter a town openly but stayed outside in lonely places" (v.45).

44 The reason Jesus didn't want the leper to tell anyone of his cure was that Jesus did not want to gain the reputation of being just another *theios anēr* ("a divine man," i.e., "a miracle-worker"). This would thwart the essential purpose of his ministry. Instead, he instructed the leper to go to those whose job it was to rule whether he was clean or not. Jesus also told the man to offer sacrifices that were required by the Mosaic Law. (These procedures are all given in detail in Lev 14:2–31). The last phrase of v.44—"as a testimony to them"—may be understood either as a testimony to the priest and the people of the reality of the cure or as a testimony against (cf. 13:9) the priests if they fail to accept the healing as having been done by Jesus. Although the latter is an attractive suggestion, it hardly seems consistent with Jesus' injunction to silence (presumably about his miraculous powers).

45 The leper acted consistent with human nature. The prohibition against telling what had happened to him made him all the more anxious to proclaim it everywhere. This resulted in curtailment of Jesus' public ministry. He avoided going into the towns and chose rather to stay in more isolated places. But even in his isolation, people managed to find him and "came to him from everywhere."

Notes

41 The translators of NIV may have been right in following the reading σπλαγχνισθείς (*splanchnistheis*, "filled with compassion") since the MS evidence strongly favors it. However, it is difficult to explain how the reading ὀργισθείς (*orgistheis*, "being angry") came into existence. It is much easier to explain the scribal origin of *splanchnistheis* as the result of embarrassment over the ascription of anger to our Lord. This solution is consistent with the use of ἐμβριμάομαι (*embrimaomai*, "speak harshly to") in v.43, which has an element of indignation or anger in it.

43 Some commentators argue that ἐμβριμάομαι (*embrimaomai*, "speak harshly to") simply expresses deep emotion and not anger. The use of the same verb, however, in Mark 14:5, in a context that clearly indicates anger, supports the element of anger here.

G. *Conflict With the Religious Leaders* (2:1–3:6)

Clearly 2:1–3:6 is a separate section in Mark's Gospel. In it Jesus comes into conflict with the Jewish religious leadership in a series of five separate incidents. It is highly unlikely that these incidents happened in chronological sequence or even come out of the same period in Jesus' ministry. Mark brought them together because they have a common theme: conflict with the religious authorities. There can be little doubt that such stories as we find here were used by the church in its ongoing struggle with Judaism.

1. *Healing a paralytic*

2:1–12

> [1]A few days later, when Jesus again entered Capernaum, the people heard that he had come home. [2]So many gathered that there was no room left, not even outside the door, and he preached the word to them. [3]Some men came, bringing to him a paralytic, carried by four of them. [4]Since they could not get him to Jesus because of the crowd, they made an opening in the roof above Jesus and, after digging through it, lowered the mat the paralyzed man was lying on. [5]When Jesus saw their faith, he said to the paralytic, "Son, your sins are forgiven."
> [6]Now some teachers of the law were sitting there, thinking to themselves, [7]"Why does this fellow talk like that? He's blaspheming! Who can forgive sins but God alone?"
> [8]Immediately Jesus knew in his spirit that this was what they were thinking in their hearts, and he said to them. "Why are you thinking these things? [9]Which is easier: to say to the paralytic, 'Your sins are forgiven,' or to say, 'Get up, take your mat and walk'? [10]But that you may know that the Son of Man has authority on

earth to forgive sins . . . ." He said to the paralytic, [11]"I tell you, get up, take your mat and go home." [12]He got up, took his mat and walked out in full view of them all. This amazed everyone and they praised God, saying, "We have never seen anything like this!"

It has often been suggested (e.g., Bultmann, Schweizer, Taylor) that vv.1–12 are the conflation of two stories. The first (vv.1–5a, 10b–12) is a miracle story, and the other (vv.5b–10a) is a separate story about the forgiveness of sins. But this dissection of the passage fails to recognize the close relationship between the healing of the body and the forgiveness of sins.

1 Jesus had been away from Capernaum and had been traveling throughout Galilee. He now returns to Capernaum, a kind of base of operations for him in the northern part of the country. His presence in town was soon discovered. "Home" was probably the house of Peter and Andrew referred to in 1:29.

2 Even the place Jesus called home afforded him no privacy. The house filled with people, and the overflow was so great that the space outside the door was blocked. They no doubt flocked to him because they wanted to see him perform more miracles (like the healing of the leper). But Jesus was not working miracles inside the house. He was preaching the gospel to the people.

3–4 In order to understand the action these verses describe, it is necessary to visualize the layout of a typical Palestinian peasant's house. It was usually a small, one-room structure with a flat roof. Access to the roof was by means of an outside stairway. The roof itself was usually made of wooden beams with thatch and compacted earth in order to shed the rain. Sometimes tiles were laid between the beams and the thatch and earth placed over them.

The four men brought the paralytic (v.3) to the house where Jesus was; but when they saw the size of the crowd, they realized it was impossible to enter by the door. So they carried the paralytic up the outside stairway to the roof (v.4). There they dug up the compacted thatch and earth (no doubt dirt showered down on those inside the house below), removed the tiles, and lowered the man through the now-exposed beams to the floor below.

5 Jesus recognized this ingenuity and persistence as faith. Mark says Jesus "saw their faith." It was evident in the actions of both the paralytic and his bearers. But instead of healing the man of his lameness, Jesus forgave his sins. This hardly seemed to be what the man needed—at least on the surface.

> It is not as if this sick man were unusually sinful, but his case makes the universal separation of man from God more conspicuous and illustrates the truth which is proclaimed over and over in the Old Testament, that all suffering is rooted in man's separation from God. For this reason, Jesus must call attention here to man's deepest need; otherwise the testimony of this healing would remain nothing more than the story of a remarkable miracle. (Schweizer, p. 61)

6 Mark has already mentioned the "teachers of the law" in 1:22 (q.v.), where their teaching is contrasted with Jesus' authoritative teaching. Here they become directly

involved with Jesus. Luke (5:17) says that they had come from "every village of Galilee and from Judea and Jerusalem." Obviously they were there out of more than curiosity; they hoped to be able to ensnare him on some theological point. Jesus' statement about forgiveness gave them their opportunity.

7 For anyone but God to claim to forgive sin was blasphemy. Since for the teachers of the law Jesus was not God, therefore he blasphemed. If they were right about who Jesus was, their reasoning was flawless. In Jewish teaching even the Messiah could not forgive sins. That was the prerogative of God alone. Their fatal error was in not recognizing who Jesus really was—the Son of God who has authority to forgive sins.

8–9 The teachers of the law had not openly expressed their misgivings about Jesus' actions. They were "thinking in their hearts" (v.8). But Jesus knew their thoughts and challenged them with the question "Which is easier: to say to the paralytic, 'Your sins are forgiven,' or to say, 'Get up, take your mat and walk'?" (v.9). Of course, as he meant the words, neither of the two was easier. Both were alike impossible to men and equally easy for God. To the teachers of the law, it was easier to make the statement about forgiveness because who could verify its fulfillment? But to say, "Get up . . . and walk"—that could indeed be verified by an actual healing that could be seen.

10–11 The first half of v.10—"But that you may know that the Son of Man has authority on earth to forgive sins"—is usually understood to be addressed to the scribes. In that case the words "he said to the paralytic" constitute a parenthesis to explain that the following words are addressed not to the teachers of the law but to the paralytic. The change of addressee seems awkward; but, if this is the correct interpretation, presumably Jesus indicated his change by some sort of gesture. Another possibility is to take the entire verse as addressed to Mark's readers. This would not only solve the problem of awkwardness stated above but also the theological one of so early a public use of the title "Son of Man" (for a discussion of "Son of Man," cf. remarks at 8:31). In Mark's Gospel the use of this title seems to be reserved until after the crucial incident of 8:29 (cf. the remarks at 2:28 and also cf. Taylor, pp. 197–98).

The healing verified the claim to grant forgiveness. As sure as actual healing followed Jesus' statement "Get up" (v.11), so actual forgiveness resulted from his "your sins are forgiven." As Hunter (p. 38) says, "He did the miracle which they could see that they might know that he had done the other one that they could not see."

12 The man responded immediately (*euthys*) (not tr. in NIV). The cure was instantaneous. And "in full view of them all" (i.e., the entire crowd and especially the teachers of the law who had challenged Jesus' authority to forgive sins), the ex-paralytic walked out. Again the response of the crowd (the "all" includes the teachers of the law) was one of amazement, and there is the added response of giving praise to God for what had happened. Never before had they seen anything like this.

The significance of this story is not to be understood in terms of Jesus' pity on a helpless cripple that moves him to heal the man's paralyzed body. The emphasis is on the forgiveness of sins. This was at the root of the paralytic's problem, and it was to this that Jesus primarily addressed himself. In his act of forgiveness Jesus was also declaring the presence of God's kingdom among men.

Notes

2 "He preached the word to them" translates ἐλάλει αὐτοῖς τὸν λόγον (elalei autois ton logon, lit., "he was speaking to them the word"). Logon is here used of the "message of salvation," "the good news," "the gospel" (BAG, p. 479).

2. Eating with sinners

2:13–17

> 13Once again Jesus went out beside the lake. A large crowd came to him, and he began to teach them. 14As he walked along, he saw Levi son of Alphaeus sitting at the tax collector's booth. "Follow me," Jesus told him, and Levi got up and followed him.
> 15While Jesus was having dinner at Levi's house, many tax collectors and "sinners" were eating with him and his disciples, for there were many who followed him. 16When the teachers of the law who were Pharisees saw him eating with the "sinners" and tax collectors, they asked his disciples: "Why does he eat with tax collectors and 'sinners'?"
> 17On hearing this, Jesus said to them, "It is not the healthy who need a doctor, but the sick. I have not come to call the righteous, but sinners."

13 This is the second incident in the series of five in which Jesus comes into conflict with the religious leaders. The incident is introduced by the story of the calling of Levi, the tax collector. The only connecting word Mark uses is palin ("once again"), which makes it clear that this is a separate unit of tradition. The scene is the shore of the Sea of Galilee. Jesus' popularity with the crowds was still very evident—"a large crowd came to him, and he began to teach them."

14 Jesus may have done his teaching on this occasion as rabbis often did theirs—"as he walked along." If so, his teaching was interrupted by his encounter with Levi, at the tax collector's booth. This Levi is almost universally identified with Matthew (in the same incident in Matt 9:9, he is called Matthew). Levi was probably his given name and Matthew ("gift of God") his apostolic name. He was employed by Herod Antipas, the tetrarch of Galilee, as a tax collector. A traveler from either Herod Philip's territory or the Decapolis would naturally pass through Capernaum on entering Galilee. Tax collectors were despised by the Jews because they were considered traitors and because they often were, in fact, extortioners.

Jesus found Levi at the "tax collector's booth." This was probably the toll booth on the road that ran from Damascus through Capernaum to the Mediterranean coast. There was much at stake for Levi in accepting Jesus' challenge. Fishermen could easily go back to fishing (as some of the disciples did after Jesus' crucifixion), but for Levi there would be little possibility of his returning to his occupation. Tax collector jobs were greatly sought after as a sure way to get rich quickly.

15-16 The dinner held in Levi's house (v.15) was probably his farewell party since he was leaving to become one of Jesus' disciples, or perhaps he simply wanted to gather his friends together so that they too could have an opportunity to meet Jesus. "Eating with Jesus ['him' NIV]" (*synanekeinto tō Iēsou*) seems to suggest that the tax collectors and sinners were having dinner with Jesus; i.e., he was the host, not Levi! "When this is understood the interest of the entire pericope centers on the significance of Messiah eating with sinners. The specific reference in v.17 to Jesus' call of sinners to the Kingdom suggests that the basis of table-fellowship was *messianic forgiveness*, and the meal itself was an anticipation of the messianic banquet" (Lane, p. 106; emphasis his).

"Sinners" (v.16) denotes those people who refuse to follow the Mosaic Law as interpreted by the Pharisees. That Jesus would include in his most intimate circle a man associated with so disreputable a profession and would sit at table (in the ancient world a sign of intimacy) with tax collectors and "sinners" was too much for the "teachers of the law" to keep quiet about.

These particular teachers of the law were also Pharisees. Little is known of either the origin or the predecessors of this sect. The probability is that they were the successors of the Hasidim, the pious Jews who joined forces with Mattathias and his sons during the Maccabean period. After religious liberty was achieved, they largely deserted the Maccabees in their struggle for political independence. They first appear under the name "Pharisee" during the reign of the Hasmonean John Hyrcanus (135-104 B.C.) (cf. EBC, 1:192).

Josephus says, "The Pharisees [are] a body of Jews with the reputation of excelling the rest of their nation in the observances of religion, and as exact exponents of the laws" (War I, 110 [v.2]). Although many of them were doubtless pious and godly men, those Jesus came into conflict with represented some of the worst elements of traditional religion: jealousy, hypocrisy, and religious formalism. "Pharisaism is the final result of that conception of religion which makes religion consist in conformity to the Law, and promises God's grace only to the doers of the Law" (Metzger, *The New Testament*, p. 41). The consorting of Jesus with people who openly refused to keep the requirements of the law prompted the question "Why does he [supposedly a 'religious' or observant Jew] eat with tax collectors and 'sinners'?"

17 No statement of Jesus in this Gospel is more profound than this one. A doctor ministers not to healthy persons but to the sick. So Jesus came not to call the "righteous" (i.e., the self-righteous) but "sinners" (i.e., not merely people who refuse to carry out the details of the law but those who are alienated from the life of God). Jesus' call is to salvation; and, in order to share in it, there must be a recognition of need. A self-righteous man is incapable of recognizing that need, but a sinner can. "It would be true to say that this word of Jesus strikes the keynote of the Gospel. The new thing in Christianity is not the doctrine that God saves sinners. No Jew would have denied that. It is the assertion 'that God loves and saves them *as sinners.*' . . . This is the authentic and glorious doctrine of true Christianity in any age" (Hunter, pp. 40-41, emphasis his).

3. *A question about fasting*

2:18-22

> [18]Now John's disciples and the Pharisees were fasting. Some people came and asked Jesus, "How is it that John's disciples and the disciples of the Pharisees are fasting, but yours are not?"

¹⁹Jesus answered, "How can the guests of the bridegroom fast while he is with them? They cannot, so long as they have him with them. ²⁰But the time will come when the bridegroom will be taken from them, and on that day they will fast.

²¹"No one sews a patch of unshrunk cloth on an old garment. If he does, the new piece will pull away from the old, making the tear worse. ²²And no one pours new wine into old wineskins. If he does, the wine will burst the skins, and both the wine and the wineskins will be ruined. No, he pours new wine into new wineskins."

18 In the law only the fast of the Day of Atonement was required (Lev 16:29, 31; 23:27–32; Num 29:7), but after the Exile four other annual fasts were observed by Jews (Zech 7:5; 8:19). In NT times the stricter Pharisees fasted twice a week (Monday and Thursday; cf. Luke 18:12). The phrase "the disciples of the Pharisees" is unique in the NT. It presents some difficulty because the Pharisees as such were not teachers and thus did not have disciples. However, a small number of them were numbered among the scribes (NIV, "teachers of the law") and they did have disciples. Or perhaps the term is used in a nontechnical sense to refer to people who were influenced by the teachings and practice of the Pharisees. It is in this latter sense that the expression "John's disciples" (the Baptist) is also to be understood.

Why these two groups were fasting, Mark does not say. John's disciples may have been fasting because he was in prison at the time, or perhaps they were fasting in anticipation of the Messianic Age. The Pharisees' disciples were probably observing one of the biweekly fasts. In both instances fasting was a sign of true piety. This being the case, "some people" (Mark does not identify them specifically) were asking why Jesus' disciples were not evidencing true religious piety by fasting.

19–20 Jesus answers in a parable. Its great emphasis is on the joy the presence of Jesus makes possible. Therefore fasting—a sign of mourning—is not appropriate. A Jewish wedding feast was a particularly joyous occasion. The guests joined in the celebration that sometimes lasted a week. To fast during that time of great joy and festivity would be unthinkable. Jesus is the bridegroom (v.19) and his disciples the guests. While he remains with them they will rejoice, not fast. However, he will not always be with them. When he is taken away (v.20), fasting will be appropriate.

The mention of the removal of the bridegroom has often been explained as reading the death of Jesus back into the text on the ground that it was unlikely that he would so early have made mention of his death. On this two comments need to be made: (1) the reference to his death is veiled, and he only speaks of the bridegroom being "taken from them" and not specifically of death (though see note on this verse); and (2) we do not know when this incident took place, but it could conceivably have been late in Jesus' ministry.

21–22 These two parables, which occur side by side, were probably spoken on different occasions; but they belong together because they deal with a single theme. Obviously they bear on the question of fasting, but beyond that they also bear on the forms of Judaism generally. In ancient times wine was kept in goatskins. New skins were soft and pliable and would stretch when wine that had not yet completed fermentation was put in them. However, old wineskins that had been stretched would become brittle and, being no longer pliable, were thus unable to stretch. The gas from the fermenting wine burst them open, destroying both wine and wine-skins. Putting new wine into old wineskins (v.22) and patching an old garment with a new cloth (v.21) are just as inappropriate as fasting at a wedding feast. A wedding, new wine, and a new garment are all symbols of the New Age. The main teaching of the parable seems to be that the newness the coming of Jesus brings cannot be confined to the old forms.

Notes

20 Ἀπαρθῇ (*aparthē*, "will be taken away") is from ἀπαίρω (*apairō*) and occurs in the NT only here and in the parallels in Matthew and Luke. It means "take away," "remove." According to Bratcher and Nida (p. 92), "the verb as such does not state whether the removal is natural, or sudden and violent. The context of the whole saying, however, implies a violent removal which will provoke sorrow (cf. the use of the verb in the LXX Isa 53:8 [where, however, the simple form αἴρω is used])."

4. *The Lord of the Sabbath* (2:23–3:6)

a. *Picking grain on the Sabbath*

2:23–28

23One Sabbath Jesus was going through the grainfields, and as his disciples walked along, they began to pick some heads of grain. 24The Pharisees said to him, "Look, why are they doing what is unlawful on the Sabbath?"
25He answered, "Have you never read what David did when he and his companions were hungry and in need? 26In the days of Abiathar the high priest, he entered the house of God and ate the consecrated bread, which is lawful only for priests to eat. And he also gave some to his companions."
27Then he said to them, "The Sabbath was made for man, not man for the Sabbath. 28So the Son of Man is Lord even of the Sabbath."

The specific time or place of this incident is not given. Nor is it clear how it relates to what precedes or what follows except that it is a conflict story. The theme of the incident, not its chronological position in the life of Jesus, is what determined its inclusion at this point in Mark's Gospel. The conflict centers on the keeping of the Sabbath, something far more important in Judaism than the question of fasting.

23-24 The main point at issue was not the act of harvesting the heads of grain (v.23). Such activity as Jesus and his disciples were involved in was explicitly allowed in the law: "If you enter your neighbor's grain field, you may pick kernels with your hands, but you must not put a sickle to his standing grain" (Deut 23:25). What the Pharisees objected to (v.24) was doing this (regarded as reaping) on the Sabbath (cf. M *Shabbath* 7.2, where one of the thirty-nine acts forbidden on the Sabbath was reaping).

25-26 Jesus meets the accusation of the Pharisees with a counterquestion (v.25). The incident he refers to is recorded in 1 Samuel 21:1–6. David and his companions were hungry and ate the consecrated bread—the twelve loaves baked of fine flour, arranged in two rows or piles on the table in the Holy Place. Fresh loaves were brought into the sanctuary each Sabbath to replace the old ones that were then eaten by the priests (cf. Exod 25:30; 35:13; 39:36; Lev 24:5–9; cf. Jos. Antiq. III, 255–56, [x.7]). Although the action of David was contrary to the law, he was not condemned for it. Jesus does not claim that the Sabbath law has not been technically broken but that such violations under certain conditions are warranted. "Human need is a higher law than religious ritualism" (Earle, p. 49).

The problem associated with the phrase *epi Abiathar archiereōs* is well known (v.26). If it means "at the time when Abiathar was high priest," it is incorrect historically. At the time the incident occurred, Ahimelech, Abiathar's father, was high priest; and it was from him David received the consecrated bread. The difficulty is revealed by the fact that neither Matthew nor Luke records the phrase in the parallel passages, and it is not found in several MSS. In some MSS a definite article is inserted before "high priest." This would make possible the translation "in the time of Abiathar, the one who [later] became high priest." It is this reconstruction that NIV's "in the days of" reflects. Another possibility is to translate the preposition *epi* "in the account of," as is done in Mark 12:26 (*epi tou batou*, "in the account of the bush"). None of these solutions is entirely satisfactory. The OT itself seems to confuse Ahimelech and Abiathar (cf. 1 Sam 22:20 with 2 Sam 8:17; 1 Chron 18:16; 24:6).

27–28 The pronouncement is preceded by the phrase "Then he said to them" (v.27). Since this seems to be a literary device used by Mark (cf. 4:2b, 11, 21, 24, 26; 6:10; 7:9; 8:21; 9:1) to insert into the account an independent saying of Jesus that is relevant to the subject at hand, it seems best so to regard the pronouncement here. The larger context out of which this authentic saying of Jesus came is not given; but the crucial line is given, and that fact has special relevance to the controversy. To Jesus the Sabbath was not created for its own sake; it was a gift of God to man. Its purpose was not to put man in a kind of straight jacket. It was for his good—to provide rest from labor and opportunity for worship. Jesus' pronouncement was not as radical for his day as some would think. Rabbi Simeon ben Menasya (c. A.D. 180) said, "The Sabbath has been committed to you and not you to the Sabbath" (Melkilta *Shabbata* 1 to Exod 31:14).

The big question in v.28 is whether this is a statement of Mark about Jesus or of Jesus about himself. The question is not whether Jesus claims to be Son of Man in Mark's Gospel. That he does this is abundantly clear from such texts as 8:31, 38; 9:9, 12, 31; 10:33; 13:26; 14:21 (bis), 41, 62. But does he claim it here? If v.27 is a separate saying of Jesus inserted by Mark to climax the teaching of Jesus about the Sabbath, then it seems best to regard this verse as Mark's comment to the church, after the same pattern as 2:10. If taken as spoken by Mark of Jesus, the pronouncement is no less true. "Since the Sabbath was made for man, He who is man's Lord . . . has authority to determine its law and use" (Taylor, p. 219).

b. *Healing on the Sabbath*

3:1–6

¹Another time he went into the synagogue, and a man with a shriveled hand was there. ²Some of them were looking for a reason to accuse Jesus, so they

watched him closely to see if he would heal him on the Sabbath. ³Jesus said to the man with the shriveled hand, "Stand up in front of everyone."

⁴Then Jesus asked them, "Which is lawful on the Sabbath: to do good or to do evil, to save life or to kill?" But they remained silent.

⁵He looked around at them in anger and, deeply distressed at their stubborn hearts, said to the man, "Stretch out your hand." He stretched it out, and his hand was completely restored. ⁶Then the Pharisees went out and began to plot with the Herodians how they might kill Jesus.

1 This is the last in a series of five conflict stories. Again Mark gives no details of time or geographical location. It is simply another incident out of Jesus' life used to show what his attitude toward the Sabbath was. The story takes place in a synagogue where there is a man with a "shriveled hand." Apparently some sort of paralysis is meant.

2 Mark does not specifically identify the opposition here. Though he uses the indefinite "some," the identity is nonetheless clear (cf. v.6, where the Pharisees are mentioned; cf. also Luke 6:7, which says that they were the "Pharisees and the teachers of law"). Since Jesus had already raised suspicions in their mind because of his unorthodox actions, these men were present in the synagogue, not to worship God, but to spy on Jesus ("they watched him closely"). They "were looking for a reason to accuse Jesus." The statement "to see if he would heal him on the Sabbath" makes it clear that the Pharisees were convinced of Jesus' power to perform miracles. The issue was not "could he" but "would he?" Rabbinic law allowed healing on the Sabbath only in the event that life was actually in danger (cf. SBK, 1:623).

3–4 Jesus was fully aware of the designs of the opposition. Instead of acting carefully in the situation, he commanded the man to stand up and come to "center stage" so that all in the synagogue could see what he was going to do to him (v.3). There is no secrecy motif here!

No question had been asked Jesus by the religious leaders, but he knew what was racing through their minds. So he asked them, "Which is lawful on the Sabbath: to do good or to do evil, to save life or to kill?" (v.4). Several interpretations of Jesus' statement are possible.

1. Calvin (2:54) took it to mean that "there is little difference between manslaughter and the conduct of him who does not concern himself about relieving a person in distress."

2. The will of God is served better by saving (i.e., restoring to health) a life than by plotting to kill (as the Pharisees were doing; cf. v.6).

3. There may be a hint here of Jesus' mission to destroy the works of Satan. Disease and disfigurement are ultimately Satan's works. Jesus came to destroy these; and, since evil works seven days a week, "the warfare against Satan must go on on the Sabbath as well as on the other six days" (T.W. Manson, *The Sayings of Jesus* [Cambridge: Cambridge University Press, 1937], p. 190). The Pharisees were silent. They refused to debate the issue with Jesus.

5 Anger is rarely directly attributed to Jesus. The only other place in the Gospels he is said to be angry is in the reading rejected by the NIV in Mark 1:41. His anger was real, but it was never the expression of injured self-concern. It was more like "righteous indignation"—what a good man feels in the presence of stark evil. Such anger was particularly appropriate to this situation. But even such justifiable anger was couched in compassion. The tenses of the verbs are important here. The looking "around at them in anger" was momentary (aorist tense), but the being "deeply distressed" was continuous (present tense). Jesus' distress was caused by their "stubborn hearts," i.e., their consistent failure to recognize who he really was. "Their opposition rested on a fundamental misunderstanding—an inability, or refusal, to see that Jesus was God's eschatological agent and that his sovereign freedom with regard to law and custom sprang from that fact" (Nineham, p. 110).

When Jesus ordered the man to stretch out his hand, he obeyed; and it was instantly and completely restored.

6 "The consequence of the healing was neither surprise or acclamation, but increased enmity" (H. Van der Loos, *The Miracles of Jesus* [Leiden: Brill, 1965], p. 438). The Pharisees, joined now by the Herodians, began to plot Jesus' death. Although it is not clear who the Herodians were, it seems fairly certain that they were neither a religious sect nor a political party. The term probably refers to influential Jews who were friends and backers of the Herodian family. This meant, of course, that they were supporters of Rome, from which the Herods received their authority. They joined the Pharisees in opposition to Jesus because they feared he might be an unsettling political influence in Palestine.

Notes

5 "He looked around" translates περιβλεψάμενος (*periblepsamenos*) and is one of many eyewitness details in Mark's Gospel (cf. 3:34; 5:32; 9:8; 10:23; 11:11).

III. The Later Galilean Ministry (3:7–6:13)

A summary statement (3:7–12) begins this new section of Mark's Gospel, and it ends with the sending out of the Twelve (6:6b–13). In between are two obvious sections: parables about the kingdom (4:1–34) and miracles of Jesus' power over hostile powers (4:35–5:43). In addition there are several units that deal with hostility and rejection (3:20–30, 31–35; 6:1–6a), and there is a brief account of the selection of the Twelve (3:13–19). The fact that the renown of Jesus reaches the Jerusalem authorities, who send their representatives up to Galilee to observe what was going on, suggests an advanced stage in the ministry of Jesus, as does the sending out of the Twelve. Most of the action takes place in the vicinity of the Sea of Galilee.

A. Withdrawal to the Lake

3:7–12

[7]Jesus withdrew with his disciples to the lake, and a large crowd from Galilee followed. [8]When they heard all he was doing, many people came to him from Judea, Jerusalem, Idumea, and the regions across the Jordan and around Tyre

and Sidon. ⁹Because of the crowd he told his disciples to have a small boat ready for him, to keep the people from crowding him. ¹⁰For he had healed many, so that those with diseases were pushing forward to touch him. ¹¹Whenever the evil spirits saw him, they fell down before him and cried out, "You are the Son of God." ¹²But he gave them strict orders not to tell who he was.

7 Why did Jesus withdraw? Mark does not say, but Matthew's use of the participle *gnous* ("knowing," i.e., about the plot to kill him) in 12:15 makes it clear that Jesus left wherever he had been (Capernaum?) because he realized that the religious authorities were determined to get him. Since the time had not yet come for a serious confrontation, he withdrew to the Lake of Genessaret. This withdrawal, however, did not separate him from the crowds.

8 The crowds that came to Jesus were not only from the regions in the vicinity of Capernaum but also from the south (Jerusalem, Idumea), the east (across the Jordan), and the northwest (Tyre and Sidon). Mark includes the whole of Jewish Palestine. Schweizer (p. 79) points out that "to some extent, the locations named form an outline of the Gospel of Mark, since Jesus is active in Galilee (chs. 1–6); Tyre, Sidon and Decapolis (ch. 7); and finally beyond the Jordan and in Jerusalem (chs. 10ff.)." The only territory mentioned here in which Jesus was not active is Idumea, the area south of Hebron.

Some of the geographical terms in this verse require comment. Idumea was invaded and conquered, after the destruction of Jerusalem in 587 B.C., by the Edomites who came from the east and settled there. Judas Maccabeus had several successful campaigns against the Idumeans, and during the reign of John Hyrcanus they were forced to adopt Judaism. Herod the Great was an Idumean, and several of his sons played important roles in the political history of Palestine. "Tyre and Sidon" are terms used virtually interchangeably for the northwestern area of Palestine. The "regions across the Jordan" probably included Perea and the Decapolis, both of which were under the political control of Herod Antipas, as was Galilee.

9–10 Only Mark includes the detail about the boat (v.9). Its purpose was, of course, to provide escape for Jesus in case the crowd began to get unruly. The picture is that of great numbers of people pressing forward just to touch Jesus in the hope that by doing so they might be healed (v.10). The crowd seems to have had little interest in Jesus other than as a miracle-worker. Despite this, he graciously healed many of them.

11–12 Here again Jesus comes into conflict with the demonic (v.11). The evil spirits recognized who Jesus was—even if the crowds did not. Their crying out "You are the Son of God" is best understood as a "futile attempt to render him harmless. These cries of recognition were designed to control him and to strip him of his power, in accordance with the conception that knowledge of the precise name or quality of a person confers mastery over him" (Lane, p. 130). "Son of God" in this context is a true designation of who Jesus is, expressed by his bitter foes, the demons. Jesus silenced the outcries of the demons (v.12) because the time for the clear revelation of who he was had not yet come, and the demons were hardly appropriate heralds of him.

41

Notes

7 The word translated "withdrew" is ἀνεχώρησεν (anechōrēsen), used only here in Mark. It is not clear whether it contains the idea of forced withdrawal or not. MM (p. 40) give examples of it from the papyri meaning "take refuge."

B. *Selection of the Twelve*

3:13–19

> 13Jesus went up on a mountainside and called to him those he wanted, and they came to him. 14He appointed twelve—designating them apostles—that they might be with him and that he might send them out to preach 15and to have authority to drive out demons. 16These are the twelve he appointed: Simon (to whom he gave the name Peter); 17James son of Zebedee and his brother John (to them he gave the name Boanerges, which means Sons of Thunder); 18Andrew, Philip, Bartholomew, Matthew, Thomas, James son of Alphaeus, Thaddaeus, Simon the Zealot 19and Judas Iscariot, who betrayed him.

13 Lightfoot has a suggestive interpretation of the significance of the appointing of the Twelve. He understands the withdrawal of 3:7 as a withdrawal from the synagogue (the only other reference in Mark's Gospel to Jesus in the synagogue is in 6:2):

> After withdrawing from the synagogue . . . he first meets a great multitude of enthusiastic followers on the shore of the lake, and proceeds to make a selection from them, with whom He withdraws to the high ground; and we then read of the appointment of the twelve, and a list is given of their names. We may see here, if we choose, the foundation of the new Israel, Israel after the flesh having proved itself unworthy." (p. 39)

Luke (6:12) says that Jesus spent a night in prayer before choosing the Twelve. Although literally *eis to oros* means "into the mountain," it is best to understand it to mean the hill country of Galilee near the lake. It was there that Jesus called "those he wanted," and they came to him. No delay in their response is indicated (cf. 1:18, 20; 2:14).

14–15 It may be (contra Lightfoot above) that the Twelve Jesus appointed (v. 14) were the same he called in v. 13. At any rate, from this point on there seem to be no persons designated "disciples" in Mark's Gospel other than the Twelve (cf. R.P. Meye, *Jesus and the Twelve* [Eerdmans: Grand Rapids, 1968], passim). The words "designating them apostles" entail textual problems and may not be original in Mark's Gospel. (UBS's apparatus assigns this a "C" rating, indicating considerable doubt as to its authenticity.) There can be little doubt that the number twelve has theological significance. The Twelve represent the new Israel in embryo.

The purpose for which the Twelve were appointed was twofold: (1) "that they might be with him"; (2) "that he might send them out to preach and to have authority to drive out demons." The Twelve were to be brought into the closest association possible with the life of the Son of God. They were to live with Jesus, travel with him, converse with him, and learn from him. Mark's Gospel indicates that much of Jesus' time was occupied with their training. The training was not an end in itself. They were to be sent out (in Mark's Gospel not until 6:7). And their ministry was to consist of preaching the Good News and driving out demons (v.15). The two are closely associated. The salvation Jesus brings involves the defeat of Satan and his demons.

16-19 There are three other lists of the apostles in the NT (Matt 10:2-4; Luke 6:14-16; Acts 1:13). The names of the Twelve as given in these lists naturally divide into four parts. Peter heads the three other names in the first section; Philip heads the second section; James the Son of Alphaeus (called "the Less" in Matthew) the third; the last section consists of the name of Judas (except in Acts since he had already committed suicide). Simon's nickname "the rock" (Peter) was given him by Jesus (v.16; cf. Matt 16:18). Why Jesus gave it to him is not clear since Peter is depicted in the Gospel narrative as anything but a rock. Perhaps Jesus saw in Peter, unreliable and fickle though he was, the potential for being firm and confident (cf. on Matt 16:18, this commentary).

James and John, the sons of Zebedee, were nicknamed "Sons of Thunder" (v.17). This was probably descriptive of their disposition; it had something of the thunderstorm in it. Since Bartholomew (v.18) is not a personal name but a patronymic, meaning "son of Talmai," he probably had another name (Nathaniel? cf. John 1:45). Matthew is doubtless to be identified with Levi (2:14), but Mark makes no point of it. Thaddaeus is probably the Judas son of James of Luke's lists (Luke 6:16; Acts 1:13). Simon is called "the Zealot." This may simply be a description of his religious zeal; but it is more likely a reference to his membership in the party of the Zealots, a Jewish sect bent on the overthrow at all costs of the Roman control of Palestine. Judas's surname is given as Iscariot (v.19), which probably means "the man from the place called Karioth." Karioth (Kerioth) is identified either with Kerioth Hezron (Josh 15:25), twelve miles south of Hebron, or with Kerioth in Moab (Jer 48:24). Judas is further identified as the man who betrayed Jesus.

It was a strange group of men our Lord chose to be his disciples. Four of them were fishermen, one a hated tax collector, another a member of a radical and violent political party. Of six of them we know practically nothing. All were laymen. There was not a preacher or an expert in the Scriptures in the lot. Yet it was with these men that Jesus established his church and disseminated his Good News to the end of the earth.

C. Jesus, His Family, and the Beelzebub Controversy (3:20-35)

The historicity of this incident can scarcely be denied. The church would not have invented a story that put the family of Jesus into such bad light. In the first verse of this section we are shown that

> ordinary, unprejudiced folk, recognizing (as we may assume) the goodness and God-given character of Jesus' power, flocked to avail themselves of it. In the rest of the section we are shown by contrast how those who might have been expected to share this attitude to the full, Jesus' own family and the religious leaders of the people, not only failed to recognize the true source and character of his actions, but insisted on attributing them to evil sources. (Nineham, p. 119)

Another feature of this section is the insertion of one incident (in this case the Beelzebub controversy) into another (the story of the relationship between Jesus and his family). This is a fairly frequent device in Mark's Gospel (cf. 5:21–43; 6:7–30; 11:12–25; 14:1–11). Mark may use this to heighten the suspense and allow for the passage of time. Lane suggests that in this incident Mark deliberately inserts the Beelzebub controversy between the earlier and later phases of the family narrative: "It suggests that those in Jesus' family who declare that he is mad (Ch. 3:21) are not unlike the scribes who attribute his extraordinary powers to an alliance with Beelzebul, the prince of the demons (Ch. 3:22)" (p. 137).

1. *Charged with insanity*

3:20–21

> [20]Then Jesus entered a house, and again a crowd gathered, so that he and his disciples were not even able to eat. [21]When his family heard about this, they went to take charge of him, for they said, "He is out of his mind."

20–21 Jesus again was being pressed by the crowds. The house (probably Peter and Andrew's; cf. 1:29) was so packed with people demanding his attention that both he and his disciples were prevented from eating (v.20). When Jesus' family heard that he was so engrossed by his work that he failed even to care for his physical needs, they decided to go to Jesus and "take charge of him" (v.21). This probably means that they wanted to take him back to Nazareth. This would remove him from the strain of having so many people constantly pressing on him to meet their physical and spiritual needs. The verb translated "take charge" is *kratēsai* and is used of arresting someone in 6:17; 12:12; 14:1, 44, 46, 49, and 51. The reason Jesus' family wanted to do this was because they feared that overwork had affected him mentally —he was "out of his mind." These are shocking words, but as C.L. Mitton says, "If they reveal his family's failure to understand him, they are also a measure of their concern for him" (*The Gospel According to Mark* [London: Epworth, 1957], p. 26).

2. *Charged with demon possession*

3:22–30

> [22]And the teachers of the law who came down from Jerusalem said, "He is possessed by Beelzebub! By the prince of demons he is driving out demons."
> [23]So Jesus called them and spoke to them in parables: "How can Satan drive out Satan? [24]If a kingdom is divided against itself, that kingdom cannot stand. [25]If a house is divided against itself, that house cannot stand. [26]And if Satan opposes himself and is divided, he cannot stand; his end has come. [27]In fact, no one can enter a strong man's house and carry off his possessions unless he first ties up the strong man. Then he can rob his house. [28]I tell you the truth, all the sins and blasphemies of men will be forgiven them. [29]But whoever blasphemes against the Holy Spirit will never be forgiven; he is guilty of an eternal sin."
> [30]He said this because they were saying, "He has an evil spirit."

Jesus' family was located in Nazareth. Jesus himself at this time was probably in Capernaum; so his family had to travel to Capernaum to get him and take him home. To allow for this time, Mark fills in the gap with the Beelzebub controversy.

22 The teachers of the law had come down from Jerusalem ("down" because Jerusalem was located at a higher elevation than Capernaum). This is a strong indication that the word about Jesus was spreading and was causing concern in high places. Their analysis of Jesus' condition was "he is possessed by Beelzebub!" (cf. John 10:20: "He is demon-possessed and raving mad"). Mark gives no account of the healing of the blind-and-dumb demoniac that prompted this statement (cf. Matt 12:22; Luke 11:14). Beelzebub is "the prince of demons," i.e., Satan. The further accusation is that Jesus and Satan are in collusion with each other.

23–27 Jesus replies to the charge "in parables" (v.23), which in this context means by making a comparison or by speaking proverbially. His argument is as follows: I have just cast out demons. Now if I am doing this by Satan's power, then Satan is actually working against himself. But that would be absurd. Just as a house (v.25) or a kingdom (v.24) cannot stand if it is divided against itself or opposes itself, so Satan will bring about his own destruction by working against himself (v.26). Furthermore, in order to enter the house of a strong man and plunder it, one must first tie up the strong man (v.27).

Two obvious conclusions may be drawn from the "parables": (1) Jesus cannot be in collusion with Satan; and (2) Jesus is actually destroying Satan's work, which means he is more powerful than Satan. The teachers of the law should have had the spiritual discernment to recognize something as obvious as this.

In v.27 it may be that *ta skeuē autou* ("his possessions") is a reference to people in bondage to Satan. Then the tying up of Satan is a reference to the coming of Jesus Christ into the world to deliver from bondage those under Satan's control. However, though "tied," Satan is on a long chain and will not be finally defeated till the End.

28–30 The pronouncement Jesus makes is meant to be a solemn one: "I tell you the truth" (v.28). Forgiveness is available for all the sins and blasphemies of men, except one. That exception is blasphemy against the Holy Spirit (v.29). What is that sin?

Verse 30—"because they were saying, 'He has an evil spirit' "—suggests an explanation for the unforgivable sin. Jesus had done what any unprejudiced person would have acknowledged as a good thing. He had freed an unfortunate man from the power and bondage of evil (cf. Matt 12:22; Luke 11:14). This he did through the power of the Holy Spirit, but the teachers of the law ascribed it to the power of Satan. Taylor (p. 244) says that the sin described here is "a perversion of spirit which, in defiance of moral values elects to call light darkness." Further, Mitton says, "To call what is good evil (Isa 5:20) when you know well that it is good, because prejudice and ill will hold you in bondage, that is the worst sin of all. The tragedy of the 'hardening of heart' (as in 3:5) is that it makes men capable of committing just this sin" (*Gospel of Mark*, p. 28).

The words of v.29—"will never be forgiven; he is guilty of an eternal sin"—have caused great anxiety and pain in the history of the church. Many have wondered whether they have committed the "unpardonable sin." Surely what Jesus is speaking of here is not an isolated act but a settled condition of the soul—the result of a long history of repeated and willful acts of sin. And if the person involved cannot be forgiven it is not so much that God refuses to forgive as it is the sinner refuses to allow him. Ryle's famous words are great reassurance to any who might be anxious

45

about this sin: "There is such a thing as a sin which is never forgiven. But those who are troubled about it are most unlikely to have committed it" (J.C. Ryle, *Expository Thoughts on the Gospels* [New York: Revell], 2:59). On the other hand, those who actually do commit the sin are so dominated by evil that it is unlikely that they would be aware of it.

3. *Jesus' true family*

3:31–35

> [31]Then Jesus' mother and brothers arrived. Standing outside, they sent someone in to call him. [32]A crowd was sitting around him, and they told him, "Your mother and brothers are outside looking for you."
> [33]"Who are my mother and my brothers?" he asked.
> [34]Then he looked at those seated in a circle around him and said, "Here are my mother and my brothers! [35]Whoever does God's will is my brother and sister and mother."

31 Mark now turns back to the family of Jesus. By inserting the account of the Beelzebub controversy, he has both heightened the suspense and allowed for travel time from Nazareth to Capernaum. The family arrived where Jesus was, but they did not enter the place where he was. Instead they stood outside and sent someone in to call him. Specifically, only Jesus' mother (the only reference to her in Mark's Gospel) and his brothers are mentioned. Joseph is not mentioned. Presumably he was not living at this time.

32–34 When Jesus was told that his mother and his brothers were looking for him (v.32), he responded by asking the queston, "Who are my mother and my brothers?" (v.33). Then with a sweep of his eyes over those seated in a circle around him, he identified his true family: "Here are my mother and my brothers" (v.34). This statement probably included only the Twelve, who were seated nearest to Jesus. They had responded to his call to be with him. There were now spiritual ties between him and them that were far closer than blood ties.

35 Jesus' true family is not limited to the Twelve. It includes all who obey the will of God. It can easily be imagined what this statement meant to the original readers of Mark's Gospel. "In place of broken family relations, ostracism and persecution, was the close and intimate relation to the Son of God" (Grant, p. 694). In view of the Jewish attitude toward one's parents—an attitude adopted by the church—the authenticity of vv.31–35 is unimpeachable.

D. *Parables About the Kingdom of God* (4:1–34)

This is one of the few sections in Mark's Gospel devoted to teaching. Although Mark frequently shows us Jesus teaching (1:21; 2:13; 6:2, 6), only here and in 13:2–37—and perhaps in 7:1–13—does he give any sustained account of the content of his teaching.

Chapter 4 contains four of Jesus' parables: the parable of the sower and its interpretation (vv.1–20), the parable of the lamp (vv.21–25), the parable of the secretly growing seed (vv.26–29), and the parable of the mustard seed (vv.30–32). Parables are the most striking feature in the teaching of Jesus. Although he did not invent this form of teaching (parables are found both in the OT and in the writings of the rabbis), he used it in a way and to a degree unmatched before his time or since.

The Sunday school definition of a parable—"an earthly story with a heavenly meaning"—is good as far as it goes. Many parables are stories taken out of ordinary life, used to drive home a spiritual or moral truth. But they are not always stories. Sometimes they are brief similes, comparisons, analogies, or even proverbial sayings. The Greek word *parabolē* (lit., "something placed along side") includes all these meanings. The word most often used in the OT is *māšal*. This can include anything from a simple metaphor to an elaborate story.

For centuries parables were interpreted allegorically; i.e., each element of the story was assigned a specific meaning. Thus Augustine found in the parable of the Good Samaritan references to Adam, Jerusalem, the Devil and his angels, the Law and the Prophets, and Christ and the church! Now we are more apt to look for the one main point a parable teaches. This is not to say that all Jesus' parables have only one point to make. Some clearly have more than one, but the principle is a generally valid one. We have also learned (from Dodd and Jeremias) that the teaching found in the parables is more than general religious truth. It is always related in a dynamic way to Jesus' message and mission, i.e., to the life situation of his ministry. This does not mean, of course, that the meaning of the parables are bound to the historical and theological situation of first-century Palestine. Like all Scripture, the parables contain truth relevant for God's people everywhere—those of the twentieth-century world as well as those of the first-century world.

1. *Parable of the sower*

4:1–9

1Again Jesus began to teach by the lake. The crowd that gathered around him was so large that he got into a boat and sat in it out on the lake, while all the people were along the shore at the water's edge. 2He taught them many things by parables, and in his teaching said: 3"Listen! A farmer went out to sow his seed. 4As he was scattering the seed, some fell along the path, and the birds came and ate it up. 5Some fell on rocky places, where it did not have much soil. It sprang up quickly, because the soil was shallow. 6But when the sun came up, the plants were scorched, and they withered because they had no root. 7Other seed fell among thorns, which grew up and choked the plants, so that they did not bear grain. 8Still other seed fell on good soil. It came up, grew and produced a crop, multiplying thirty, sixty, or even a hundred times."

9Then Jesus said, "He who has ears to hear, let him hear."

1–2 Mark gives us no information as to when the situation in which Jesus spoke this parable took place but uses the indefinite "again" (v.1). The place was by the Lake of Galilee. The presence of the large crowd shows Jesus' popularity as a teacher. In fact, the crowd was so large that he found it convenient to use a small boat pushed out from the shore as his lectern (actually he sat while teaching). Whether the boat mentioned here is the same one "made ready" for him (3:9) is uncertain; if it is, the teaching reported in chapter 4 may have been given on that occasion and is only summarized in 3:9–11. What is contained in 4:1–34 is only part of Jesus' teaching in parables; for Mark says, "He taught them many things by parables" (v.2).

3–9 The parable of the "sower" (*ho speirōn;* NIV, "farmer") begins and ends with a call for careful attention. This suggests that its meaning may not be self-evident. Alert minds are needed to comprehend its truth. The background of the parable is rural life in Palestine. Seed was sown in broadcast fashion (v.3). The sower deliberately sowed it on the path (v.4), in rocky places (v.5), and among the thorns (v.7) because sowing preceded plowing. However, if plowing was delayed for any time at all, the consequences Jesus mentioned inevitably resulted.

The great emphasis in the parable is on the act of sowing the seed rather than on the soils into which it is sown. "The Kingdom of God breaks into the world even as seed which is sown on the ground. In the details about the soils there is reflection on the diversity of response to the proclamation of the Word of God, but this is not the primary consideration" (Lane, p. 154). Although difficulties face God's kingdom, it grows and ultimately produces an abundant harvest (v.8). This is no self-evident truth; so "he who has ears to hear, let him hear" (v.9), or as Moule paraphrases it: "Now think that one out for yourself, if you can!" (*Gospel of Mark*, p. 35).

2. *Secret of the kingdom of God*

4:10–12

> 10When he was alone, the Twelve and the others around him asked him about the parables. 11He told them, "The secret of the kingdom of God has been given to you. But to those on the outside everything is said in parables 12so that,
>
> > " 'they may be ever seeing but never perceiving,
> > and ever hearing but never understanding;
> > otherwise they might turn and be forgiven!' "

10 The question about the parables must have been, in view of the answer given by Jesus, directed toward their purpose in his teaching. The plural "parables" is used because more is in view in Jesus' answer than the parable of the sower. Jesus had spoken other parables, and the disciples were inquiring into the purpose of parables generally. Mention is made of "others around him." These are followers of Jesus whom Mark distinguishes from the Twelve. This indicates that Jesus' teaching is not narrowly limited to the Twelve. He is no gnostic revealer whose esoteric teaching is only for the fortunate few. He came to reveal the truth to all who were open to receive it.

11–12 These verses are among the most difficult in the entire Gospel. It is important to look carefully at the terminology. The word translated "secret" (v.11) is *mystērion*. Although it occurs only here and in the parallels (Matt 13:11; Luke 8:10) in the Gospels, Paul uses it frequently in his epistles (twenty-one times); and it is found in the Book of Revelation four times (1:20; 10:7; 17:5, 7). In the NT it does not mean something only for the initiated few. The emphasis is on God's disclosure to man of what was previously unknown. It is proclaimed to all, but only those who have faith really understand. Here in Mark the mystery is the disclosure that the kingdom of God has drawn near in the person of Jesus Christ, or perhaps as G.E. Ladd suggests, the mystery "is that the Kingdom that is to come finally in apocalyptic power, as foreseen in Daniel, has in fact entered into the world in advance in a hidden form to work secretly within and among men" (*A Theology of the New Testament* [Grand Rapids: Eerdmans, 1974], p. 94).

The secret has been given to the disciples because they have responded in faith, but to "those on the outside" (i.e., men hardened by unbelief; cf. ch. 3), "all things," i.e., the entire significance of Jesus' person and mission, are "in parables." Here the word *parabolē* takes on the meaning of "riddle," a meaning well within the range of the word.

12 The introductory conjunction (*hina*, "so that") is Mark's. The quotation that follows is from Isa. 6:9–10, which in the MT is a command; this is not surprising, since in Semitic thought a command may be used to express a result.

Mark follows the LXX text. However, he omits the strong statements of the first part of v.10: "Make the heart of this people calloused, make their ears dull, and close their eyes," and changes the LXX's "and I heal them" (*kai iaomai autous*) to "and be forgiven" (*kai aphethē autois*). In doing this, Mark follows the Targum—an indication of the authenticity of the statement.

Taken at face value, the statement seems to be saying that the purpose of parables is that unbelievers ("those on the outside," v.11) may not receive the truth and be converted. That this statement was thought to be difficult theologically may be seen in Matthew's change of *hina* ("in order that") to *hoti* ("with the result that" NIV translates *hina* with the ambiguous, "so that"), and in Luke's dropping of the *mēpote* ("otherwise") clause.

Several recent attempts have been made to weaken the telic force of *hina:*

1. It is held that *hina* is used in the text to mean the same thing as *hoti*. Thus Jesus is not speaking of the purpose of parables but their result.

2. Mark has mistranslated the original Aramaic word *de*. It means "who," not "in order that." Thus the text should read, "The secret of the kingdom of God has been given to you. But to those on the outside *who* are ever seeing but never perceiving . . . everything is said in parables" (emphasis mine).

3. The purposive idea (expressed both by *hina* and *mēpote*) is not authentic with Jesus but represents Mark's theology.

4. *Hina* is an introductory formula to the free translation of Isa. 6:9–10. On this understanding *hina* would be almost equivalent to *hina plērōthē*, "in order that it might be fulfilled."

All of these attempts have their defects. Although 1 and 2 alleviate the problem of *hina*, they do not address that of *mēpote* ("otherwise"), which also suggests purpose (also cf. BAG, p. 378, which after discussing the possibility of *hina* meaning "with the result that," flatly rejects it for this passage). Solution 3 has no support at all, while 4, clearly the best choice of the four, founders on the fact that Mark elsewhere does not use *hina* to mean "in order that it might be fulfilled."

Perhaps the best way to understand v.12 is as an authentic saying that simply teaches that one reason Jesus taught in parables was to conceal the truth to "outsiders" (which I take to mean "persistent unbelievers"). Even a cursory reading of the Gospels reveals that Jesus' parables were not always clear. The disciples themselves had difficulty understanding (cf. Mark 7:17). So Jesus taught in parables (at least on some occasions) so that his enemies might not be able to comprehend the full significance of his words and bring false accusations or charges against him. He knew that in some cases understanding would result in more sin and not in accepting the truth. Furthermore, it is not foreign to the teaching of Scripture that God in his wisdom hardens some (again, I understand these to be "persistent unbelievers") in order to carry out his sovereign purposes (cf. Rom. 11:25–32). Marshall strikes a good balance when he says, "By this method of teaching in parables Jesus not only invited his audiences to penetrate below the surface and find the real meaning; at the same time he allowed them the opportunity—which many of them took—of turning a blind eye and a deaf ear to the real point at issue" (*Commentary on Luke*, p. 323). For an in-depth treatment of the purpose of parables in the teaching of Jesus, cf. R. Stein, *An Introduction to the Parables of Jesus* (Philadelphia: Westminster, 1981), pp. 25–35.

3. Interpretation of the parable of the sower

4:13–20

> [13]Then Jesus said to them, "Don't you understand this parable? How then will you understand any parable? [14]The farmer sows the word. [15]Some people are like seed along the path, where the word is sown. As soon as they hear it, Satan comes and takes away the word that was sown in them. [16]Others, like seed sown on rocky places, hear the word and at once receive it with joy. [17]But since they have no root, they last only a short time. When trouble or persecution comes because of the word, they quickly fall away. [18]Still others, like seed sown among thorns, hear the word; [19]but the worries of this life, the deceitfulness of wealth and the desires for other things come in and choke the word, making it unfruitful. [20]Others, like seed sown on good soil, hear the word, accept it, and produce a crop—thirty, sixty or even a hundred times what was sown.

Many modern scholars reject this passage as authentic because it allegorizes the parable. It is thought to be the work of the early church rather than the authentic teaching of Jesus. This is a good example of allowing unproved presuppositions to dominate exegesis: Jesus never used allegory; this is allegory; therefore it must not be from Jesus. The logic is sound, but the presupposition is faulty. Moule's word is to the point: "There is no evidence that Jesus never used allegory; and this is such a good and natural allegory, in which each point is itself a quite straightforward miniature parable, that Jesus may well have used it" (*Gospel of Mark*, p. 36). There is nothing in the interpretation of the parable that is contrary to the teachings of Jesus. Thus there is no reason to reject it as not having come from him.

13 There is a slight rebuke in Jesus' statement. The implication is that the meaning of the parable of the sower was clear and understandable. If the disciples could not understand this clear parable, how would they understand more obscure ones? Cranfield comments, "The blindness of men is so universal that even the disciples are not exempt from it" (*Gospel of Mark*, p. 97).

14–15 The "farmer" (v. 14), though not specifically identified here, is Christ himself; and the "word" is the word of the kingdom (cf. Matt 13:19), i.e., the coming of the reign of God in the person and work of Jesus. Whereas in the parable itself the emphasis is on the sowing of the word, in the interpretation it is on its reception. This must be understood in the historical setting of the parable in the ministry of Jesus. Jesus had already received negative responses to his proclamation (chs. 2–3). Mark clearly contrasts the belief of the disciples with "those on the outside" (4:11).

In the interpretation of the parable, Jesus describes in more detail the kind of reception the word of the kingdom receives. By some it receives a shallow reception. They are like seed sown on the hard-beaten path (v.15). Satan snatches the word from them before it has had an opportunity to take root.

16-17 Another hindrance to proper reception of the word is to be found in persecution and trials. This word of Jesus must have been particularly relevant to the Roman church and probably sounded a warning to any who, because of persecution and trials, may have been thinking of defecting from the faith. Those who do defect have no root in "themselves" (Gr.); they are "like seed sown on rocky places" (v.16). The word translated "fall away" (v.17) is *skandalizomai*. A *skandalon* was originally a stick placed in a trap or snare that, when touched by an animal, caused the trap to spring. In the NT it means "cause to stumble" or "fall away."

18-19 The third group of hearers are "like seed sown among thorns" (v.18). At first they seem to make good progress, but the word is choked out by "the worries of this life" (v.19)—a reference to whatever distracts people from the really important things—what Taylor (p. 260) calls "anxiety arising out of the times"; by "the deceitfulness of wealth"—deceitful because it gives to its possessor a false sense of security —a problem particularly evident in society today; and "the desires for other things" —an all-inclusive statement that includes everything that would choke out the sown word and prevent it from being productive.

20 Some seed does fall on good soil and is productive. The kind of person spoken of here is open and receptive to the word of the kingdom. He is neither hard, shallow, nor preoccupied. So the message gets through to him and issues forth in a productive life. In him truth becomes virtue. Moule sums up the meaning of the parable as follows:

> Words may be sound and lively enough, but it is up to each hearer to let them sink in and become fruitful. If he only hears without responding—without doing something about it and committing himself to their meaning—then the words are in danger of being lost, or of never coming to anything. The whole story thus becomes a parable about the learner's responsibility, and about the importance of learning with one's whole will and obedience, and not merely with one's head. (*Gospel of Mark*, p. 36)

Notes

19 Αἰών (*aiōn*) in αἱ μέριμναι τοῦ αἰῶνος (*hai merimnai tou aiōnos*, "the worries of this life") means "this age" and is often contrasted in the NT with the "age to come."

NIV translates ἀπάτη (*apatē*) as "deceitfulness." In Hellenistic Greek it can have the meaning "pleasure" or "delight" and may mean that here (cf. BAG, p. 81).

4. Parables of the lamp and the measure

4:21-25

21He said to them, "Do you bring in a lamp to put it under a bowl or a bed? Instead, don't you put it on its stand? 22For whatever is hidden is meant to be disclosed, and whatever is concealed is meant to be brought out into the open. [23]If anyone has ears to hear, let him hear."

[24]"Consider carefully what your hear," he continued. "With the measure you use, it will be measured to you—and even more. [25]Whoever has will be given more; whoever does not have, even what he has will be taken from him."

The sayings in vv.21-25 occur in different contexts in Matthew and Luke, but in each case they follow Mark's order. This group of sayings seems to be composite, being made up of two trilogies, both introduced by *kai elegen autois* ("and he said to them"). What the original contexts were, we do not know.

21-23 Only Mark has *erchetai* (lit., "does come") speaking of the "lamp" (*lychnos*); and he alone has the definite article (*ho*) before it (v.21). These may be keys for understanding the parable. The lamp represents Jesus who "comes," and the definite article "the" serves to identify him. As the purpose of the lamp is to be put on a lampstand and not under a bowl or a bed, so the present hiddenness of Jesus will not always be—hidden things are meant to be brought out into the open (v.22)—and God intends that one day Jesus will be manifested in all his glory, at the Parousia. But who Jesus really is, is now hidden. It is therefore of utmost importance for us to be careful hearers (v.23), i.e., to have spiritual perception.

24 The second trilogy of parables begins with an exhortation to spiritual perception. The proverb Jesus quotes occurs in other contexts (cf. Matt 7:2; Luke 6:38) with different applications. Here the meaning is that the more one listens to the word of Jesus with spiritual perception and appropriates it, the more the truth about Jesus will be revealed.

25 This proverb also occurs in other contexts (cf. Matt 13:12; 25:29; Luke 19:26). Here the meaning is that the more one appropriates the truth now, the more one will receive in the future (a reference to salvation in the End?); and whoever does not lay hold of the word now, even the little spiritual perception he has will be taken from him.

5. Parable of the secretly growing seed

4:26-29

[26]He also said, "This is what the kingdom of God is like. A man scatters seed on the ground. [27]Night and day, whether he sleeps or gets up, the seed sprouts and grows, though he does not know how. [28]All by itself the soil produces grain—first the stalk, then the head, then the full kernel in the head. [29]As soon as the grain is ripe, he puts the sickle to it, because the harvest has come."

26-29 Only Mark records this parable. Its emphasis is different from the parable of the sower. There the importance of proper soil for the growth of the seed and the success of the harvest is stressed. Here the mysterious power of the seed itself to produce a crop is emphasized.

The parable relates to the kingdom of God (v.26) and, more particularly, how that kingdom grows. All the farmer can do is plant the seed on suitable ground. He cannot make the seed grow. He does not even understand how it grows (v.27). But it does grow, and "all by itself the soil produces grain" (v.28). The point of the parable is as follows: "As seedtime is followed in due time by harvest, so will the present hiddenness and ambiguousness of the kingdom of God be succeeded by its glorious manifestation" (Cranfield, *Gospel of Mark*, p. 168).

A similar emphasis is suggested by J. Jeremias:

> The fruit is the *result* of the seed; the end is implicit in the beginning. The infinitely great is already active in the infinitely small. In the present, and indeed in secret, the event is already in motion. . . . Those to whom it has been given to understand the mystery of the Kingdom (Mark 4:11) see already in its hidden and insignificant beginnings the coming kingdom of God. (*The Parables of Jesus* [London: SCM, 1963], pp. 152–53; emphasis his).

The last part of the parable calls to mind Joel 3:13. The harvest spoken of (v.29) is the eschatological judgment.

6. *Parable of the mustard seed*

4:30–32

30Again he said, "What shall we say the kingdom of God is like, or what parable shall we use to describe it? 31It is like a mustard seed, which is the smallest seed you plant in the ground. 32Yet when planted, it grows and becomes the largest of all garden plants, with such big branches that the birds of the air can perch in its shade."

30–32 This is the third and last of the parables about the seed sown. The mustard seed is "the smallest seed you plant in the ground" (v.31). NIV has interpreted the Greek, which really reads "which is smaller than any seed in the ground at its sowing" (NEB). The mustard seed was proverbial for its smallness (cf. SBK, 1:669), but it is not in fact the smallest known seed (e.g., the seed of the black orchid is smaller). Jesus obviously was not giving a lesson in botany. The mustard seed was the smallest seed his audience was familiar with. When grown, it becomes a huge treelike shrub (v.32). I myself have seen one about ten feet high, in front of the monastery on top of Mount Tabor, and another almost that size, near the Pool of Bethesda in Jerusalem.

The main point of the parable is that the kingdom of God (v.30) is like what happens to the mustard seed. It has insignificant and weak beginnings, but a day will come when it will be great and powerful. It is doubtful whether the detail in the parable about the birds taking shelter in the branches of the tree has any significance, though some interpreters see in it a mention of the inclusion of the Gentiles in the kingdom. Nineham (p. 144) makes a general practical application of the truth the parable teaches: "The example of the mustard seed should prevent us from judging the significance of results by the size of the beginnings."

7. *Summary statement on parables*

4:33–34

33With many similar parables Jesus spoke the word to them, as much as they could understand. 34He did not say anything to them without using a parable. But when he was alone with his own disciples, he explained everything.

33–34 Mark ends this section with its collection of parables with a statement about Jesus' use of them. Parables (here the word has its broad meaning to include similitudes, riddles, etc.) constituted one of Jesus' primary methods of speaking the word (i.e., the word of the kingdom—God's reign revealed in Jesus himself) to "them"— the crowd (v.33). He did this in order to help them understand by means of a veiled confrontation with the truth. It was his gracious means to stimulate their thinking and awaken their spiritual perception. The crowd was not ready for a direct revelation of the truth. In contrast, when Jesus was alone with his disciples (v.34), he could speak more directly with them; but even they needed his explanation to understand.

E. *Triumph Over Hostile Powers* (4:35–5:43)

1. *Calming the storm*

4:35–41

35That day when evening came, he said to his disciples, "Let us go over to the other side." 36Leaving the crowd behind, they took him along, just as he was, in the boat. There were also other boats with him. 37A furious squall came up, and the waves broke over the boat, so that it was nearly swamped. 38Jesus was in the stern, sleeping on a cushion. The disciples woke him and said to him, "Teacher, don't you care if we drown?"

39He got up, rebuked the wind and said to the waves, "Quiet! Be still!" Then the wind died down and it was completely calm.

40He said to his disciples, "Why are you so afraid? Do you still have no faith?"

41They were terrified and asked each other, "Who is this? Even the wind and the waves obey him!"

The calming of the storm on the Lake of Galilee is a classic example of a nature miracle. Miracles of this kind seem to present the greatest problem to contemporary man. The NT, however, makes clear that Jesus Christ is not only Lord over his church but also Lord of all creation. "For by him all things were created: things in heaven and on earth, visible and invisible, whether thrones or powers or rulers or authorities; all things were created by him and for him"(Col 1:16). The Creator-Lord also controls what he has created. "He is before all things, and in him all things hold together" (Col 1:17). It is completely inadequate to explain this miracle of the sovereign Lord by coincidence or to relegate it to myth or imagination. One's conclusion about the historicity of this and similar stories in the Gospels will inevitably depend on one's christology. If Jesus was, as he claimed to be, the strong Son of God, a miracle of this kind is not inconsistent with that claim. If, on the other hand, he was less than God, there is a serious problem.

35–36 Note the details in the story: the mention of the time of day (v.35), the reference to Jesus "just as he was" (v.36), the statement about the "other boats," the position of Jesus in the boat (v.38), the mention of the cushion, the sharp rebuke made by the disciples, and their terror and bewilderment. Taken together these suggest the report of an eyewitness.

Jesus had been teaching the people from a boat pushed out from the shore a short distance (4:1). Evening had come; so Jesus decided to go over to the other side of the lake (v.35). Mark mentions no reason for this decision. Perhaps Jesus simply wanted to escape from the crowds for a little while and renew his strength. The disciples responded to Jesus' request by taking Jesus "just as he was, in the boat" (v.36). This presumably means "without going to shore." That is, Jesus wanted to go directly to the other side of the lake in the same boat he had been teaching the people from and without the delay his first going ashore might have caused.

The mention of "other boats with him" (v.36) seems to be a pointless detail and strongly suggests an eyewitness account. We are not told what happened to the other boats. Perhaps they were lost in the storm or driven back to the western shore of the lake.

37 The geographic location of the Sea of Galilee makes it particularly susceptible to sudden, violent storms. It is situated in a basin surrounded by mountains. Though at night and in the early morning the sea is usually calm, when storms come at those times, they are all the more treacherous. The storm is described as a "furious squall" (*lailaps megalē anemou*) that was driving the waves into the boat so that it was being swamped. Smith's description of the Sea of Galilee's susceptibility to storms is illuminating: "The atmosphere, for the most part, hangs still and heavy, but the cold currents, as they pass from the west, are sucked down in vortices of air, or by the narrow gorges that break upon the lake. Then arise those sudden storms for which the region is notorious" (G.A. Smith, *The Historical Geography of the Holy Land* [New York: Armstrong and Son, 1909], pp. 441–42).

38 Jesus, tired from a long day's teaching, was in the stern of the boat, asleep on a "cushion" (*proskephalaion*). Lagrange (p. 231) says that "in these boats, which will no doubt always have been the same, the place for any distinguished stranger is on the little seat placed at the stern, where a carpet or cushions are arranged." The cushion (the definite article is used) was apparently the only one on board, and Jesus used it as a pillow for his head. This is the only place in the Gospels where Jesus is said to have slept; but he did, of course, get tired and need sleep like any other man. He must have been very tired to have slept through such a violent storm.

The disciples' rebuke of Jesus—"Teacher, are we to drown for all you care?" (Mof)—indicates that they did not know who he really was. Such a rebuke of the Son of God was entirely inappropriate. Both Matthew and Luke eliminate the rebuke. "The rudeness of the Mk form, which is no doubt more original, is an eloquent pointer to the messianic veiledness—the Son of God subject to the rudeness of men" (Cranfield, *Gospel of Mark*, p. 174).

39–40 Jesus rebuked the wind and spoke to the waves. The result was that "the wind died down and it was completely calm" (v.39). The sovereign Lord spoke and his creation immediately responded. Mark alone records the words Jesus used.

Jesus also rebuked his disciples for their lack of faith (v.40). The preferred reading (*oupō*, "not yet"; NIV, "still") indicates that Jesus had expected them by this time to have demonstrated more mature faith. "Faith" here means faith in God's saving power as it is present and active in the person of Jesus. This is the first of several rebukes of the disciples by Jesus for their lack of understanding and faith (cf. 7:18; 8:17–18, 21, 32–33; 9:19).

41 "Were terrified" describes the feeling of awe that came over the disciples as the result of Jesus' mighty act. There was something about him revealed to them on this occasion that they had not experienced before. Thus they raised the rhetorical question "Who is this? Even the wind and the waves obey him!" The implied answer is "He is the strong Son of God."

It is not difficult to imagine what effect this story had on the members of the persecuted Roman church Mark wrote his Gospel for. It assured them that the strong Son of God would go with them into the storm of opposition and trial.

Notes

39 It has often been pointed out that the verbs ἐπιτιμᾶν (*epitiman*, "to rebuke") and φιμοῦν (*phimoun*, "to muzzle") are also found in the description of the exorcism of Mark 1:25. Lane (p. 177) sees in the use of these words evidence of "cosmic overtones in Mark's Gospel. The raging storm is an evil "force" threatening Jesus and his disciples. Jesus muzzled it by his sovereign word of authority.

2. *Healing the demon-possessed man*

5:1–20

¹They went across the lake to the region of the Gerasenes. ²When Jesus got out of the boat, a man with an evil spirit came from the tombs to meet him. ³This man lived in the tombs, and no one could bind him any more, not even with a chain. ⁴For he had often been chained hand and foot, but he tore the chains apart and broke the irons on his feet. No one was strong enough to subdue him. ⁵Night and day among the tombs and in the hills he would cry out and cut himself with stones.

⁶When he saw Jesus from a distance, he ran and fell on his knees in front of him. ⁷He shouted at the top of his voice, "What do you want with me, Jesus, Son of the Most High God? Swear to God that you won't torture me!" ⁸For Jesus had said to him, "Come out of this man, you evil spirit!"

⁹Then Jesus asked him, "What is your name?"

"My name is Legion," he replied, "for we are many." ¹⁰And he begged Jesus again and again not to send them out of the area.

¹¹A large herd of pigs was feeding on the nearby hillside. ¹²The demons begged Jesus, "Send us among the pigs; allow us to go into them." ¹³He gave them permission, and the evil spirits came out and went into the pigs. The herd, about two thousand in number, rushed down the steep bank into the lake and were drowned.

¹⁴Those tending the pigs ran off and reported this in the town and countryside, and the people went out to see what had happened. ¹⁵When they came to Jesus, they saw the man who had been possessed by the legion of demons, sitting there, dressed and in his right mind; and they were afraid. ¹⁶Those who had seen it told the people what had happened to the demon-possessed man—and told about the pigs as well. ¹⁷Then the people began to plead with Jesus to leave their region.

¹⁸As Jesus was getting into the boat, the man who had been demon-possessed begged to go with him. ¹⁹Jesus did not let him, but said, "Go home to your family and tell them how much the Lord has done for you, and how he has had mercy on you." ²⁰So the man went away and began to tell in the Decapolis how much Jesus had done for him. And all the people were amazed.

1 Jesus had demonstrated his power over the forces of nature by stilling the winds and the waves. Now he demonstrates his power over the forces of evil by casting out demons from a possessed man. The two stories go together. They reveal that Jesus is truly divine.

"Across the lake" means on the eastern side. That the population of this region was largely Gentile is shown by the name Decapolis (v.20) and the presence of a large herd of pigs, animals considered unclean by Jews and therefore unfit to eat (Lev 11:7–8).

The name of the place where the miracle was done is disputed. The correct reading in Mark is "the region of the Gerasenes" (so NIV). The textual variants (cf. Notes) arose because Gerasa, located about thirty miles southeast of the lake, seemed too far removed. However, Mark says the "region" of the Gerasenes, and this apparently included the entire district extending down from the city to the lake. Another possibility is that Gerasa is to be identified with the ruins of Kersa (Koursi), a village on the eastern shore. Not far from this site there is a cliff within forty meters of the shore and some old tombs.

2 From this verse it would appear that Jesus, on stepping out of the boat, was immediately confronted by the possessed man. Verse 6 clarifies the situation. The man actually saw Jesus from a distance and came running to him. Since it was already evening (cf. 4:35) when they started across the lake, by the time they reached the other side it was probably dark.

3–5 The possessed man lived in the tombs (v.3). Often in Palestine people were buried in natural caves or in tombs cut out of the limestone rock. These provided good shelter for anyone desiring to live in them. It was a natural place for a possessed man to dwell because of the popular belief that tombs were the favorite haunts of demons. This wretched man had probably been driven from ordinary society into the tombs. Efforts had been made to control him, but without success. Although bound "hand and foot," he had broken the chains; and no one was strong enough to subdue him (v.4). Verses 3–5 "give a vivid picture of the manic stage of a manic depressive psychosis" (Johnson, p. 101).

6 NIV correctly translates *prosekynēsen autō* as "fell on his knees in front of him" rather than "worshipped" (KJV). It was an act of homage rather than worship. The demon shows respect because he recognizes that he is confronted with one greatly superior to him.

7–8 The demon addresses Jesus (v.7) by shouting "at the top of his voice." His cry, "What do you want with me?" was a way of saying, "What have we in common?" The demon recognizes that he is in the presence of one who threatened his very existence. In addressing Jesus the demon uses his personal name. Had he heard it from the lips of the disciples? Or had Jesus' fame already spread into this territory? The demon also uses the title "Son of the Most High God," a title that implies that the demon recognized Jesus' deity. The demon, however, uses the title, not to express his belief in the dignity of Jesus, but in the hope of controlling him (cf. Mark 1:24). The demon fears that he will be exorcised; so he says to Jesus, "Swear to God that you won't torture me." The tormentor now changes his role; he pleads exemption from torment. This may be a reference to eschatological punishment (cf. 1:24: "Have you come to destroy us?").

Verse 8 seems to be an explanatory statement by Mark to make clear why the demon was acting so excitedly. Jesus had ordered him to come out of the man. Understood this way, there is no need to suggest that v.8 originally preceded v.7, perhaps in place of v.6, as does O. Bauernfeind (*Die Worte der Dämonen im Markusevangelium* [Stuttgart, 1927], pp. 48–49).

9 To Jesus' inquiry about his name, the demoniac replied, "Legion." The significance of his name is not clear. Perhaps he had had an unfortunate experience with a Roman legion and this had caused his madness. Or perhaps he felt as if he was possessed by thousands of demons (a legion consisted of over six thousand men). Perhaps the many demons in him combined to form one aggregate force, thus the name "Legion" (SBK, 2:9). Jesus may have asked him his name to help him establish an identity apart from the demons. So fully did they possess the man that he seemed to be unable to act apart from them.

10 Both the singular and the plural occur here: "He begged . . . not to send them." This is probably Mark's way of indicating that the demons are speaking through the lips of the demoniac. What they request is that they not be sent "out of the area." In Luke (8:31) the request is that they not be sent into the Abyss (Rev 20:1–3), the place of confinement before judgment.

11–13 The presence of a large herd of swine (v.11) in the Decapolis is not surprising. This region, on the eastern shore of the Sea of Galilee, was largely Gentile. Mark's account shows that what caused the stampede of the pigs (v.13b) was the entrance of the demons into them (vv.12–13a). The demons were bent on destroying. Not having been able to destroy the man, they destroyed the pigs. Demons are emissaries of Satan, the Destroyer. But why did Jesus, having exorcised the demons, allow them to enter the pigs, an act that ultimately resulted in the destruction of the entire herd? A tentative answer is that Jesus wanted to give tangible evidence to the man and to the people that the demons had actually left him and that their purpose had been to destroy him even as they destroyed the pigs.

14–15 The result of the stampede and destruction of the pigs was the flight of the herdsman to "the town" (probably the chief town of the district) and "countryside" to tell what had happened (v.14). This brought the people to the scene of the miracle. When they arrived, they could scarcely believe their eyes! The man who had been known as "crazy," who had been so violent that he could not even be controlled by chains, they saw now sitting quietly (v.15). Before he had roamed naked through the tombs (cf. Luke 8:27); now he was "dressed." Before he had been possessed by powerful evil forces; now he was in his "right mind." Calvin (2:436) makes a pointed application: "Though we are not tortured by the devil [I wonder?], yet he holds us as his slaves, till the Son of God delivers us from his tyranny. Naked, torn, and disfigured, we wander about, till he restores us to soundness of mind."

Instead of rejoicing because of the marvelous deliverance of the man from his pathetic state, the people "were afraid." Their fear was no doubt caused by the presence of one with power to perform such a miracle.

16–17 When those who had been eyewitnesses to the event reported what had happened (v.16), both to the man and to the pigs, the people decided it was time for Jesus to leave their region (v.17). In fact, they pleaded with him to leave. Why? They were afraid (v.15). They recognized that a mighty force was at work in Jesus that they could neither understand nor control. If it destroyed an entire herd of pigs, might not this power strike again with even more serious consequences? Fear, ignorance, and selfishness because of the material loss through the destruction of the pigs dominated their considerations rather than compassion for the former demoniac. So they asked Jesus to leave, and he did. He does not stay where he is not wanted.

18–19 Jesus had come to the east side of the lake by boat (5:2). Now he was about to return the same way. The man who had been possessed wanted to go with him (v.18)—a perfectly natural reaction. He was eager for Jesus' company, for no one had ever showed him such love and compassion. But our Lord did not allow it. Instead he gave him the much more difficult task of returning home to his family to bear testimony to what Jesus in his mercy had done for him (v.19). The command "Tell them how much the Lord has done for you" is in marked contrast to Jesus' instructions to the cleansed leper in 1:44—"See that you don't tell this to anyone." This is probably because in the case of the demoniac Jesus was in Gentile territory where there would be little danger that popular messianic ideas about him might be circulated. It was in Jewish territory that this possibility was always present. Or perhaps in the case of this man, Jesus realized that the true nature of his person and mission was perceived; therefore this man could be trusted to convey to others the truth about Jesus.

20 The man obeyed without argument and began to bear testimony of what "Jesus had done for him." The Decapolis was a league of ten originally free Greek cities located (except Scythopolis) on the east of the Sea of Galilee and the Jordan River. They had been organized on the Greek model during the Seleucid period, brought under Hasmonean control by John Hyrcanus, and liberated by the Roman general Pompey. These cities heard the testimony of the former demoniac and responded with amazement. Anderson (p. 150) says that Mark may have regarded this incident "as the inauguration of the mission to the Gentiles (whereas foreigners from beyond Jordan came to him (Mark 3:8), it is only now Jesus has moved out into their territory (cf. 5:1)."

Notes

1 There are three different readings of the place name: Γερασηνῶν (Gerasēnōn, "Gerasenes"), original in Mark; Γαδαρηνῶν (Gadarēnōn, "Gadarenes"), found in Matthew; Γεργεσηνῶν (Gergesēnōn, "Gergasenes"), a reading attributable to Origen. "The textual variations are due to the fact that Gerasa (30 miles to the S.E.) and Gadara (6 miles to the S.E.) are too far from the lake, and to the necessity of finding a site where the mountains run down steeply into the lake" (Taylor, p. 278).

3. *Jairus's plea in behalf of his daughter*

5:21-24

> 21When Jesus had again crossed over by boat to the other side of the lake, a large crowd gathered around him while he was by the lake. 22Then one of the synagogue rulers, named Jairus, came there. Seeing Jesus, he fell at his feet 23and pleaded earnestly with him, "My little daughter is dying. Please come and put your hands on her so that she will be healed and live." 24So Jesus went with him.
> A large crowd followed and pressed around him.

It is possible that Mark brought together the stories of the woman with the hemorrhage and the healing of Jairus's daughter with the story of the healing of the demoniac because they all have to do with ritual uncleanness. According to Jewish law contact with graves, blood, or death made one ceremonially unclean.

The account of the healing of the woman with a hemorrhage occurs within the story of the healing of Jarius's daughter. Both Cranfield (p. 182) and Taylor (p. 289) hold that the events actually occurred in the sequence in which Mark has them. But in view of the fact that Mark elsewhere uses the method of insertion (cf. 3:22-30; 6:14-29; 11:15-19) and that he frequently seems more interested in theology than in chronology, thematic interests here probably have determined the sequence of events (cf. Anderson, p. 151; Lane, p. 189). This seems to be a better solution than to understand the sandwiching of the two narratives as an artificial intercalation to allow for the passage of time or to heighten the suspense. Both incidents read like eyewitness accounts.

21 Again the scene shifts. Jesus has returned to the west side of the lake. On the east side he had been asked to leave. Here great crowds greeted him. The specific place where the incident occurred is not given, but most commentators conjecture that it was near Capernaum.

22-24 Jesus was probably busy teaching when he was interrupted by the plea of "one of the synagogue rulers" (v.22). This does not mean that Jairus was one of several rulers in a particular synagogue (though some synagogues did have more than one; cf. Acts 13:15), but that he belonged to that particular group called "synagogue rulers." These were laymen whose responsibilities were administrative, not priestly, and included such things as looking after the building and supervising the worship. Sometimes the title was honorary, given to prominent members of the congregation with no administrative duties attached. At Antioch Paul and Barnabas were invited by the synagogue rulers to participate in the service (Acts 13:15). Jairus's need was so urgent that he jettisoned all dignity and pride, fell at Jesus' feet, and begged for help (v.23). Jairus had apparently heard about Jesus and believed that he could heal his child. Mark records no oral reply by Jesus to Jairus's request. Here Jesus does not speak; he acts. He set out with Jairus to go to the child, and a large crowd—probably of curiosity seekers—followed along (v.24).

4. *Healing a woman with a hemorrhage*

5:25-34

> 25And a woman was there who had been subject to bleeding for twelve years.
> 26She had suffered a great deal under the care of many doctors and had spent all

she had, yet instead of getting better she grew worse. ²⁷When she heard about Jesus, she came up behind him in the crowd and touched his cloak, ²⁸because she thought, "If I just touch his clothes, I will be healed." ²⁹Immediately her bleeding stopped and she felt in her body that she was freed from her suffering.

³⁰At once Jesus realized that power had gone out from him. He turned around in the crowd and asked, "Who touched my clothes?"

³¹"You see the people crowding against you," his disciples answered, "and yet you can ask, 'Who touched me?' "

³²But Jesus kept looking around to see who had done it. ³³Then the woman, knowing what had happened to her, came and fell at his feet and, trembling with fear, told him the whole truth. ³⁴He said to her, "Daughter, your faith has healed you. Go in peace and be freed from your suffering."

25-26 The story of the healing of the woman with a hemorrhage is sandwiched between the report of Jairus's daughter's illness and Jesus' action in raising her to life. The precise nature of the woman's ailment is not stated. Probably some sort of uterine disease caused the bleeding that had persisted for twelve years (v.25). Luke (8:43) says of her condition that "no one could heal her." Mark includes vivid details: she had suffered much, had been treated by many doctors, had spent all she had; and, instead of getting better, her condition had gotten worse (v.26). Luke understandably tones down this verse.

27-29 The reports the woman had heard about Jesus' healings and her belief that he could help her led her to come to him. But her faith seemed to be mixed with a measure of superstition. She apparently shared the belief, common in her day, that the power of a person was transmitted to his clothing (v.27). So she went into the crowd and, because of her ceremonial uncleanness, approached Jesus surreptitiously from the rear. She thought, If I just touch his clothes, I will be healed (v.28). At once her faith, even though mixed with superstition, was rewarded. The bleeding was stopped, and she felt a soundness in her body that assured her that she had been healed (v.29).

30-32 Not only had something happened to the woman when she touched Jesus' clothes, he too was aware that something had happened to him (v.30). Healing energy had gone out of him for someone's benefit; and, insisting on knowing who it was, he asked, "Who touched my clothes?" To his disciples this seemed like a stupid question in view of the crush of the crowd all about him (v.31). Both Matthew and Luke soften the harshness of the disciples' response to Jesus—strong evidence of the historicity of Mark's account. The lack of understanding on the part of Christ's disciples and their harsh reply may have been caused by their concern to get Jesus to Jairus's daughter where a real emergency existed. The question raised by Jesus would only cause delay. But Jesus' spiritual sensitivity told him that someone had touched his clothes, and he "kept looking around" to find who it was (v.32). His purpose was not to rebuke her but to make personal contact with her. She needed to know that it was her faith, not her superstitious belief, that had caused God to heal her.

33-34 The woman responded to Jesus' searching eyes. She knew what had happened to her; and, though "trembling with fear," she came forward, prostrated herself before Jesus, and "told him the whole truth" (v.33). This must have taken great courage, especially since she was regarded as ceremonially unclean. Jesus addressed her as "daughter" (v.34)—the only occurrence in the Gospels of Jesus' addressing a woman by that word. He made clear to her that it was her faith (in Jesus, or God) that had healed her. The word translated "healed" is *sesōken* ("saved"). Here both physical healing and theological salvation are in mind. In Mark's Gospel the two go closely together (cf. 2:1–12).

The phrase "Go in peace" is a traditional Jewish formula of leave-taking (cf. *šālôm*, "shalom" [cf. Judg 18:6; 1 Sam 1:17]). The word *peace* here "means not just freedom from inward anxiety, but that *wholeness* or *completeness* of life that comes from being brought into a right relationship with God" (Anderson, p. 154, italics his; cf. also TDNT, II: 911).

By Jesus' last statement to the woman—"be freed from your suffering"—he actively participated in her healing and confirmed God's will to make her well.

5. Raising Jairus's daughter

5:35–43

> 35While Jesus was still speaking, some men came from the house of Jairus, the synagogue ruler. "Your daughter is dead," they said. "Why bother the teacher any more?"
> 36Ignoring what they said, Jesus told the synagogue ruler, "Don't be afraid; just believe."
> 37He did not let anyone follow him except Peter, James and John the brother of James. 38When they came to the home of the synagogue ruler, Jesus saw a commotion, with people crying and wailing loudly. 39He went in and said to them, "Why all this commotion and wailing? The child is not dead but asleep." 40But they laughed at him.
> After he put them all out, he took the child's father and mother and the disciples who were with him, and went in where the child was. 41He took her by the hand and said to her, *"Talitha koum!"* (which means, "Little girl, I say to you, get up!"). 42Immediately the girl stood up and walked around (she was twelve years old). At this they were completely astonished. 43He gave strict orders not to let anyone know about this, and told them to give her something to eat.

35–37 While Jesus was still speaking to the woman, "some men" brought Jairus the news of the death of his daughter (v.35). Since death is final, they advised him not to bother Jesus any longer. But Jesus ignored what the messengers said (v.36). In an effort to encourage Jairus, Jesus turned to him and said, "Don't be afraid; just believe." This word of assurance must have been just what he needed. He in no way tried to dissuade Jesus from resuming his journey to the child's bedside. At this point Jesus decided to separate himself from the crowd following him (v.37). A momentous miracle was about to take place, and he would have only a chosen few witness it. Peter, James, and John had a particularly close relationship to Jesus. This, no doubt, is why he selected them to see this miracle.

38 When Jesus arrived at Jairus's house, a great commotion was taking place. Swete (p. 107) puts it succinctly: "The Lord has dismissed one crowd only to find the house occupied by another." As was the custom, professional mourners had been secured; and they were already at work. "The lamentations consisted of choral song or antiphony, accompanied by hand-clapping" (Van der Loos, *Miracles of Jesus*, p. 568; cf. SBK, 1:521ff.). Since Jairus occupied a prominent position in the Jewish community, the number of professional mourners was large. So along with members of his family, they were making a great uproar.

39–40 On entering the house, Jesus asked why they were making such a commotion since the child was not dead but only asleep (v.39). On the surface this statement is enigmatic. It could mean that she had slipped into a comatose state. From this he would awake her. Or it could be Jesus' way of indicating that he proposed to bring her back from the dead. Since her death was not final, he spoke of it as sleep. Luke's account clearly indicates that Jesus resurrected the girl from the dead: "Her spirit returned, and at once she stood up" (Luke 8:55). A careful reading of the text reveals that Mark too "intended his account to be understood in the same way" (Lane, p. 197; cf. Taylor, p. 295).

The mourners, however, misunderstood Jesus' reference to sleeping to mean that she was not really dead. So they laughed him to scorn (v.40). Tears were quickly changed to laughter—a clear indication of the superficiality of the grief of the professional mourners. Jesus did not want any noisy crowd present when he performed this stupendous miracle; so he put the mourners out. Their lack of sensitivity disqualified them from being present at such a beautiful event. Only Jesus' three most intimate disciples and the mother and father were allowed to enter the room where the dead child lay.

41 Jesus stood by the side of the child, took her hand, and spoke the Aramaic words *"Talitha koum,"* which Mark conveniently translates for his Gentile readers: "Little girl, I say to you, get up!" Mark is the only Evangelist who preserves the original Aramaic here. Aramaic was the language of Palestine in the first century A.D. and was probably the language Jesus and his disciples normally spoke. However, since they came from Galilee, which was surrounded by the Gentile Decapolis and by Syrian Phoenicia, it seems highly likely that they also knew Greek and on occasion spoke Greek. The suggestion that the original Aramaic words were preserved because Mark wanted to provide Christian healers with certain verbal prescriptions in the original language is farfetched and must be rejected. Mark usually uses foreign words in nonmiracle story contexts (cf. 3:17; 7:11; 11:9; 14:36; 15:22, 34). The only exceptions are this passage and 7:34 (the healing of the deaf mute).

42–43 The young girl (Mark tells us she was twelve years old) responded immediately to Jesus' words (v.42). She not only stood up, she began to walk around. "Strength returned as well as life" (Swete, p. 109). The reaction of the five witnesses to the miracle (Peter, James, John, and the parents) was one of complete amazement.

Jesus gave two orders to the witnesses (v.43). First, they were not to reveal the facts about the miracle. It has been suggested that since this was impossible (too many people had known of the death of the girl, and it was not likely that her parents could hide her), we have here an example of the artificiality of the Markan messianic-secret motif. Cranfield rightly replies that Jesus did not think that the miracle could be kept "absolutely private, but simply that he wanted it kept as private as possible—no one was to know about it who need not. There was at least a chance of avoiding unnecessary publicity" (*Gospel of Mark*, p. 191). Jesus' messianic dignity is revealed to some (the five witnesses to the miracle) who can be entrusted with it but veiled to those (like the raucous mourners) who cannot. Jesus' second order was that they should give the girl something to eat—beautiful evidence of his concern for man's ordinary needs.

Ellis sums up the theological meaning of this miracle: "Like its younger brother, sickness, death is an enemy. But it must yield to the powers of the messianic kingdom present in Jesus. In the presence of Christ, death becomes a 'sleeping.' . . . 'Finis' is transformed into prelude. Until the *parousia* its sting remains, but its ultimate threat is broken. If we 'believe,' we need not live in dread: 'fear not!' " (E. Earle Ellis, *The Gospel of Luke*, NCB [Greenwood, S.C.: Attic, 1966], p. 134).

Notes

---

39 The word καθεύδω (*katheudō*) has three meanings in the NT: "sleep" in the literal sense (cf. Matt 8:24; 13:25; 25:5; 26:40, 43, 45; Mark 4:27, 38; 13:36; 14:37, 40–41; Luke 22:46; 1 Thess 5:7); "sleep" in the figurative sense (1 Thess 5:6); and "sleep" in the sense of death (1 Thess 5:10). It is in the last sense that it is used here. Jesus says that she is not dead (in the sense that she will not be brought back to life), but she is asleep (dead, but only briefly, because she is soon to be raised to life).

F. Rejection at Nazareth

6:1–6a

[1]Jesus left there and went to his hometown, accompanied by his disciples. [2]When the Sabbath came, he began to teach in the synagogue, and many who heard him were amazed.

"Where did this man get these things?" they asked. "What's this wisdom that has been given him, that he even does miracles! [3]Isn't this the carpenter? Isn't this Mary's son and the brother of James, Joseph, Judas and Simon? Aren't his sisters here with us?" And they took offense at him.

[4]Jesus said to them, "Only in his hometown, among his relatives and in his own house is a prophet without honor." [5]He could not do any miracles there, except lay his hands on a few sick people and heal them. [6]And he was amazed at their lack of faith.

1 If Capernaum was the scene of the healing of Jairus's daughter, the movement of Jesus described here was to the southwest through the hill country of Galilee. Nazareth is not specifically mentioned here or in Matthew, but it is obviously meant. The Greek word *patris* usually means "home country" but may also be used of one's hometown. That Jesus was considered by the Galileans as a Nazarene is implied by Mark 1:9, 24; John 1:46. Even though he was born in Bethlehem, since his family lived in Nazareth and he had been brought up there, it was natural to regard it as his hometown. The incident Mark records here should not be thought of as a personal visit by Jesus to his family. Rather, he comes as a rabbi accompanied by his disciples, "a detail dropped in Mt., but important for Mark, because in this part of the gospel he is concerned with their training" (Cranfield, *Gospel of Mark*, p. 193).

2 On the Sabbath, Jesus went into the synagogue and began to teach. (On the custom that allowed visiting teachers to give the scriptural exposition in the synagogue, see comment at 1:21.) This probably was the first time his fellow townsmen had actually heard Jesus teach, and many of them were amazed. But with some of them, there was an undercurrent of doubt as their questions imply: "Where did this man get these things?" and "What's this wisdom that has been given him, that he even does miracles!" What was the source of his teaching and his miracles? They were either from God or from Satan. Which? Although we do not know of any miracles Jesus had done in Nazareth, his reputation as a miracle-worker had been spread abroad.

3 The hostility of Jesus' townspeople toward him comes out more clearly in the rhetorical questions in this verse. "Isn't this the carpenter?" i.e., Isn't he just a common ordinary fellow who makes his living with his hands like the rest of us? How is it that he's parading as a rabbi and miracle-worker? The second question, "Isn't this Mary's son?" seems also to be derogatory since it was not customary among Jews to describe a man as the son of his mother even when the father was not alive (cf. Taylor, pp. 299–300). Behind this question may be the rumor, circulated during Jesus' lifetime, that he was illegitimate (cf. John 4:41; 9:29; SBK, 1:39–43; Origen *Contra Celsum* 1. 28).

The brothers and sisters of Jesus mentioned here were not cousins (Jerome's view) or Joseph's children by a previous marriage (Epiphanius's view). Both Jerome and Epiphanius were greatly influenced by the Roman Catholic dogma of the perpetual virginity of Mary (Jerome's theory also made possible the virginity of Joseph!). But neither Epiphanius's nor Jerome's view finds support in Scripture. The children mentioned here were more probably children born to Mary and Joseph according to natural biological processes subsequent to the virgin birth of Jesus (Helvidius's view). James was probably the oldest and was certainly the best known of Jesus' brothers. He was closely identified with the church of Jerusalem (Acts 12:17; 15:13; 21:18; 1 Cor 15:7; Gal 1:19; 2:9, 12) and was probably the author of the Epistle of James (James 1:1). Both Josephus (Antiq. XX, 200 [ix.1]) and Eusebius (*Ecclesiastical History* 2.33) preserve accounts of his violent death. Jude was probably the author of the Book of Jude. We know nothing of Joseph and Simon.

The word translated "they took offense" is from *skandalizomai*, from which the English word "scandal" is derived. The difficulty the word presents is reflected in the versions: "are repelled" (Mof); "fall away" (RSV); "stumble" (ASV); "fell foul of him" (NEB). "The idea conveyed by the Greek verb is that of being offended and repelled to the point of abandoning (whether temporarily or permanently, the word does not specify) belief in the Word (cf. Lk 8:13) or one's relation with Jesus (14:27, 29)" (Bratcher and Nida, pp. 139–40).

4 Jesus responded to the doubts raised about the legitimacy of his teaching and his miracles by a proverb that has parallels in both Jewish and Greek literature. One of these proverbs states the principle on which all of them are based: Familiarity breeds contempt. The basic difference between Jesus' proverb and the Jewish and Greek ones is his use of the word "prophet" (here it probably means "inspired teacher"). This word is not found in any of the Jewish or pagan proverbs. The people of Nazareth were incapable of appreciating who Jesus was because, like Jesus' own family, they identified him with themselves so closely.

5–6a Verse 5 opens with "one of the boldest statements in the Gospels, since it mentions something that Jesus could not do" (Taylor, p. 301). It was not, of course, that he did not have the power to do more miracles than he did at Nazareth. The inability was related to the moral situation. In the climate of unbelief he chose not to exercise his miraculous power. One of the great emphases of Mark's Gospel is that Jesus performs his miracles in response to faith.

Jesus expressed amazement at their lack of faith (v.6a). Apparently he did not expect such a response from his neighbors. It was their deep lack of faith that amazed him. It is significant that only here in Mark's Gospel is amazement ascribed to Jesus.

Notes

3 Matthew calls Jesus "the carpenter's son" (13:55), but only Mark says he was a "carpenter" (τέκτων, *tektōn*). The variant reading "son of a carpenter" is an obvious assimilation to Matthew. Origen (*Contra Celsum* 6.36) says that nowhere in the Gospels current in his day is Jesus called a carpenter. This statement apparently was due to either (1) a lapse of memory or (2) his acceptance of a Markan text assimilated to Matthew (probably because he preferred not to think of the Son of God as involved in so menial an occupation). The word *tektōn* can be used of masons or smiths but seems to have its usual meaning "carpenter" here.

G. *Sending Out the Twelve*

6:6b–13

> Then Jesus went around teaching from village to village. [7]Calling the Twelve to him, he sent them out two by two and gave them authority over evil spirits.
> [8]These were his instructions: "Take nothing for the journey except a staff—no bread, no bag, no money in your belts. [9]Wear sandals but not an extra tunic. [10]Whenever you enter a house, stay there until you leave that town. [11]And if any place will not welcome you or listen to you, shake the dust off your feet when you leave, as a testimony against them."
> [12]They went out and preached that people should repent. [13]They drove out many demons and anointed many sick people with oil and healed them.

6b There is some question whether 6b should go with vv.1–6 or vv.7–13. If with the former, it means that as a result of his rejection at Nazareth, Jesus decided to inaugurate a village ministry. If, with the latter, it was as a result of the village ministry that he decided to send out the Twelve, presumably to increase his own ministry through them. NIV and NEB take v.6b with vv.7–13. RSV is noncommittal; it sets off the verse by itself.

7 Jesus had carefully prepared his disciples for this mission. He had called them with the promise "I will make you fishers of men" (1:17). He had withdrawn on several occasions to give them special attention (3:7, 13; 4:10). And, all the while they had been with him, they had witnessed his mighty acts and had listened to his wise words. Now it was time for them to be sent out (cf. 3:14–15: "that he might send them out to preach and to have authority to drive out demons").

The verb translated "sent" is *apostellein* and carries with it the idea of official representation. "Jesus authorized the disciples to be his delegates with respect to both word and power. Their message and deeds were to be an extension of his own" (Lane, p. 206). The Twelve were sent "two by two," apparently a Jewish custom (cf. Mark 11:1; 14:13; Acts 13:2, 4; 16:40). The purpose of their going in pairs was so that the truthfulness of their testimony about Jesus might be established "on the testimony of two or three witnesses" (Deut 17:6).

"Authority over evil spirits" was a part of the Twelve's commission. Mark especially highlights Jesus' power to exorcise demons. Here that power is given to the Twelve.

8–9 Inherent in the commission of the Twelve was absolute trust in God to supply all their needs. Here the physical needs are emphasized. They were to take only what they had on their backs. The only exception was a staff (v. 8). (The account in Matthew does not even allow this.) No bread (i.e., food of any kind), no bag ("knapsack," "traveler's bag," or perhaps the passage has in mind the more specialized meaning of "beggar's bag" [BAG, p. 662]), and no money (the word is *chalkos*, a small copper coin, which BAG [p. 883] translates as "small change") were allowed.

Clothing, too, was to be minimal. Sandals were allowed and only one tunic (v. 9). An extra tunic would come in handy at night because it could be used as a covering from the chilly night air. Jesus probably made this prohibition because he wanted the disciples to trust God for the provision of hospitality for each night. The total impression one receives from Jesus' instructions is that the mission he is about to send the Twelve on is extremely urgent.

The message Jesus gave them to preach was the same as the one he brought: "The kingdom of God is near. Repent and believe the good news!" (Mark 1:15). Cranfield rightly comments: "The particular instructions apply literally only to this brief mission during Jesus' lifetime; but in principle, with the necessary modifications according to climate and other circumstances, they still hold for the continuing ministry of the Church. The service of the Word of God is still a matter of extreme urgency, calling for absolute self-dedication" (*Gospel of Mark*, p. 200).

10–11 Jesus gave the instruction in this verse to protect the good reputation of the disciples. Whenever they accepted the hospitality of a home, they were to stay there until they left that town (v. 10), even if more comfortable or attractive lodgings were offered them.

Jesus knew that the mission of the Twelve would not always be accepted. Had not he too been rejected by many? So he instructed them how to act in such circumstances. The shaking off the dust from their feet (v. 11) may be understood in the light of the Jewish custom of removing carefully the dust from both clothes and feet before reentering Jewish territory (cf. SBK, 1:571). For the Jews heathen dust was defiling. The significance of the act here is to declare the place to be heathen and to make it clear that those who rejected the message must now answer for themselves. This seems to be the meaning of the phrase "as a testimony against them." The disciples' message, like that of Jesus, brings judgment as well as salvation. This always happens when the gospel is preached.

12–13 Mark now describes the actual mission of the Twelve. It was clearly patterned after Jesus' own ministry. Three activities are described: (1) preaching repentance (v.12), (2) driving out demons (v.13), and (3) healing the sick—all of them associated with Jesus' ministry. By these activities they were demonstrating that the kingdom of God had come with power. But the mission of the Twelve is a mere extension of the ministry of Jesus that completely overshadows it. Their independent mission waits till after Jesus' resurrection.

IV. Withdrawal From Galilee (6:14–8:30)

This fourth section of Mark's Gospel finds Jesus withdrawing from the territory of Galilee for the primary purpose of further instructing his disciples. Though one incident of public teaching occurs in the section 7:1–23, the focus of Jesus' teaching is now on the Twelve. The section begins with an account of the various views that people held as to Jesus' identity (6:14–16), including the view of Herod Antipas, followed parenthetically with the story of the death of John the Baptist (6:17–29). The section ends with the healing of a blind man at Bethsaida (8:22–26) and the disciples' recognition of Jesus as the Messiah (8:27–30). In between are several complexes of incidents including two stories of Jesus' feeding the multitudes: the five thousand (6:30–44) and then the four thousand (8:1–10). Jesus moves from Galilee into the territory of Tyre and Sidon and then back through Galilee to the Decapolis.

A. Popular Views of Jesus' Identity

6:14–16

> [14]King Herod heard about this, for Jesus' name had become well-known. Some were saying, "John the Baptist has been raised from the dead, and that is why miraculous powers are at work in him."
> [15]Others said, "He is Elijah."
> And still others claimed, "He is a prophet, like one of the prophets of long ago."
> [16]But when Herod heard this, he said, "John, the man I beheaded, has been raised from the dead!"

14 The Herod mentioned here is Antipas, son of Herod the Great and Malthace. When his father died, he became tetrarch ("ruler of the fourth part") of Galilee and Perea. He was not officially granted the title of "king." It was, in fact, his ambition to secure that title for himself that led to his downfall in A.D. 39 under Caligula. Mark may be using the title of "king" here ironically, or perhaps he is reflecting local custom (cf. Taylor, p. 308).

If the paragraph that begins with v.14 goes with the one that precludes it, then the "this" refers to the mission of the Twelve. Herod heard about this. It is possible that the disciples of Jesus traveled as far as Tiberias on the southwestern shore of the Lake of Galilee, where Herod had built his capital and had named it after the ruling Caesar, Tiberias. On the other hand, the "this" of v.14 may be a reference to the mighty works of Jesus. This latter view seems likely because the entire discussion focuses on the question of Jesus' identity.

Since NIV, correctly in my view, accepts the reading *elegon* ("some were saying") instead of *elegen* ("he [Herod] was saying"), what follows are popular views of who Jesus was. That some thought Jesus to be John the Baptist raised from the dead shows that they knew nothing of Jesus prior to his ministry in Galilee. John the Baptist did not perform miracles while he was alive, but apparently his resurrection status was thought to give him that power.

15 Another popular view identified Jesus with Elijah. John the Baptist had spoken of Jesus as "the Coming One"; and though he did not specifically identify who that was, to anyone who knew the OT it could be no one else but Elijah (cf. Mal 3:1; 4:5). Perhaps this popular view of Jesus owed its origin to John.

A third view was that "he is a prophet, like one of the prophets of long ago." This seems to be a lower estimate of Jesus than the previously mentioned one. He is just an ordinary prophet, not the Prophet foretold in Deuteronomy 18:15–19.

16 Herod's view—that Jesus was John the Baptist raised from the dead—arose not so much from what he had heard about Jesus as from the proddings of a guilty conscience, since Herod had been directly responsible for John's death. This view of Jesus suggests that Herod knew nothing about Jesus prior to the death of John. Otherwise he would hardly have viewed him as John redivivus. The mention of the death of John causes Mark to interrupt the account of the mission of the Twelve in order to tell the story of John's murder.

B. *Death of John the Baptist*

6:17–29

> [17]For Herod himself had given orders to have John arrested, and he had him bound and put in prison. He did this because of Herodias, his brother Philip's wife, whom he had married. [18]For John had been saying to Herod, "It is not lawful for you to have your brother's wife." [19]So Herodias nursed a grudge against John and wanted to kill him. But she was not able to, [20]because Herod feared John and protected him, knowing him to be a righteous and holy man. When Herod heard John, he was greatly puzzled, yet he liked to listen to him.
> [21]Finally the opportune time came. On his birthday Herod gave a banquet for his high officials and military commanders and the leading men of Galilee. [22]When the daughter of Herodias came in and danced, she pleased Herod and his dinner guests.
> The king said to the girl, "Ask me for anything you want, and I'll give it to you." [23]And he promised her with an oath, "Whatever you ask I will give you, up to half my kingdom."
> [24]She went out and said to her mother, "What shall I ask for?"
> "The head of John the Baptist," she answered.
> [25]At once the girl hurried in to the king with the request: "I want you to give me right now the head of John the Baptist on a platter."
> [26]The king was greatly distressed, but because of his oaths and his dinner guests, he did not want to refuse her. [27]So he immediately sent an executioner with orders to bring John's head. The man went, beheaded John in the prison, [28]and brought back his head on a platter. He presented it to the girl, and she gave it to her mother. [29]On hearing of this, John's disciples came and took his body and laid it in a tomb.

17–18 Lane (p. 215) points out that in the scheme of Mark's Gospel there are two "passion narratives": the passion of John and the passion of Jesus. The passion of the Forerunner is a precursor to the passion of the Messiah. It is significant that Mark devotes fourteen verses to the death of John but only three to his ministry.

Numerous historical questions have been raised about Mark's account of John's death. Most of them arise out of his differences with Josephus. (For a complete discussion of these problems, see Cranfield, *Gospel of Mark*, pp. 208–9; Lane, pp. 215–16; and Taylor, pp. 310–11.)

John the Baptist had been arrested by Herod (v.17), who put him in prison because he had denounced Herod's adulterous union with Herodias, his brother Philip's wife (v.18). Josephus (Antiq. XVIII, 119 [v.2]) says that John was put in prison at Machaerus, the fortress situated in Perea, on the eastern side of the Dead Sea. Mark does not identify the place of John's imprisonment. Herodias was the daughter of Aristobolos, one of the sons of Herod the Great; so she was a niece of Herod Antipas. The Mosaic Law prohibited marriage to one's brother's wife while the brother was still alive (cf. Lev 18:16).

Josephus emphasizes the political motives behind the action of Herod against John. These were no doubt real. In order to marry Herodias, Herod had to rid himself of the daughter of King Aretas IV, whose kingdom lay just to the east of Perea. The situation there was already sensitive, and John's preaching had the potential to cause real trouble. Mark emphasizes the moral considerations. Calvin (2:222) comments: "We behold in John an illustrious example of that moral courage, which all pious teachers ought to possess, not to hesitate to incur the wrath of the great and powerful, as often as it may be found necessary: for he, with whom there is acceptance of persons, does not honestly serve God."

19–20 Herodias had not taken John's condemnation of her marriage lightly. In fact, she was infuriated by him and wanted to kill him (v.19). Herodias knew that "the only place where her marriage certificate could safely be written was on the back of the death warrant of John" (T.W. Manson, *The Servant Messiah* [London: Cambridge University Press, 1953], p. 40). She was thwarted in her design because Herod protected John (v.20). Motivated by fear and a recognition of John's righteous and holy character, Herod refused to allow him to be put to death. "Herod was awed by the purity of John's character, feared him as the bad fear the good" (Swete, p. 123). Yet "he liked to listen to him"; but he did not understand, being "greatly puzzled" by what he said.

21–23 Herodias finally got the opportunity she was waiting for (v.21). Herod celebrated his birthday with a banquet that he invited the military and political leaders of his tetrarchy to. At this festive occasion Herodias's daughter went before the guests to dance (v.22). A reading of the entire account suggests that Herodias sent her into the banquet hall to dance as part of her scheme to get rid of John the Baptist.

The dance was probably a lewd one. Objections to the historicity of the account have been raised on the basis of the unlikelihood of such a performance, but the low morals in Herod's court would not be inconsistent with it. Herod and his dinner guests were pleased with her performance—so much so that Herod offered her up to half his kingdom (v.23). The words "up to half my kingdom" may have been a kind of proverbial way of expressing openhanded generosity and were not to be taken literally.

24–25 The girl left the banquet hall to seek the advice of her mother (v.24). Herodias's quick reply betrayed the premeditated nature of her homicidal plan. Mark does not mention any surprise on the daughter's part when her mother made the request. In fact, when she went to convey the request for the head of John the Baptist, the daughter added two things: she wanted John's head "right now" and she wanted it "on a platter" (v.25).

26–28 Herod was in a quandary (v.26). Up to this point he had been able to protect John; but now, "because of his oaths and his dinner guests," he could hardly refuse the girl. Reluctantly (v.26 says he "was greatly distressed" about the whole thing) he ordered an executioner to be sent to the prison to decapitate John (v.27). John's head was brought to Herod (v.28), who presented it to Salome; and she gave it to her mother.

29 Mark ends the shocking story with John's disciples coming for the body to give it proper burial. Herod no doubt thought that he was now finished with the righteous prophet he both feared and respected. But this was not to be. The ministry of Jesus stirred up Herod's memories of John and his fears returned once more. Josephus says that when Herod's army was defeated by the Nabataeans in A.D. 30, the Jews thought it was a "punishment upon Herod and a mark of God's displeasure against him" (Antiq. XVIII, 119 [v.2]).

Notes

20 Some MSS read πολλὰ ἐποίει (polla epoiei, "he did many things"), but the reading adopted by NIV, πολλὰ ἠπόρει (polla ēporei, "he was greatly puzzled"), has the stronger MS support. It also seems consistent with what we know of Herod's character.

22 The external evidence supports the reading αὐτοῦ (autou, "his"). This identifies the girl as Herodias, the daughter of Herod. In v.24, however, she is identified as the daughter of Herodias; and we know from other sources that her name was Salome. The best solution seems to be to regard autou as an early scribal error and αὐτῆς (autēs, "her" as the original reading. In that case autēs would be used intensively to mean "herself" (cf. ASV: "When the daughter of Herodias herself came in").

26 The depth of the distress experienced by Herod at Salome's request for the head of John the Baptist is expressed graphically by the Greek word περίλυπος (perilypos, "greatly distressed"). This is the same word used to describe Jesus' agony in Gethsemane (Mark 14:34).

C. Feeding the Five Thousand

6:30–44

> 30The apostles gathered around Jesus and reported to him all they had done and taught. 31Then, because so many people were coming and going that they did not even have a chance to eat, he said to them, "Come with me by yourselves to a quiet place and get some rest."
> 32So they went away by themselves in a boat to a solitary place. 33But many who saw them leaving recognized them and ran on foot from all the towns and got there ahead of them. 34When Jesus landed and saw a large crowd, he had compassion on them, because they were like sheep without a shepherd. So he began teaching them many things.

³⁵By this time it was late in the day, so his disciples came to him. "This is a remote place," they said, "and it's already very late. ³⁶Send the people away so they can go to the surrounding countryside and villages and buy themselves something to eat."

³⁷But he answered, "You give them something to eat."

They said to him, "That would take eight months of a man's wages! Are we to go and spend that much on bread and give it to them to eat?"

³⁸"How many loaves do you have?" he asked. "Go and see."

When they found out, they said, "Five—and two fish."

³⁹Then Jesus directed them to have all the people sit down in groups on the green grass. ⁴⁰So they sat down in groups of hundreds and fifties. ⁴¹Taking the five loaves and the two fish and looking up to heaven, he gave thanks and broke the loaves. Then he gave them to his disciples to set before the people. He also divided the two fish among them all. ⁴²They all ate and were satisfied, ⁴³and the disciples picked up twelve basketfuls of broken pieces of bread and fish. ⁴⁴The number of the men who had eaten was five thousand.

In Mark's Gospel the story of the feeding of the five thousand plays an important role. It begins with an elaborate introduction (6:35–38), is looked back to on two different occasions (6:52; 8:17–21), and has a sequel in the feeding of the four thousand (8:1–10). Its position immediately following the account of Herod's feast also serves a function. It contrasts the "sumptuous oriental aura of the Herodian court with the austere circumstances in which Jesus satisfied the multitude with the staples of a peasant's diet" (Lane, p. 227).

30 Mark now continues the account of the mission of the Twelve after having interrupted it by a flashback to the death of John the Baptist. The disciples returned to Jesus from their mission of preaching, casting out demons, and healing and reported to him "all they had done and taught." Only here does Mark use the word "apostles" for the disciples. (Its occurrence in 3:14 is highly doubtful textually.) The word is particularly appropriate because the Twelve were returning from doing their apostolic work (cf. Gould, p. 115).

31–32 The disciples had just returned from what was apparently an intensive mission. Their activities had created much interest. So many people were coming and going that the disciples had no time even to eat (v.31; cf. 3:20). Since the disciples were doubtless tired from their missionary activities and from the demands of the crowds, Jesus decided to seek rest for them. Where specifically they went we are not told. Mark merely says it was a "quiet" and "solitary place [*erēmos*, 'desert']" (v.32).

In addition to seeking rest, it is possible that there was another purpose in the withdrawal of Jesus to the wilderness. Mark seems to have in mind the "rest in the wilderness" theme in Scripture (for a full treatment of this theme in Mark, see Lane; Mauser, passim). It was in the wilderness that God gave rest to his ancient people in the Exodus from Egypt. In the preaching of the prophets Isaiah (63:14) and Jeremiah (31:2), this became a type of a second rest promised to the new people of God in a second exodus. Jesus and his disciples fulfill this promise. Jesus is God's presence (instead of the pillar and the cloud), and the Bread (instead of the manna) is God's provision of sustenance.

The best way for Jesus and his disciples to get away from the crowds was by boat. They probably went to the northeast side of the lake. Although the crowd that followed by land would have had to cross the Jordan where it flows into the Lake of Galilee, this, according to Dalman, could have been possible: "On October 10, 1921, I saw that it was almost possible to cross over the Jordan dry-shod, just where it enters into the lake. An absolutely dry bar lay before the mouth" (G. Dalman, *Sacred Sites and Ways* [London: SPCK, 1935], p. 161). However, in the spring of the year, when this event apparently took place (cf. v.39: "green grass"), the Jordan had more water in it.

33–34 Perhaps the little boat faced a strong headwind, which slowed it down. At any rate the crowd was able to walk around the lake and arrive at the landing place ahead of the boat (v.33).

Jesus had every right to be annoyed with the crowd. They had prevented him and his disciples from having a much needed rest. But instead of being irritated, he responded compassionately and in love (v.34). He saw the multitude as "sheep without a shepherd" (cf. Num 27:17; Ezek 34:5). It is significant that in the context of these two OT passages the shepherd theme is associated with the wilderness. Mark seems to be working with these themes. Jesus, like Moses, leads his people into the wilderness; and, like David (cf. Ezek 34:23, 25), Jesus provides rest for them (cf. Lane, p. 226; Mauser, p. 135).

35–36 Jesus' disciples became concerned for the crowd (v.35). It was late in the day; and, since they were in a desolate place, there was little possibility of obtaining food. Their suggestion was that the crowd be dismissed so that they could get food for themselves in the neighboring towns and villages (v.36). This seemed to be a simple way for them to satisfy their hunger.

37 Jesus did not concur with the suggestion of his disciples that the food needed to feed the crowd was to be supplied from the resources of the neighboring towns and villages. The disciples themselves were to supply it! Jesus uses the emphatic personal pronoun to make the message plain: "*You* give them something to eat" (emphasis mine).

The reply of the disciples indicates how startled they were at Jesus' command. They could only think of the impossible amount of money it would take to feed a crowd like this one. Two hundred denarii represented the pay a common laborer earned in a period of about eight months (cf. Matt 20:2–15, where the usual pay for a day's wage is one denarius). Not even that amount of money would buy enough bread for all to eat (cf. John 6:7: "for each one to have a bite").

38 Jesus was not thinking of bread bought in the neighboring villages for two hundred denarii or whatever it might cost to supply the people. Before proceeding with his approach to the problem, he asked his disciples what the present status of the supply was. When they inquired, they found it to be meager: five loaves and two fish—a mere pittance in view of the number of people to be fed. The loaves, John tells us (6:9), were barley loaves. Unlike our modern loaves of bread, these were small and flat. One could easily eat several of them at a single meal.

39–40 At Jesus' direction (v.39), the disciples arranged the crowd into groups of hundreds and fifties (v.40). The words used to describe this arrangement mean literally "drinking parties by drinking parties" and "vegetable plots by vegetable plots" (cf. BAG, pp. 787, 705). Here they are used to describe the orderly arrangement of the crowd in order to facilitate the distribution of the food. Beyond that there may be a symbolic meaning. The arrangement may suggest the teacher-student relationship. The "rabbis compared their classes to vineyards because they were arranged in rows, 'shuroth shuroth'; and we may compare our own use of the word 'seminary,' which means a 'seed-plot'" (P. Carrington, *According to Mark* [Cambridge: Cambridge University Press, 1960], p. 136). Lane, in keeping with the wilderness motif, finds in this arrangement a recalling of the Mosaic camp in the wilderness. Thus the people taught by Jesus are shown to be the new people of God and Jesus is "the eschatological Saviour, the second Moses who transforms the leaderless flock into the people of God" (p. 230).

Mark notes that the grass was green (v.39). This shows that the incident took place in the late winter or early spring, when the grass in Galilee turns green after the rains.

41 Jesus did what any pious Jew would have done before eating—he prayed. The usual form of the prayer was a thanksgiving or eucharist: "Blessed art thou, O Lord our God, King of the Universe, who bringeth forth bread from the earth." As to how the miracle was performed, Mark does not give us so much as a hint. He simply says that Jesus broke the loaves, divided the fish, and gave them to the disciples to distribute among the people.

42–44 There can be no question but that Mark understood the actions of Jesus to have been miraculous. Temple correctly observes: "Every Evangelist supposed our Lord to have wrought a creative act; and for myself, I have no doubt that this is what occurred. This, however, is credible only if St. John is right in his doctrine of the Lord's Person. If the Lord was indeed God incarnate, the story presents no insuperable difficulties" (W. Temple, *Readings in St. John's Gospel* [London: Macmillan, 1940], p. 75). Not only were all the people fed and their hunger satisfied (v.42), but there was more left over at the end than there had been at the beginning—twelve basketfuls (v.43). These were the small wicker baskets (*kôphinōn*) every Jew took with him when away from home. In it he carried his lunch and some needed essentials so that he would not have to eat defiling Gentile food.

Mark says that the number of the men who had eaten was about five thousand (v.44)—a number that could easily have been calculated because of the division of the crowd into groups of hundreds and fifties.

Notes

40 The word πρασιαί (*prasiai*, "groups") is etymologically "leek beds." J.D.M. Derrett points out that leeks need a great deal of water and because of their need for irrigation must be planted in straight rows. Thus the explanation of arrangement of the crowd like leek beds was "to show that in the World to Come the righteous will be sated like the well-irrigated vegetables which the stupid and unbelieving Israelites lusted for in the desert" ("Leek Beds and Methodology," *Biblische Zeitschrift* 19, no. 1 [1975]: 102).

44 The word used for "men" here is not ἄνθρωποι (*anthrōpoi*), the generic sense, i.e., "human beings," but ἄνδρες (*andres*), "men" as opposed to women or children. Matthew makes this clear by adding "besides women and children" (14:21), though there probably were not many of them present. The number five thousand is very large when one realizes that the neighboring towns of Capernaum and Bethsaida had only two-to-three thousand people.

D. *Walking on the Water*

6:45–52

45Immediately Jesus made his disciples get into the boat and go on ahead of him to Bethsaida, while he dismissed the crowd. 46After leaving them, he went on a mountainside to pray.

47When evening came, the boat was in the middle of the lake, and he was alone on land. 48He saw the disciples straining at the oars, because the wind was against them. About the fourth watch of the night he went out to them, walking on the lake. He was about to pass by them, 49but when they saw him walking on the lake, they thought he was a ghost. They cried out, 50because they all saw him and were terrified.

Immediately he spoke to them and said, "Take courage! It is I. Don't be afraid." 51Then he climbed into the boat with them, and the wind died down. They were completely amazed, 52for they had not understood about the loaves; their hearts were hardened.

45 Mark records no reaction of the crowd to the multiplication of the loaves and fish, but there must have been one. The hurried departure of the disciples suggests that there was danger of a messianic uprising as a result of the miracle. (John's Gospel [6:15] refers specifically to this.) The suggestion that the crowd did not know a miracle had taken place and that Jesus wanted to get the disciples out of there before they divulged that one had happened seems farfetched. Bethsaida is on the northeast shore of the Lake of Galilee and could not have been far from the place where the miracle took place. Herod Philip elevated the village to the status of a city and named it after Julias, the daughter of the Roman emperor Augustus (cf. Jos. Antiq. XVIII, 28 [ii.1]). After sending his disciples away in the boat, Jesus stayed to dismiss the crowd. No doubt his purpose was to calm the people down.

46 Mark's mention of Jesus' praying is further evidence of the crisis nature of the situation. There are only three occasions in this Gospel in which Jesus withdraws to pray, and each time some sort of crisis is involved: after the excitement and activity of a busy Sabbath in Capernaum (1:35), after the multiplication of the loaves (6:46), and in Gethsemane after the Lord's Supper (14:32–36). Each incident involves the temptation not to carry out God's mission for him—a mission that would ultimately bring suffering, rejection, and death. These crises seem to represent an ascending scale and reach their climax in the agony of Gethsemane.

47–48 The time of this incident is "evening" (v.47). Since it was "already very late" (v.35) before the feeding of the five thousand, "evening" here must mean late at night. The Lake of Galilee is only about four miles wide. Thus a boat in the middle of the lake could easily be seen in the full moon of Passover time (assuming that the incident took place at that time) from the shore.

Apparently the wind was blowing from the north or northeast and had blown the disciples off their course. They were "straining at the oars" (v.48)—an indication of a stiff headwind. Jesus came to them "walking on the lake," about the fourth watch. According to Roman reckoning (and Mark follows this), the night was divided into four watches: 6–9 P.M., 9–12 P.M., 12–3 A.M., and 3–6 A.M. "He was about to pass by them" translates *kai ēthelen parelthein autous,* which literally means "and he was desirous to pass by them." NIV probably catches the correct meaning, showing that we have here not the intention of Jesus but the impression of an eyewitness as to what was happening.

49–50 To try to rationalize this incident by suggesting that what the disciples really saw was Jesus wading through the shallows at the edge of the shore is ridiculous. Although they did not recognize him at first—they thought they had seen some sort of water spirit (v.49)—Jesus calmed their fears with words of assurance: "Take courage! It is I. Don't be afraid" (v.50). It has sometimes been suggested that the statement "It is I" points to Mark's understanding this incident as a theophany (cf. the "I am who I am" of Exod 3:14). It is, however, simplest and best to regard the expression as a way by which Jesus was identifying himself ("It is I—Jesus").

51 Here another miracle is presupposed. When Jesus climbed into the boat, "the wind died down." Then Mark says, "They were completely amazed." There was unmistakenly some relationship between his getting into the boat and the calming of the wind. Only this explains the attitude of the disciples.

52 Mark relates his explanation of the disciples' panic at seeing Jesus walking on the water and their amazement at the calming of the wind to their failure to understand about the multiplication of the loaves. Had they understood about the loaves, i.e., that the sovereign Lord of the universe was in action there, they would have been prepared to understand walking on water and calming waves. Their problem was a christological one. Not unlike Jesus' opponents, "their hearts were hardened."

E. *Healings Near Gennesaret*

6:53–56

> [53]When they had crossed over, they landed at Gennesaret and anchored there. [54]As soon as they got out of the boat, people recognized Jesus. [55]They ran throughout that whole region and carried the sick on mats to wherever they heard he was. [56]And wherever he went—into villages, towns or countryside—they placed the sick in the marketplaces. They begged him to let them touch even the edge of his cloak, and all who touched him were healed.

53 Jesus stayed with the disciples in the boat and crossed over with them to Gennesaret, referring either to the plain north of Magdala on the western side of the lake or to a city in the plain (cf. Dalman, *Sacred Sites,* p. 128). The great fertility of the soil in the plain of Gennesaret enabled it to support a relatively large population. Josephus says of it, "One may call this place the ambition of nature, where it forces those plants that are naturally enemies to one another to agree together" (War III, 518 [x.8]).

54–56 This section serves as a summary of Jesus' work in Galilee before he withdrew to other regions. It resembles the summaries in 1:32–34 and 3:7–12, except that no mention is made of exorcising demons. In it we see the widespread fame of Jesus as a healer (vv.54–55). As a good Jew, he wore the fringes and tassels commanded by God in Numbers 15:37–39 and Deuteronomy 22:12. It was not the mere touch of the fringes of Jesus' garments that produced the healings (v.56). Though in some instances superstition was probably involved, it was the faith of those who came to touch Jesus' clothes that he responded to (cf. 5:25–34).

F. Commands of God and Traditions of Men

7:1–13

¹The Pharisees and some of the teachers of the law who had come from Jerusalem gathered around Jesus and ²saw some of his disciples eating food with hands that were "unclean," that is, unwashed. ³(The Pharisees and all the Jews do not eat unless they give their hands a ceremonial washing, holding to the tradition of the elders. ⁴When they come from the marketplace they do not eat unless they wash. And they observe many other traditions, such as the washing of cups, pitchers and kettles.)

⁵So the Pharisees and teachers of the law asked Jesus, "Why don't your disciples live according to the tradition of the elders instead of eating their food with 'unclean' hands?"

⁶He replied, "Isaiah was right when he prophesied about you hypocrites; as it is written:

" 'These people honor me with their lips,
    but their hearts are far from me.
⁷They worship me in vain;
    their teachings are but rules taught by men.'

⁸You have let go of the commands of God and are holding on to the traditions of men."

⁹And he said to them: "You have a fine way of setting aside the commands of God in order to observe your own traditions! ¹⁰For Moses said, 'Honor your father and your mother,' and 'Anyone who curses his father or mother must be put to death.' ¹¹But you say that if a man says to his father or mother: 'Whatever help you might otherwise have received from me is Corban' (that is, a gift devoted to God), ¹²then you no longer let him do anything for his father or mother. ¹³Thus you nullify the word of God by your tradition that you have handed down. And you do many things like that."

This incident appears to be linked with vv. 14–19 and vv. 20–23 by the common theme of "cleanness." It is similar to the conflict stories found in 2:1–3:6 but is placed here (along with vv.14–19 and vv.20–23) to function as an introduction to the extension of the ministry of Jesus to the Gentiles in vv.24–30 (the Syrophoenician woman), in vv.31–37 (the deaf-and-dumb man in the Decapolis) and, less obviously, in 8:1–10 (the feeding of the four thousand). No hint is given as to when or where the incident took place.

1–2 Another delegation of fact-finding theologians (Pharisees and teachers of the law) came down from Jerusalem (cf. 3:22) to investigate the Galilean activities of Jesus (v.1). What they discovered was that Jesus' disciples did not wash their hands before eating (v.2). Their complaint was not, of course, that the disciples by this failure were being unhygenic. The Pharisees had no concern with that. The question was one of ceremonial purity versus ceremonial defilement. We know that the Jews placed great importance on this as is shown by the fact that an entire division of the Mishnah (*Tohoroth*, "cleannesses") is devoted to this subject.

3–4 Verses 3–4 are a parenthesis (as in NIV). Mark felt it necessary to explain to his Gentile readers the Jewish custom of ceremonial handwashing, a custom based on the "tradition of the elders" (v.3). This consisted in a great mass of oral tradition that had arisen about the law. About A.D. 200 it was written down in the Mishnah, but in Jesus' day it was still in oral form. Its purpose was to regulate a man's life completely. If the law was silent or vague about a particular subject, one could be sure that the tradition would be vocal and explicit. The tradition, created and promulgated by the great rabbis, was passed on from one generation to the next and was considered binding.

Mark gives an example of the custom. Some versions translate v.4 as if what the Jews brought from the marketplace was washed before they ate it. But NIV is probably correct because the verb *baptisōntai* is middle voice ("wash themselves"). After being in the marketplace and coming into contact with Gentiles or even nonobservant Jews, the Pharisees would wash themselves to ensure their ritual cleanness. By way of further explanation, Mark adds that the Pharisees "observe many other traditions, such as the washing of cups, pitchers, and kettles."

5–7 To the question asked Jesus as to why his disciples acted as they did (v.5), he answered by quoting a passage from Isaiah, preceded by his own comment: "Isaiah was right when he prophesied about you hypocrites" (v.6). The word "hypocrite" (*hypokritēs*) means "play actor" and refers here to people whose worship is merely outward and not from the heart. In saying that Isaiah had prophesied about them, Jesus did not mean that Isaiah had in mind the Pharisees and the teachers of the law when he originally wrote these words but that his denunciation of the religious leaders of his day fitted those of Jesus' day. The quotation (Isa 29:13) is from the LXX, which, though differing somewhat from the MT, makes essentially the same point—viz., that in carrying out all their traditions and regulations, they were heartless hypocrites. Their outward appearance of piety was a lie, because it was not accompanied by a "total life commitment to the one who is the true object of religious devotion" (Anderson, p. 185). Jesus goes on (v.7) to equate neglect of true holiness to submission to man-made rabbinic tradition.

8–9 Here Jesus contrasts the "commands of God" with the "traditions of men" (v.8). It is clear that this great body of Jewish tradition had failed to get to the heart of God's commands. It was supposed to fence in the law so that the people would not infringe on it. Actually, however, the tradition distorted and ossified the law (v.9). In fact, it had even become a means of getting around God's law.

10–13 Jesus now cites a specific example of how the tradition was used to set aside God's commands. The first quotation is from the LXX of Exodus 20:12 and is a statement of the fifth commandment. The second quotation is from the LXX of Exodus 21:16 [17 MT]. In the latter the seriousness of failure to keep the fifth commandment is underscored—death is the penalty for anyone who curses his father or mother (v.10). But by means of the tradition, the responsibility of children to their parents could be easily circumvented (v.11). A son need only declare that what he had intended to give his father and mother be considered "Corban," i.e., a gift devoted to God, and it could no longer be designated for his parents. By devoting the gift to God, a son did not necessarily promise it to the temple nor did he prevent its use for himself. What he did do was to exclude legally his parents from benefiting from it (v.12). So the very purpose for which the commandment was given was set aside by the tradition. This is what is meant by "nullifying" (*akyrountes*) the word of God (v.13).

Notes

2 The word κοινός (*koinos*, "unclean") occurs again in v.5 and the verb form κοινόω (*koinoō*) in vv. 15, 18, 20, 23. It appears to be the theme word for the entire section (vv.1–23). In classical Greek, *koinos* means "common" in contrast to ἴδιος (*idios*, "private"). It sometimes has the classical meaning in the LXX, but in 1 Macc 1:47, 62 it has the sense of "ritually unclean," which is its meaning here in Mark (cf. Acts 10:14, 28; 11:8; Rev 21:27).

3 NIV translates the Greek phrase ἐὰν μὴ πυγμῇ νίψωνται (*ean mē pygmē nipsōntai*) "unless they give their hands a ceremonial washing." *Pygmē* means literally "with a [the] fist." Taylor (p. 335) says that no satisfactory explanation of this difficult word can be given. The difficulty prompted some copyists to omit it (Δ syr[s] cop[sa] Diatessaron[p]) and others to substitute another word that to them made better sense, such as πυκνά (*pykna*, "often" or "thoroughly") (א W it[b,1] vg al) or *momento* ("in a moment," it[a]) or *primo* ("fist," it[d]) (cf. Bruce Metzger, *A Textual Commentary on the Greek New Testament*, corrected ed. [New York: UBS, 1975], p. 93). The preferred reading (*pygmē*) has been taken to mean (1) with the clenched fist of one hand rubbing the palm of the other, (2) up to the wrist or elbow, or (3) with a handful of water (cupped hand). The RSV translation committee found the expression so difficult that they did not translate it at all.

6 Ὑποκριτής (*hypokritēs*, "hypocrite")—"The thought here is probably not so much that the people concerned were consciously acting a part as that there was a radical inconsistency in their lives. . . . If they were themselves deceived as well as deceiving others, their situation was more, not less serious" (Cranfield, *Gospel of Mark*, p. 235).

G. *True Defilement*

7:14-23

14Again Jesus called the crowd to him and said, "Listen to me, everyone, and understand this. 15Nothing outside a man can make him 'unclean' by going into him. Rather, it is what comes out of a man that makes him 'unclean.' "

17After he had left the crowd and entered the house, his disciples asked him about this parable. 18"Are you so dull?" he asked. "Don't you see that nothing that enters a man from the outside can make him 'unclean'? 19For it doesn't go into his heart but into his stomach, and then out of his body." (In saying this, Jesus declared all foods "clean.")

20He went on: "What comes out of a man is what makes him 'unclean.' 21For from within, out of men's hearts, come evil thoughts, sexual immorality, theft, murder, adultery, 22greed, malice, deceit, lewdness, envy, slander, arrogance and folly. 23All these evils come from inside and make a man 'unclean.' "

These verses form a part of the section vv.1–23 and are not to be regarded as a separate, unconnected pericope. Their connection with what precedes is evident from Jesus' statement in v.15 that directly answers the question the Pharisees and teachers of the law raised (v.5).

14–15(16) Jesus has been speaking directly to the Pharisees and the teachers of the law. Now he calls the crowd around him (v.14) because he wants them to hear the crux of his teaching about what is clean. He prefaces his statement with a prophetic call to hear his words.

Jesus states clearly what does and does not make a person unclean (v.15). What is external cannot defile a person. Food, for example, cannot do this—not even if it is eaten with unwashed hands or declared unclean by kosher food laws. (This must have come as a startling statement to Jesus' hearers.) What really makes a person unclean comes from within, out of the heart and the will—what one thinks, says, desires, and does—these only can make a person unclean.

Verse 16 does not appear in NIV because, though it is present in the majority of the MSS, it does not occur in the important Alexandrian witnesses. "It appears to be a scribal gloss (derived perhaps from 4:9 or 4:23), introduced as an appropriate sequel to ver. 14" (Metzger, *Textual Commentary*, p. 95).

17–19 After leaving the crowd, Jesus entered a house (some have suggested it was Peter's house at Capernaum; but since the noun is without the definite article, no specific house is intended) and was teaching the disciples privately (v.17). Here, as in 9:28, 33 and 10:10, the place where Jesus reveals the true meaning of his teaching is in a "house." The explanation was prompted by the question of his disciples.

Although the disciples had already spent considerable time with Jesus and belonged to the inner circle of his concern, they were slow to grasp the meaning of his teaching. Jesus expressed surprise at this: "Are you so dull?" (v.18), i.e., "After all the time I have spent with you, do you still not comprehend spiritual truth?"

The reason nothing entering a person from the outside defiles him is because it enters into the stomach, not the heart (v.19). And it is in the heart that the true issues of life lie. In Semitic expression the heart is the center of human personality that determines man's actions and inaction (cf. Isa 29:13: "These people come near to me with their mouth and honor me with their lips, but their hearts are far from me").

In v.19b Mark explains for his readers the significance of Jesus' teaching about ceremonial purity.

> This statement clearly has its eye on a situation such as developed in the Pauline mission churches in which questions of clean and unclean foods (cf. Acts 10:9–16; 11:5–10 and see Rom 14:13ff.) and idol-meats became live issues (as we know from I Cor 8:10). This chapter in Mark 7 is perhaps the most obvious declaration of Mark's purpose as a Christian living in the Graeco-Roman world who wishes to publicize the charter of Gentile freedom by recording in the plainest terms Jesus' detachment from Jewish ceremonial and to spell out in clear tones the application of this to his readers. (Martin, *Mark*, p. 220). If Peter stands behind Mark's Gospel, these words are particularly apropos in the light of Acts 10:15.

20–23 Since v.20 is introduced by an indirect statement (*elegen de hoti*, "and he was saying that"; NIV, "he went on") and not a direct quotation, it is taken by some commentators to be Mark's further interpretation (cf. v.19b) or explanation of Jesus' teaching in vv.15–19a. The catechistical structure of section 19b–23 seems to lend support to this possibility. If it is Mark's interpretation, it is not inconsistent with Jesus' teaching in vv. 15–19a.

The main force of the passage is the same as in v.15b, which, in fact, is repeated in v.20. The source of uncleanness in anyone is the heart (v.21), for it is there that the true issues of life lie. The list that follows is "without parallel in the sayings of Jesus" (Taylor, p. 345), but it is typically Jewish (cf. Rom 1:29–31; Gal 5:19–23; 1 QS 4.9–11). The list is difficult to classify; it seems to move from overt sins to sinful attitudes or dispositions. "Evil thoughts" stand first, which suggests that what follows arises from these. *Porneia* ("sexual immorality") is a broader term than *moicheia* ("adultery") since it describes illegitimate sexual relations generally, while adultery is limited to illicit sex within marriage. *Aselgeia* ("lewdness") suggests open and shameless immorality. *Pleonexiai* ("greed," v.22) may have sexual overtones since it is frequently associated (as here) with words indicating sexual sins (e.g., Eph 4:19, 5:3; Col 3:5; 2 Peter 2:3). *Ophthalmos ponēros* ("envy") is literally "evil eye," a Semitic term for "stinginess" (cf. Deut 15:9; Ecclus 14:10; 31:13) or perhaps better, "envious jealousy." *Blasphēmia* ("slander") includes speaking evil of either God or man, and *aphrosynē* describes "the stupidity of the man who lacks moral judgment" (Taylor, p. 346). The meanings of the rest of the words in the list are obvious.

Notes

15 Rawlinson (p. 96) tones down this statement of Jesus by arguing that since the Hebrew and Aramaic know no comparative degree, what Jesus is saying is that "pollutions from within are more serious than pollutions from without." But this fails to see the revolutionary nature of Jesus' teaching concerning the oral law.

H. *The Faith of the Syrophoenician Woman*

7:24–30

24Jesus left that place and went to the vicinity of Tyre. He entered a house and did not want anyone to know it; yet he could not keep his presence secret. 25In fact, as soon as she heard about him, a woman whose little daughter was possessed by an evil spirit came and fell at his feet. 26The woman was a Greek, born in Syrian Phoenicia. She begged Jesus to drive the demon out of her daughter.

27"First let the children eat all they want," he told her, "for it is not right to take the children's bread and toss it to their dogs."

28"Yes, Lord," she replied, "but even the dogs under the table eat the children's crumbs."

29Then he told her, "For such a reply, you may go; the demon has left your daughter."

30She went home and found her child lying on the bed, and the demon gone.

Why does Mark place this incident here? It seems to be a natural sequence to the preceding incidents in which Jesus breaks with the Jewish oral law and particularly the law of ceremonial cleanness. Jews normally had no relationship with Gentiles because associations with them made Jews ritually unclean. Jesus now shows by example that those oral laws are invalid and deliberately associates himself with a Gentile woman. Another purpose is to emphasize the mission to the Gentiles. The gospel of the kingdom is not limited to Israel, even though historically it came to her first (cf. v.27). Mark regards this story of the Syrophoenician woman as a natural consequence of Jesus' attitude toward the ceremonial law (vv. 1–23); and by including it here, Mark wants to assure his Gentile readers that the "good news" is for them as it was for the Syrophoenician woman.

24 "Left that place" translates *ekeithen* (lit., "from here") and may refer to the house (7:17), to Gennesaret (6:53), or to some other place. The historical setting of the story is not known. Mark puts it here because of its theme ("the Gentiles hear the Good News") and not because it actually followed the preceding incident.

Phoenicia (now Lebanon), in which the city of Tyre was located, bordered on Galilee to the northwest. Why Jesus went there or how far he penetrated into this territory we are not told. Mark usually leaves such details up to the imagination of the reader. Apparently Jesus did not go there for public ministry. He went into a house "and did not want anyone to know it." This suggests that he went there to get out of the public eye, perhaps to rest and to prepare himself spiritually for what he knew lay ahead of him. But his hope of a time of quiet retirement was thwarted. His fame had apparently spread beyond the borders of Galilee into the territory of Phoenicia, and "he could not keep his presence secret."

25–26 One of the persons who sought out Jesus was a Gentile woman. No doubt she had heard about his healing powers and came to him because her daughter was possessed by an evil spirit (v.25). Mark says that the woman was "a Greek, born in Syrian Phoenicia" (v.26). Since she obviously was not a Greek by nationality, "Greek" is probably equivalent here to "Gentile" (in distinction from Jew) or to "Greek-speaking." By nationality the woman was a Syrophoenician. In those days Phoenicia belonged administratively to Syria. So Mark probably used Syrophoenician to distinguish this woman from the Libyo-Phoenicians of North Africa.

27–28 Jesus' conversation with this woman must have been in Greek, not Aramaic. There is no reason why Jesus, raised in Galilee, would not have known Greek. In the villages and towns of Palestine, he would ordinarily have used Aramaic. But in the coastal cities of the Gentiles, he spoke Greek.

Jesus' reply is in the form of a comparison between the children of the household and the little dogs (*kynarioi*, "puppies") that were kept as household pets (v.27). The contrast is between the privileged position of Israel ("children") and the less-privileged Gentiles ("little dogs"). First (*prōton*) the children are to be fed. Martin (*Mark*, p. 222) rightly attaches an eschatological sense to this verse, as in Mark 13:10, and treats the insertion of *prōton* "as a note required to indicate the passing of the exclusive privilege of Israel. The period immediately following the birth of the Jerusalem church saw the time of Israel's opportunity when the children 'first' would be fed; but this is no exclusive right belonging to the Jews. Later (ὕστερον) there would be provision made for Gentile dogs." So far as this woman was concerned, the "later" time had already come, because Jesus responded compassionately to her needs.

The reply of the woman (v.28) was remarkable. She admitted her status ("Yes, Lord"—the only time Jesus is called "Lord" in Mark) but refused to believe she was thereby excluded from any benefits. "Quite so, Lord; and in that case I may have a crumb" (Plummer, p. 189).

29–30 Jesus was pleased with the woman's reply (v.29). It revealed to him not only her wit but also her faith and humility, and he responded by declaring that her daughter had been healed ("the demon has left your daughter"). This is the only instance of healing at a distance found in Mark's Gospel. The woman returned home and discovered the truth of what Jesus had said (v.30). She found her daughter lying on the bed, perhaps as the result of the final convulsion of the demon as he came out of her (cf. Mark 9:26), and the demon gone.

I. Healing a Deaf and Mute Man

7:31–37

> [31]Then Jesus left the vicinity of Tyre and went through Sidon, down to the Sea of Galilee and into the region of the Decapolis. [32]There some people brought to him a man who was deaf and could hardly talk, and they begged him to place his hand on the man.
>
> [33]After he took him aside, away from the crowd, Jesus put his fingers into the man's ears. Then he spit and touched the man's tongue. [34]He looked up to heaven and with a deep sigh said to him, "*Ephphatha!*" (which means, "Be opened!"). [35]At this, the man's ears were opened, his tongue was loosened and he began to speak plainly.
>
> [36]Jesus commanded them not to tell anyone. But the more he did so, the more they kept talking about it. [37]People were overwhelmed with amazement. "He has done everything well," they said. "He even makes the deaf hear and the mute speak."

31 None of the other evangelists record this story. Mark includes it because it gives an account of another healing on Gentile territory, and this is its connection with the preceding story. The geographic references are difficult. Jesus journeys north from Tyre through Sidon and then apparently in a southeasterly direction through the territory of Herod Philip to the eastern side of the Sea of Galilee and into the territory of the Decapolis. The textual tradition indicates that the copyists had problems with this circuitous journey (cf. Notes). Yet the journey is not geographically impossible. Mark gives us no information as to what Jesus was doing during the journey. The Decapolis (the territory of the ten Greek cities) was largely Gentile, but there were also a significant number of Jews living there.

32 Mark says that the man brought to Jesus was "deaf and could hardly talk" (NEB has "had an impediment in his speech"). The adjective is *mogilalos* and is far from being a common word. This is its only occurrence in the entire NT; and it appears only once in the LXX, where its use is of great importance to the meaning of this story. Certainly Mark must have had Isaiah 35:6 in mind, which is a poetical description of the Messianic Age: "Then will the lame leap like a deer, and the tongue of the dumb [*mogilalos*] shout for joy." (For the rabbinic understanding of this text as fulfilled in the age of the Messiah, see R *Genesis* 95; Midrash *Tehillim* 146.8.)

The people brought the deaf mute to Jesus and begged him to lay his hands on him. Although they did not explicitly say so, they obviously wanted Jesus to heal the man. "They begged" (*parakalousin*) shows their concern for him, and Jesus responds to it. The deaf mute could make no intelligible request for himself.

33 In order to deal more personally with the mute, Jesus took him apart from the crowd. Mark emphasizes Jesus' desire to have personal contact with the people he heals. Here his actions seem to be done to help the man exercise faith—the fingers placed in his ears apparently indicate they were to be unblocked and the saliva on the tongue indicates it was going to be restored to normal use. Calvin (2:271–72) comments:

> The laying on of hands would of itself have been sufficiently efficacious, and even, without moving a finger, he might have accomplished it by a single act of his will; but it is evident that he made abundant use of outward signs, when they were found to be advantageous. Thus, by touching the tongue with spittle, he intended to point out that the faculty of speech was communicated by himself alone; and by putting his fingers into the ears, he showed that it belonged to his office to pierce the ears of the deaf.

(See also SBK, 2:17, where a similar understanding of the use of the fingers and spittle is offered.)

34–35 Jesus' looking up to heaven (v.34) is best understood as an attitude of prayer (cf. John 11:41; 17:1), and perhaps it was also a way of showing the man that God was the source of his power. The "deep sigh" should be interpreted together with the looking up into heaven. It was

> the "sighing" of the prayer, the sighing that accompanied the concealed communion of Jesus with the Father. If this looking up and sighing had been permanent technical aspects cf the modus operandi of Jesus, we should definitely find references to them in early Christianity, but what we find there is that it is repeatedly stated that healing was simply performed only "in the name of Jesus"! (Van der Loos, *Miracles of Jesus*, p. 327)

Jesus' prayer consisted of only a single word—*Ephphatha*. According to his custom, Mark explains the meaning of this Aramaic word to his readers: "Be opened!" When Jesus spoke, as in this case, to the peasant people of Palestine, he used Aramaic (cf. Mark 5:41). To the Syrophoenician woman, he almost certainly spoke Greek.

The effect of the command was instantaneous (v.35). The man's ears were opened, his tongue loosed, and he spoke "plainly" (*orthōs*). He had not been completely mute; he had a speech impediment in his voice—"could hardly talk" (v.32).

36–37 Jesus again ordered the crowd not to divulge the miracle, but this had no effect at all (v.36). The more he insisted on their not talking about it, the more they blazed the miracle abroad. This is very much in contrast to the attitude of the crowd when, also in the Decapolis, he healed the Gadarene demoniac. Then the crowd was afraid and wanted to get rid of Jesus. His reason for enjoining silence here was probably the same as in 1:44. He did not want a false concept of him as only a miracle worker to spread lest it touch off a messianic insurrection and prevent him from accomplishing his God-appointed mission.

Another result of the healing was that the people were "overwhelmed" (*hyperperissōs*, a true *hapax legomenon*—i.e., a word occurring only once in Greek literature—that means "beyond measure," "in the extreme"). The statement "he has done everything well" reminds us of Genesis 1:31: "God saw all that he made, and it was very good." The reminder is not unsuitable, for in a profound sense Jesus' work is indeed "a new creation." And again we are reminded of the messianic significance of this miracle by words that reflect Isaiah 35:5–6 (already anticipated by the use of *mogilalon* ["hardly speak"] in v.32):

> Then will the eyes of the blind be opened and the ears of the deaf unstopped.
> Then will the lame leap like a deer, and the mute tongue shout for joy.

There can be no doubt that for Mark the significance of this miracle was the proclamation of the gospel in the territory of the Gentiles, a sign of the messianic activity of Jesus.

Notes

31 The best representatives of the Alexandrian and the Western texts, in addition to important Caesarean witnesses, support the reading ἦλθεν διὰ Σιδῶνος (*ēlthen dia Sidōnos*, "he went through Sidon"). This means that Jesus took a circuitous route, traveling from Tyre north through Sidon and thence southeast across the Leontes and south past Caesarea Philippi to the east of the Jordan and into the territory of the Decapolis on the east of the Lake of Galilee. The alternate reading καὶ Σιδῶνος ἦλθεν (*kai Sidōnos ēlthen*, "and he went to Sidon") arose because copyists either had difficulty with Mark's geography and deliberately changed the text or introduced it accidentally, being influenced by the well-known expression "Tyre and Sidon" (cf. Metzger, *Textual Commentary*, pp. 95–96).

J. *Feeding the Four Thousand*

8:1–10

¹During those days another large crowd gathered. Since they had nothing to eat, Jesus called his disciples to him and said, ²"I have compassion for these people; they have already been with me three days and have nothing to eat. ³If I send them home hungry, they will collapse on the way, because some of them have come a long distance."

⁴His disciples answered, "But where in this remote place can anyone get enough bread to feed them?"

⁵"How many loaves do you have?" Jesus asked.

"Seven," they replied.

⁶He told the crowd to sit down on the ground. When he had taken the seven loaves and given thanks, he broke them and gave them to his disciples to set before the people, and they did so. ⁷They had a few small fish as well; he gave thanks for them also and told the disciples to distribute them. ⁸The people ate and were satisfied. Afterward the disciples picked up seven basketfuls of broken pieces that were left over. ⁹About four thousand men were present. And having sent them away, ¹⁰he got into the boat with his disciples and went to the region of Dalmanutha.

Interest in Mark as an author in his own right, not merely a scissors-and-paste editor of the tradition, has focused attention lately on the structural arrangement of his Gospel. A study of the section 8:1–30 has revealed some important parallels with the section 6:31–7:37. Lane (p. 269) sets these out as follows:

6:31–44	Feeding the Multitude	8:1–9
6:45–56	Crossing the Sea and Landing	8:10
7:1–23	Conflict With the Pharisees	8:11–13
7:24–30	Conversation About Bread	8:13–21
7:31–36	Healing	8:22–26
7:37	Confession of Faith	8:27–30

The motif that seems to be behind this arrangement of the tradition is spiritual understanding—or lack of it. Jesus sounds a call to spiritual understanding in 7:14–18, but the disciples fail to understand after each feeding miracle (6:52; 8:14–21). The miracles of healing—the opening of the ears of the deaf man (7:31–36) and the eyes of the blind man (8:22–26)—are symbolic of and prepare the way for the opening of the spiritual understanding of the disciples. Mark's arrangement of the tradition to carry out his motif in no way decreases the historical reliability of the tradition.

The striking similarity between this story and the one in 6:34–44 raises the question whether there was one or two feedings of the multitude. The majority of scholars think there was only one and take 8:1–9 as a doublet of 6:34–44. Particularly important to this view is the disciples' apparent failure to remember the first feeding (cf. 8:4). Nonetheless there are strong reasons to support the view that 6:34–44 and 8:1–9 are indeed accounts of two separate events.

1. The language in the two accounts though similar also has significant differences (see commentary for details).

2. Jesus himself clearly refers to two feedings (8:18–21).

3. Verse 4 does not seem to be an insurmountable problem since it would be presumptuous to assume that the disciples always expected Jesus to meet a crisis situation by performing a miracle (cf. commentary for additional interpretations of 8:4).

The accounts certainly are similar. Yet their differences suggest that on two different occasions Jesus fed a multitude. There can be little doubt that Mark thought them to be two separate events.

1–3 "During those days" (v.1) probably connects this incident with the preceding one (7:31–37). Jesus remained in the Decapolis, on the east side of the Lake of Galilee. The presence of a large crowd is implied. They had been with Jesus for three days, probably receiving instruction from him. Taylor (p. 358) points out that "the reference to 'three days' is peculiar to the narrative, distinguishing it from 6:35–44, in which the crossing, the meal, and the recrossing all take place on the same day." Jesus, not the disciples (as in 6:35–36), recognized the physical needs of the crowds (v.2). He was moved with compassion for them because they had not had anything to eat for three days. Another difference in this amount is that Jesus immediately dismisses the idea that the crowd should be sent away for food ("If I send them home hungry, they will collapse on the way" [v.3]), whereas in 6:36 the disciples definitely ask him to send them away. The "long distance" that "some of them" had come may imply that the crowd was partly made up of local people.

4 The disciples' reply may indicate that they had completely forgotten the feeding of the five thousand. This is perhaps the strongest argument against the view that there were two separate feedings. But the argument is not so strong as it appears. Several things may be said in rebuttal (cf. Cranfield, *Gospel of Mark*, p. 205).

1. A considerable period of time may have elapsed between the two events.

2. Even mature Christians (which the disciples were not), having experienced God's power and provision, have subsequently acted in unbelief.

3. The reluctance of Jesus to perform miracles must have so impressed itself on the disciples that they did not expect to meet every crisis in that fashion.

4. Some allowance must be made for the assimilation of the language of the two accounts because of their repeated use in teaching and worship.

The disciples' answer here is in terms of the difficulty of finding enough food for such a huge crowd rather than sending them away to get their own as in 6:36.

5-7 Only seven loaves were available to feed the crowd (v.5). Again the details differ from the account in chapter 6. There is no ordering of the people into groups of hundreds and fifties. They are simply asked to sit down where they are on the ground (v.6). Jesus gives thanks separately for the bread and the fish—there were a few small ones, Mark tells us—and after each prayer the disciples distributed the food to the people. NIV does not distinguish between *eucharistein* ("to give thanks," v.6) and *eulogein* ("to bless," v.7), translating both as "give thanks." The difficulty copyists had with the idea of Jesus' "blessing" the fish is reflected by the variant *eucharistēsas* ("having given thanks") in v.7 and by the omission of *auta* ("them," referring to the fish) in the same verse. Mark's "having blessed them [in God's name]" is tantamount to giving thanks.

8 As always Jesus' provision was sufficient—"the people ate and were satisfied." But it was not merely sufficient. Seven (there were twelve in ch. 6) basketfuls of fragments were left over and collected by the disciples. The use of *spyris* for "basket" here instead of *kophinos* (6:43) is striking and suggests two different occasions. A *spyris* is a large basket—Paul was lowered from the wall of Damascus in one (Acts 9:25)—whereas a *kophinos* is a wicker basket in which Jews ordinarily carried their food when journeying.

9-10 Again the details are different. The crowd numbered "about four thousand" (v.9; five thousand in ch. 6). Jesus got into the boat with his disciples (v.10; in ch. 6 he had the disciples get into the boat and go to Bethsaida, while he stayed back to dismiss the crowd).

The identity of Dalmanutha is unknown. Matthew (15:39) says Jesus went to the vicinity of Magadan." Dalmanutha and Magadan (or Magdala), located on the western shore of the Lake of Galilee, may have been names for the same place or two places located near each other. This is the only reference anywhere to the name Dalmanutha.

K. *Requesting a Sign From Heaven*

8:11-13

11The Pharisees came and began to question Jesus. To test him, they asked him for a sign from heaven. **12**He sighed deeply and said, "Why does this genera-

tion ask for a miraculous sign? I tell you the truth, no sign will be given to it."
¹³Then he left them, got back into the boat and crossed to the other side.

11 This paragraph seems quite separate from the one immediately preceding it. If it is to be understood as completing the pericope found in 3:22–30, a context would be provided that would be helpful for its interpretation. It seems best, however, to consider the paragraph as an isolated section Mark places here to form a parallel in this section (8:1–30) with 7:1–23 in the previous section (6:31–7:37). Both incidents relate to conflict with the Pharisees.

The request for a sign by the Pharisees was not sincere. It was "to test him." The word is *peirazō*, and in this context it probably should be translated "tempt" (cf. its use in 1:13 of Jesus' temptation). Jesus' temptation in the wilderness was not a once-for-all experience. The Devil came back again and again to tempt him. Here the temptation was for Jesus to produce a "sign from heaven." Two interpretations commend themselves. First, since the word *sēmeion* is used, a word by which the Synoptists denote an outward compelling proof of divine authority, what the Pharisees were asking was for more proof than Jesus' miracles (*dynameis*) afforded. Jesus resolutely refused the request for such a sign because it arose out of unbelief. Second, since the word *dynameis* ("mighty acts") is regularly used for Jesus' miracles in the Synoptics, and since the Pharisees ask for *semeia* ("signs"), what they are requesting is evidence of Jesus' trustworthiness, not of his supernatural power (Lane, p. 277). The former interpretation seems more likely and is in keeping with how NIV translates *sēmeion apo tou ouranou* ("a sign from heaven"). The mighty acts of Jesus are not clear enough for the Pharisees. Indeed, they had on one occasion ascribed them to Satan's power. They want a higher level of sign—from heaven, i.e., clearly from God.

12 Jesus responded to their request by sighing deeply. Here the word *anastenazō*, found only here in the NT, is used. It describes Jesus' grief and disappointment when faced with the unbelief of those who, because of their spiritual privileges, ought to have been more responsive to him. There is a note of impatience in Jesus' question "Why does this generation ask for a miraculous sign?" The designation "this generation" (*hē genea hautē*) is the equivalent of the rabbinic *ha-dôr ha-zeh* and includes more than the Pharisees. Jesus has in mind the entire people, i.e., the Jewish people. To them no sign will be given. This is a particularly strong statement by Jesus. It is introduced by the solemn asseveration "I tell you the truth," and the statement itself represents in Greek a shortened form of the Hebrew self-imprecation: "If I do such a thing may I die" (cf. Taylor, p. 136). Thus Jesus, with deep feeling and with an oath, flatly refuses to give any sign.

As to why Jesus refused to do this, Martin (*Mark*, p. 174) cogently says: "For Mark and Paul the answer to this wrongful instance is the same. There is no legitimating sign—save the ambiguity of the humiliated and crucified Lord; and to see in his cross the power and wisdom of God is to be shut up to the exercise of faith, which by definition can never rest in proofs or signs, or else its character would be lost." This teaching of Jesus was doubtless what the church in Rome needed to hear, especially if they had been too engrossed in an exalted-Lord christology.

13 Having so emphatically made his point, Jesus left the Pharisees, got into the boat, and, with his disciples (cf. v.14), crossed over to the east side of the lake.

L. *The Yeast of the Pharisees and Herod*

8:14–21

¹⁴The disciples had forgotten to bring bread, except for one loaf they had with them in the boat. ¹⁵"Be careful," Jesus warned them. "Watch out for the yeast of the Pharisees and that of Herod."

¹⁶They discussed this with one another and said, "It is because we have no bread."

¹⁷Aware of their discussion, Jesus asked them: "Why are you talking about having no bread? Do you still not see or understand? Are your hearts hardened? ¹⁸Do you have eyes but fail to see, and ears but fail to hear? And don't you remember? ¹⁹When I broke the five loaves for the five thousand, how many basketfuls of pieces did you pick up?"

"Twelve," they replied.

²⁰"And when I broke the seven loaves for the four thousand, how many basketfuls of pieces did you pick up?"

They answered, "Seven."

²¹He said to them, "Do you still not understand?"

14 For some reason the disciples (the Greek merely says "they," but NIV correctly assumes that the pronoun refers to the disciples) had forgotten to bring an adequate supply of bread with them for the trip across the lake. Had their quick departure from the Pharisees caused this? At any rate, their failure sets the stage for the teaching of our Lord in this pericope. Some commentators see in the "one loaf" a symbolic reference to Jesus. The disciples failed to see that the one loaf they had with them was none other than Jesus himself, and that was sufficient.

15 The connection of this verse with vv. 11–12 is clear, but its connection with the immediately preceding verses is obscure. Jesus warns his disciples about the yeast of the Pharisees and of Herod. Here, as generally in Scripture, yeast is a symbol of evil; and, as only a very small amount of it is necessary to leaven a loaf of bread, so evil has a permeating power. Here the yeast of the Pharisees clearly refers to their desire for a sign from God to validate the actions of Jesus. The yeast of Herod is mentioned because he too (cf. Luke 23:8) desired a sign, Jesus is warning his disciples not to make the same mistake the Pharisees and Herod did. He is appealing to them to understand that the authority he possesses cannot be proved by a sign. Only by faith can they recognize him as the bringer of God's salvation.

16 Since the meaning of v. 16 turns on which reading is adopted, that must be the first consideration in interpreting it. KJV, RSV, NEB, and NIV follow the majority of Greek MSS and read *echomen* ("we have"). However, *echousin* ("they have") has good attestation and is adopted as a "C" rated reading by the third edition of the UBS Greek text (a change of heart from the second edition). The rationale is that the reading *echomen* seems to be an accommodation to the following context and probably was also influenced by Matthew 16:7 (cf. Metzger, *Textual Commentary*, p. 98). If, following the reading *echousin*, *hoti* is taken as an indirect interrogative ("why"), the translation would be thus: "They discussed with one another why they had no bread." According to this reading, the disciples were so concerned to find out who was to blame for not bringing more bread that they completely ignored

Jesus' warning about the yeast of the Pharisees and of Herod. Such an understanding of this verse heightens Mark's depiction of the disciples' lack of understanding.

17–21 Jesus rebuked his disciples for their lack of understanding (v.17). They were like those on the outside (cf. 4:11–12) who had eyes but did not see and ears but did not hear (v.18). They should not have been so concerned over the bread. That concern had prevented them from profiting from the warning about the leaven of the Pharisees and of Herod. They should have remembered how abundantly Jesus had provided for them on two occasions—so much so that on both occasions they had leftover bread to collect (vv.19–20). He, the Provider, was with them in the boat. What else could they want or need? Almost pleadingly Jesus asks, "Do you still not understand?" (v.21).

Notes

11 The verb ζητεῖν (zētein, "ask") is used consistently in Mark in a negative sense (cf. 11:18; 12:12; 14:1). Here it is used in the same way. The asking was wrongheaded and misguided.

12 The introductory formula ἀμὴν λέγω ὑμῖν (amēn legō hymin, "I tell you the truth") is evidence that the form we have of the saying in Mark's Gospel, which allows for no exception in sign giving, "stands at the furthest recoverable point of the tradition. Indeed it may be claimed that we hear a true accent of ipsissima vox Jesu" (Martin, Mark, p. 165).

12 Εἰ δοθήσεται (ei dothēsetai, "will not be given") is a very strong negation, ei being equivalent to the Hebrew אִם (im), which introduces an oath (cf. Ps 7:4–5 LXX). Also, the fact that the verb is in the passive voice, thus indicating that Mark is using a circumlocution for the name of God, strengthens the statement even more. The meaning is "Surely God will not give a sign to this generation."

15 In the rabbinical writings, yeast is usually a symbol for "the evil influence" (יֵצֶר הָרַע yēṣer haraʿ) or the wicked ways and dispositions of men (cf. SBK, 1:728). Paul also uses yeast in a negative sense (1 Cor 5:6–8).

19 As already noted in 8:8, two different words are used for basket in the two stories of the feeding of the multitude. Κόφινος (kophinos, "lunch basket") is used in all six references to the feeding of the five thousand (Matt 14:20; 16:9; Mark 6:43; 8:19; Luke 9:17; John 6:13), while σπυρίς (spyris, "hamper") is used in all four references to the feeding of the four thousand (Matt 15:37; 16:10; Mark 8:8, 20). This consistency argues powerfully in favor of two separate incidents.

M. Healing a Blind Man at Bethsaida

8:22–26

22They came to Bethsaida, and some people brought a blind man and begged Jesus to touch him. 23He took the blind man by the hand and led him outside the village. When he had spit on the man's eyes and put his hands on him, Jesus asked, "Do you see anything?"

24He looked up and said, "I see people; they look like trees walking around."

25Once more Jesus put his hands on the man's eyes. Then his eyes were opened, his sight was restored, and he saw everything clearly. 26Jesus sent him home, saying, "Don't go into the village."

22 This incident, which is recorded only in Mark, takes place at Bethsaida ("house of the fish") located on the east bank of the Jordan River, where it flows into the Sea of Galilee. At this place "some people" (Mark does not identify them) brought a blind man to Jesus for healing. The fact that the initiative seems to have come more from the people who brought him than from the man himself may account for the way Jesus dealt with him (cf. Mark 7:32ff.).

23–24 Why did Jesus lead the blind man out of the village (v.23)? Was it to avoid the clamor and excitement of the people or perhaps to make personal contact with the man apart from the distraction of the crowd? Most of the miracles in Mark were done in public. Only on three occasions did Jesus withdraw from the people to heal: viz., the raising of Jairus's daughter (5:35–43), where Jesus' motive is clearly to rid himself of the commotion caused by the professional mourners; the healing of the deaf mute (7:31–37), where Jesus wanted to establish a personal contact with the man to help his faith; and the present incident, where the motive seems to be the same as in the healing of the deaf mute.

Jesus performs a double action: he spits on the man's eyes and lays his hands on him. The only parallel anywhere near this double treatment occurs in the incident in John 9, where the blind man has his eyes anointed with clay and then washed in the Pool of Siloam. To Jesus' question "Do you see anything?" the answer of the blind man here in Mark is essentially "Yes, but not clearly" (v.24). Two things require comment: (1) the man had probably not been born blind or else he would not have been able to identify trees as trees and (2) the return of his sight was gradual. As to why Jesus abandoned his usual method of instantaneous healing, Calvin (2:285) said: "He did so most probably for the purpose of proving, in the case of this man, that he had full liberty as to his method of proceeding, and was not restricted to a fixed rule. . . . And so the grace of Christ, which had formerly been poured out suddenly on others, flowed by drops, as it were, on this man."

25–26 The second laying on of hands is unique in the healing ministry of Jesus (v.25). The result was a complete cure. Mark's account of it graphically records that fact: "his eyes were opened, his sight was restored, and he saw everything clearly." The word translated "clearly" (*tēlaugōs*) means "clearly at a distance" and indicates the completeness of the restoration of the man's sight. As for the reason why Jesus did this healing gradually, Mark gives us no hint. Jesus may have moved only as quickly as the man's faith would allow (in Mark's Gospel faith as a requisite for healing is emphasized). But Calvin's suggestion that Jesus was demonstrating his sovereign freedom seems more likely. One thing is certain. The early church did not make up this story!

In v.26 Jesus orders the man to go home directly without first going into the town of Bethsaida. The variant reading "Don't go and tell anybody in the city" is an attempt to clarify the reason why Jesus ordered the man not to go into the town. Doubtless it was influenced by other passages in Mark in which Jesus does enjoin silence.

The importance of this story for Mark is that it anticipates the opening of the eyes of understanding of the disciples. It is the second in a pair of incidents that only Mark records (the first one is 7:24–37) and that fulfill the OT messianic expectations of Isaiah 35:5–6. Mark uses both incidents to lead up to the revelation of the messianic dignity of Jesus to the disciples (8:27–30). Their eyes too are opened, not by human perception, but by the miracle of God's gracious revelation, which was as much a miracle as the opening of the blind man's eyes.

N. *Recognizing Jesus as Messiah*

8:27–30

27Jesus and his disciples went on to the villages around Caesarea Philippi. On the way he asked them, "Who do people say I am?"
28They replied, "Some say John the Baptist; others say Elijah; and still others, one of the prophets."
29"But what about you?" he asked. "Who do you say I am?
Peter answered, "You are the Christ."
30Jesus warned them not to tell anyone about him.

This incident is usually taken to mark the beginning of the second half of Mark's Gospel. While it is true that 8:27–30 has a close connection with 8:31–9:1, its relationship to 8:22–26 is even closer. This may be seen by the remarkable parallelism in the two stories—a parallelism that may be set out like this:

8:22	Circumstances	8:27
8:23–24	Partial Sight—Partial Understanding	8:28
8:25	Sight—Understanding	8:29
8:26	Injunction to Silence	8:30

Assuming that this arrangement is not by chance, Mark uses the account of the opening of the blind man's eyes to symbolize and anticipate the opening of the understanding of the disciples as to the true nature of the messiahship of Jesus. To be sure, their understanding was not complete, as 8:32 makes clear; yet the two accounts are generally parallel. Where the parallelism breaks down is at the point of partial understanding (8:28), for this is a partial understanding on the part of the people, not the disciples. Mark could have changed the story to force parallelism. That he did not do so supports the historicity of the account.

27 The first half of Mark's Gospel mounts to a climax with the story of the disciples' recognition of Jesus' messiahship. Caesarea Philippi was at the foot of Mount Hermon, on a shelf of land 1,150 feet above sea level and overlooking the north end of the Jordan River Valley. Originally the city was called Paneas (the name survives today as Banias) in honor of the Roman god Pan, whose shrine was located there. Herod Philip had rebuilt the ancient city and named it in honor of Tiberias Caesar and himself. Thus it was known as Caesarea Philippi and was distinguished from Caesarea, the Roman city on the Mediterranean coast. It was somewhere in the vicinity of Caesarea Philippi that Jesus put to his disciples the crucial question "Who do people say that I am?"

Cranfield is certainly right when he says:

To argue that the content of the question and the fact that Jesus takes the initiative with it shows that the material is secondary, since according to Jewish custom it was the disciple, not the Rabbi, who asked the questions, and since Jesus would not have asked a question concerning something about which he must have been as well informed as those whom he is supposed to question, is surely unimaginative. (*Gospel of Mark,* p. 268).

Jesus was no ordinary rabbi and did not ask the question simply to get information. He used it as preliminary to his second question (v.29).

28 The answers all reflect an inadequate view of Christ. John the Baptist had a preparatory role. He looked for another messenger far greater than himself (cf. Mark 1:7–8). A common Jewish concept of the day was that of "Elijah redivivus" (Elijah returned or revived), based on Malachi 3:1; 4:5; but he too was only a forerunner of the Messiah (cf. 6:14–15, where the same opinions are expressed about Jesus). "One of the prophets" reflects an even lower view of Jesus. He is merely one of many prophets who have come on the scene of Israel's history. It is surprising that the disciples do not report that anyone said that Jesus was the Messiah, especially since the demons recognized who he was and said so publicly (1:24; 3:11, 5:7). But his messiahship was veiled from the crowd.

29 Jesus now directs the question at the disciples. His use of *hymeis* ("you"), the emphatic pronoun, is particularly important. NIV catches this nuance by repeating the "you": "But what about you? . . . Who do you say I am?" In other words Jesus is asking, "Who do you, my most intimate and trusted friends—in contrast to the other people who neither know me nor understand me—think I am?"

Peter, true to form, had a ready answer: "You are the Christ." Peter speaks not only for himself. He is the spokesman for the Twelve, and in his confession one of the themes of this Gospel (cf. 1:1; "The beginning of the gospel about Jesus Christ") is stated.

The Greek word *Christos* ("Christ") translates the Hebrew *māšîaḥ* ("Messiah") and means the "Anointed One" of God. In the OT the word is used of anyone who was anointed with the holy oil, as, for example, the priests and kings of Israel (cf. Exod 29:7, 21; 1 Sam 10:1, 6; 16:13; 2 Sam 1:14, 16). The word carries with it the idea of chosenness by God, consecration to his service, and enduement with his power to accomplish the task assigned.

Toward the close of the OT period, the word "anointed" assumed a special meaning. It denoted the ideal king anointed and empowered by God to deliver his people and establish his righteous kingdom (Dan 9:25–26). Particularly important in the development of the concept was its use in the pseudepigraphal Psalms of Solomon (chs. 17–18). There the coming ruler is spoken of as restoring David's kingdom to its former prosperity and greatness. The ideas that clustered around the title "Messiah" tended to be political and national in nature. It is probably for that reason that Jesus seldom used the term. Of its seven occurrences in Mark, only three of them are in sayings of Jesus (9:41; 12:35; 13:21); and in none of these does he use the title of himself.

Because Jesus was reluctant to speak of himself as the Messiah does not mean that he did not believe himself to be the Messiah. In this passage (8:29) and in 14:6–62, he accepted it as used of him by others (cf. John 4:25–26).

> And this is hardly surprising; for the title, in spite of all the false and narrow hopes which had become attached to it, was peculiarly fitted to express his true relation both to the OT and to the people of God. . . . the title, applied to Jesus,

designates him as the true meaning and fulfillment of the long succession of Israel's anointed kings and priests, the King and Priest . . . ; the Prophet anointed with the Spirit of God, who fulfills the long line of Israel's prophets; and the One in whom the life of the whole nation of Israel finds its fulfillment and meaning, in whom and for whose sake the people of Israel were, and the new Israel now is, the anointed people of God. (Cranfield, *Gospel of Mark,* pp. 270–71)

Peter's confession revealed real insight into the nature of Christ's person and mission, but his concept of Jesus' messiahship was far from being perfect. Peter still had much to learn of Messiah's suffering, rejection, and death, as the immediately following incident reveals.

30 Jesus' injunction of silence arose out of his knowledge of the disciples' defective view of his messiahship. They still needed instruction about it before they would be given permission to proclaim it without restraint.

V. The Journey to Jerusalem (8:31–10:52)

A new section in Mark's Gospel begins with 8:31. Its structure centers around three predictions Jesus makes of his passion (8:31; 9:31; 10:33–34). What had previously been veiled is now stated openly: the Son of Man must go up to Jerusalem, suffer and die, and on the third day be raised from the dead. This is the secret of Jesus' messiahship, and it is now revealed. Mark also stresses what this will mean for Jesus' followers. Throughout the section (cf. 8:34–38; 9:35; 10:29–30, 38–39) there are sayings about what true discipleship is, with the stress on suffering. Another purpose of this middle section of Mark's Gospel is to provide for Jesus' move from Galilee (where almost his entire ministry took place) to Jerusalem for the climactic events of his ministry. Mark does this by means of a travel narrative. Jesus progressively moves closer and closer to the Holy City. The final event, the healing of blind Bartimaeus (10:46–52), takes place when Jesus is coming out of Jericho with the crowds of people on the way to the Passover Feast in Jerusalem. Chapter 11 opens with the Triumphal Entry into the city.

This section with its emphasis on the suffering of the Messiah and of those that follow him must have had special meaning for the persecuted Christians in Rome. Mark is reminding them that to follow Jesus is to follow the path of suffering and even death.

A. *First Prediction of the Passion*

8:31–33

> [31]He then began to teach them that the Son of Man must suffer many things and be rejected by the elders, chief priests and teachers of the law, and that he must be killed and after three days rise again. [32]He spoke plainly about this, and Peter took him aside and began to rebuke him.
>
> [33]But when Jesus turned and looked at his disciples, he rebuked Peter. "Get behind me, Satan!" he said. "You do not have in mind the things of God, but the things of men."

31 Jesus now begins to teach his disciples what messiahship really meant. However he does not refer to himself as Messiah but as the Son of Man. Since this title is so important theologically, extended comment is in order.

"Son of Man" is by far the favorite expression Jesus uses in the Gospels to refer to himself. It occurs eighty-one times; and, with the possible exceptions of Mark 2:10 and 28—where the title "Son of Man" seems to be part of Mark's editorial comments—no one else, neither his friends nor his foes, refers to Jesus as the Son of Man.

"Son of Man" occurs in the OT. In the Psalms it means simply "man" (cf. Pss 8:4; 80:17); and in Ezekiel, where it occurs over ninety times, it is the particular name by which God addresses the prophet. These OT passages throw some light on the NT usage. The most helpful text, however, is Daniel 7:13–14:

> In my vision at night I looked, and there before me was one like a son of man, coming with the clouds of heaven. He approached the Ancient of Days and was led into his presence. He was given authority, glory and sovereign power; all peoples, nations and men of every language worshiped him. His dominion is an everlasting dominion that will not pass away, and his kingdom is one that will never be destroyed.

This passage, depicting the Son of Man as a heavenly figure who at the end time brings the kingdom to the oppressed on earth, is especially reflected in the sayings of Jesus in Mark's Gospel that speak of the coming of the Son of Man "in his Father's glory with the holy angels" (8:38; 13:26; 14:62). The title has, however, been infused with additional meaning, especially in those passages that associate the Son of Man with suffering and death (8:31; 9:9, 12, 31; 10:33, 45; 14:21, 41). The combining of the motif of eschatological glory with that of suffering and death is what characterizes the Son-of-Man idea in Mark's Gospel as elsewhere in the Synoptics. It is evident that Jesus considered "Son of Man" a messianic title because, immediately following Peter's confession of him as the Christ, he began to teach them that the Son of Man (equivalent to Christ in v.29) must suffer, etc. Son of Man was the title Jesus preferred in referring to himself because, unlike "Messiah," it was not freighted with connotations that might prove harmful to his God-appointed mission.

The Son of Man "must" (*dei*) suffer. Gould (p. 153) remarks: "The necessity arises, first, from the hostility of men; secondly, from the spiritual nature of his work, which made it impossible for him to oppose force to force; and thirdly from the providential purpose of God, who made the death of Jesus the central thing in redemption." If *dei* refers to God's will in Scripture, the most likely reference is to the Suffering Servant passage in Isaiah 52:13–53:12. The Targum to Isaiah shows how difficult it was for the Jews to associate suffering with the Messiah. There the sufferings are referred to the people and the other statements in the passage to the Messiah. However, the common view that Jesus was the first to associate sufferings with the Messiah is questionable. Cranfield (*Gospel of Mark*, p. 277) says that evidence for a suffering Messiah existed in Judaism before Jesus' day, and its rareness was due to Anti-Christian polemic.

Jesus predicted that the rejection of the Messiah would be by three groups: the elders, the chief priests, and the teachers of the law. The elders were the lay members of the Sanhedrin; the chief priests included not only Caiaphas, the high priest, and Annas, the emeritus high priest, but the members of the high priestly families; the teachers of the law were the professional scribes. These three groups made up the Sanhedrin, the Jewish high court.

The death of the Son of Man would be followed by his vindication: after three days he would be raised from the dead. "After three days" occurs also in Mark 9:31;

10:34. In Matthew 16:21; 17:23; 20:19; Luke 9:22; 18:33, "on the third day" is used. This change may indicate a difficulty with the Markan expression. Actually the two expressions are identical in meaning. Taylor (p. 378) points out that, contrary to English usage, in a Jewish context "after three days" can mean a period of less than seventy-two hours. Another possibility is that "after three days" is another way of saying "after a short period of time."

Verse 31 is particularly important because it is the only explanation in Mark's Gospel of "the messianic secret." Jesus did not want his messiahship to be disclosed because it involved suffering, rejection, and death. Popular expectations of messiahship would have hindered, if not prevented, the accomplishment of his divinely ordained (*dei*, "must") messianic mission.

32 Jesus now spoke plainly about his suffering role as Son of Man and Messiah. Before he had veiled it. The message got through to Peter, but he refused to accept it. Peter had the greatest difficulty in conceiving of messiahship in any other than the popular theological and political categories. A suffering Messiah! Unthinkable! The Messiah was a symbol of strength, not weakness. So Peter took Jesus aside and, amazingly, rebuked him. The word translated "rebuked" (*epitimaō*) is the same one used for the silencing of the demons (cf. 1:25; 3:12).

33 Jesus' words to Peter were not only very severe, they were deliberately spoken in the presence of the other disciples ("Jesus turned and looked at his disciples"). They probably shared Peter's views and needed the rebuke, too. The severity of the rebuke arises from Jesus' recognition in Peter's attempt to dissuade him from going to the Cross the same temptation he had experienced from Satan at the outset of his ministry. Satan offered him the option of using the world's means of accomplishing his mission (cf. Matt 4:8–10). On that occasion Jesus rebuked him, "Away from me, Satan! For it is written: 'Worship the Lord your God, and serve him only' " (Matt 4:10). Here, too, Jesus recognized the satanic opposition in Peter. " 'Get behind me, Satan!' he said. 'You do not have in mind the things of God, but the things of men.' " Peter was opposing the divine will. He had in mind a popular messiahship. That was the way the world thought; it was not how God had planned Jesus' ministry and mission.

B. *Requirements of Discipleship*

8:34–9:1

> ³⁴Then he called the crowd to him along with his disciples and said: "If anyone would come after me, he must deny himself and take up his cross and follow me. ³⁵For whoever wants to save his life will lose it, but whoever loses his life for me and for the gospel will save it. ³⁶What good is it for a man to gain the whole world, yet forfeit his soul? ³⁷Or what can a man give in exchange for his soul? ³⁸If anyone is ashamed of me and my words in this adulterous and sinful generation, the Son of Man will be ashamed of him when he comes in his Father's glory with the holy angels."
> ⁹:¹And he said to them, "I tell you the truth, some who are standing here will not taste death before they see the kingdom of God come with power."

This section is composed of separate sayings already brought together in the tradition Mark received or, more probably, brought together by Mark himself. The purpose of the section is to encourage and strengthen the Roman Christians who are faced with persecution and trials. Mark is saying to them that such experiences are normal in the life of discipleship. "Jesus had called his own disciples to the realization that suffering is not only his destiny but theirs" (Lane, p. 306).

34 Now Jesus addresses the crowd as well as his disciples. The requirements for following him are not just for the Twelve but for all Christians. Two requirements of discipleship are (1) denial of self and (2) taking up one's cross and following Jesus. By denial of self, Jesus does not mean to deny oneself something. He means to renounce self—to cease to make self the object of one's life and actions. This involves a fundamental reorientation of the principle of life. God, not self, must be at the center of life.

Cross bearing does not refer to some irritation in life. Rather, it involves the way of the cross. The picture is of a man, already condemned, required to carry his cross on the way to the place of execution, as Jesus was required to do (cf. Luke 23:26). Although the cross was a Roman method of execution, it was well known to the Jews of Jesus' day. Certainly the Christians in Rome were acquainted with it. To bear the cross is to follow Jesus. This means suffering and death—a message especially relevant to the Roman Christians.

35 This statement relates to a situation in which Christians faced the alternatives of confessing Christ or denying him. Jesus warns that by denying him, one's physical life may be saved; but one's eschatological life—i.e., his eternal life, his salvation—will be lost. Conversely, to lose one's physical life by remaining true to Christ—i.e., by confessing him under duress—is to be assured of eternal life and salvation. This seems to be the meaning of the verse in this context in Mark. Thus it would have sounded a warning to any in Mark's church who might be thinking of defecting under trial. "For me" stresses the absoluteness of Jesus' claim for allegiance, and "for the gospel" is probably a reference to the preaching of the gospel for which men are to give their lives.

36–37 These two verses emphasize the incomparable worth of the *psychē* ("eschatological life," "soul"). Not even "the whole world" compares in value to it (v.36). And once a man has forfeited his share in eternal life (in this context, by a denial of Jesus), there is no way he can get it back (v.37). Even the whole world, if he had it, could not buy back eternal life for him—another stern warning against recanting the Christian faith.

38 Here is the climax of the warning. To be ashamed of Jesus and his words (the equivalent of saving one's life in v.35) has serious consequences. In the End, at the Judgment, the Son of Man will be ashamed of that person. The Hebrew parallelism in this verse clearly identifies the "of me" (Jesus) in the first part with the Son of Man in the second part. The mention of "his Father's glory with the holy angels" suggests the final judgment (cf. 2 Thess 1:7).

9:1 Since "and he said to them" is often used in Mark as an editorial link, the verse is probably an independent saying Mark has placed here. If this is true, then Mark's placement of this saying is for the purpose of making a transition between the

Transfiguration (9:2–8), a momentary manifestation of the power of the kingdom, and the Parousia (8:38), the full manifestation of it. On this understanding the Transfiguration anticipates and guarantees the Parousia.

Jesus prefaces his announcement with the solemn "I tell you the truth." The metaphor "taste death," is a reference to violent death for the sake of Jesus. Before that happens to some of them, they will see God's kingdom come in power. As the above interpretation suggests, it is not necessary to interpret this verse to mean that Jesus taught the Parousia would come in the lifetime of the disciples. Nowhere in the Gospels does Jesus say that.

C. The Transfiguration

9:2–8

> [2]After six days Jesus took Peter, James and John with him and led them up a high mountain, where they were all alone. There he was transfigured before them. [3]His clothes became dazzling white, whiter than anyone in the world could bleach them. [4]And there appeared before them Elijah and Moses, who were talking with Jesus.
> [5]Peter said to Jesus, "Rabbi, it is good for us to be here. Let us put up three shelters—one for you, one for Moses and one for Elijah." [6](He did not know what to say, they were so frightened.)
> [7]Then a cloud appeared and enveloped them, and a voice came from the cloud: "This is my Son, whom I love. Listen to him!"
> [8]Suddenly, when they looked around, they no longer saw anyone with them except Jesus.

The Transfiguration is a revelation of the glory of the Son of God, a glory now hidden but to be manifested completely and openly at the end of the age, when the Son of Man will come in the glory of his Father to render judgment on the world (cf. Mark 8:38).

The purpose of the Transfiguration is directed toward the disciples (observe the expressions "before them" [vv.2, 4] and "enveloped them" [v.7] and observe also that the Voice from the cloud speaks to them [v.7]). Mark places the Transfiguration here as a confirmation of the difficult teaching Jesus had given the disciples about his suffering and death (cf. 8:31–38). Six days had elapsed since that startling disclosure. So additional revelation of God's purpose in his Son was needed. To a select group of Jesus' disciples, this comes in the Transfiguration with God's voice booming out of the cloud: "This is my Son, whom I love. Listen to him!" (v.7). This was a direct order given to Peter, James, and John—and through them to the rest of the Twelve—to heed Jesus' disclosure at Caesarea Philippi.

2 "After six days" suggests that the Transfiguration is historical, connected with the previous event and not a throwback to a legendary postresurrection account of Jesus (Bultmann et al.). The revelation was given to Peter, James, and John, the inner circle of the disciples. The same three were present at the raising of Jairus's daughter and were with Jesus in Gethsemane. The high mountain is not identified. The traditional site is Mount Tabor, a loaf-shaped mountain in the middle of the Plain of Jezreel. But Tabor is not a "high mountain" (1,843 feet above sea level) and so is an unlikely site. Mount Hermon, which is over 9,000 feet high, is a more probable site. It is located near Caesarea Philippi, where the event Mark has just recorded took place. The word *metamorphoō* (on which see J. Behm, TDNT 4:755–59) means "to change into another form" and is used only here, in the parallel in Matthew 17:2, and in Romans 12:2 and 2 Corinthians 3:18, where it describes the believer's progressive change into the moral likeness of Christ.

3 It is difficult to know exactly what happened at the Transfiguration. Jesus' clothes became "dazzling white"—only Mark adds "whiter than anyone in the world could bleach them." If the event took place at night, its dazzling nature was enhanced. For a moment they saw the human appearance of Jesus "changed into that of a heavenly being in the transfigured world" (Behm, TDNT, 4:758).

4 Why the appearance of Elijah and Moses? (Matthew and Luke have Moses and Elijah, the more natural order.) If what the disciples saw was a glimpse of Jesus' final state of glory, then Moses and Elijah's function is to announce the End. In Jewish expectation, Elijah clearly played that role (cf. Mal 4:5; Mark 9:11–12). But what of Moses? The reappearance of Moses seems to have been a later Jewish idea (cf. Plummer, p. 214). Perhaps that is why he is mentioned second. Or Elijah and Moses may have been at the scene as representatives of the Law and the Prophets— i.e., the OT, which was being superseded, or at least fulfilled, by Jesus. Moses well represents the Law, but one would have expected one of the great writing prophets such as Isaiah or Jeremiah, instead of Elijah, to represent the Prophets. How Peter, James, and John recognized these men is not said. "The fact that both figures were, in the Old Testament, described as having ended their lives on earth in a mysterious way (Deut 34:6; II Kings 2:11) adds to the appropriateness of their mysterious reappearance in this preview of the glorious climax of Jesus' ministry" (Moule, *Gospel of Mark*, p. 70).

5 True to form, Peter responded impulsively. His words "Rabbi, it is good for us to be here" show that he was greatly moved by the experience yet did not understand it. He wanted to prolong it by erecting three shelters—"one for you [Jesus], one for Moses and one for Elijah." Lane (p. 319) says, "The desire to erect new tents of meeting where God can again communicate with men implies that Peter regards the time of the second exodus as fulfilled and the goal of the Sabbath rest achieved." But before that rest is achieved, the suffering and death of the Messiah must take place. Peter again stumbles at the necessity of a suffering Messiah.

6 This endeavor to excuse Peter's inept remark shows Mark's sensitive concern for Peter. He was frightened and at a loss as to what to say. So he impulsively spoke, and what he said was not worth saying.

7–8 The OT background of verse 7 lies in the passages where the cloud is "the vehicle of God's presence (Exod 16:10; 19:9; 24:15f.; 33:9; Lev 16:2; Num 11:25), the abode of His glory, from which He speaks" (Taylor, p. 391). The cloud "enveloped them"—viz., Elijah, Moses, and probably Jesus. At Jesus' baptism, the Voice had spoken to him (1:11); here the disciples are addressed. The Transfiguration experience was for their spiritual instruction. God's voice spoke authoritatively out of the cloud, and "this Voice assured the disciples that, although the Jews might reject Him and the Romans put Him to death (8:31), yet He was accepted and beloved by God" (Plummer, p. 215).

"Listen" must be given its full sense of obedience. The only true listening known in the Bible is obedient listening (cf. James 1:22–24). Calvin (2:314) rightly points out that when God "enjoins us to *hear him,* he appoints him to be the supreme and only teacher of his Church. It was his design to distinguish Christ from all the rest, as we truly and strictly infer from these words, that by nature he was God's *only Son*" (emphasis his). This uniqueness of Christ is highlighted by the fact that suddenly—as suddenly as they had appeared—Moses and Elijah were gone; and the three disciples "no longer saw anyone with them except Jesus" (v.8).

Notes

2 Another possible site for the Transfiguration has recently been suggested by W. Liefield, "The Transfiguration Narrative" (*New Dimensions in New Testament Study,* edd. R.N. Longenecker and M.C. Tenney [Grand Rapids: Zondervan, 1974], p. 167). His suggestion is Mount Meron, rising to the height of 3,926 feet, and located to the west of the Sea of Galilee. But Liefeld's evidence is not convincing. Since the name of the mountain on which the Transfiguration took place is not given in the Gospels, its clear identification is not possible.

D. The Coming of Elijah

9:9–13

⁹As they were coming down the mountain, Jesus gave them orders not to tell anyone what they had seen until the Son of Man had risen from the dead. ¹⁰They kept the matter to themselves, discussing what "rising from the dead" meant.
¹¹And they asked him, "Why do the teachers of the law say that Elijah must come first?"
¹²Jesus replied, "To be sure, Elijah does come first, and restores all things. Why then is it written that the Son of Man must suffer much and be rejected? ¹³But I tell you, Elijah has come, and they have done to him everything they wished, just as it is written about him.

9 On the way down the mountain, Jesus gave the three disciples orders to keep their experience of the Transfiguration secret till after the resurrection of the Son of Man. The Transfiguration was a revelation of the glory of the Son of Man. To proclaim this before the Cross would have been too much in keeping with current popular ideas of messiahship. First must come suffering and death. Then after the Resurrection (in itself a manifestation of the glory of the Son of Man), divulging the Transfiguration experience would be appropriate. But until that time Jesus enjoined the disciples to keep what they had seen a secret.

In Mark's Gospel on numbers of occasions, especially after Jesus performs a miracle, he commands those involved to keep the matter quiet (cf. 1:34, 43–44; 3:11–12; 5:43, 7:36; 8:30). Based on these texts, William Wrede (*The Messianic Secret* (1901; reprint ed., Cambridge: James Clarke, 1971) developed his "messianic secret" theory. He held that the tradition about Jesus was nonmessianic; i.e., Jesus never actually claimed to be the Messiah. It was the post-Easter church that came to believe and teach that Jesus was the Messiah. In order to resolve this contradiction,

Mark, according to Wrede, created incidents in which Jesus commands that his messiahship be kept secret. This was Mark's way of accounting for the tradition being nonmessianic. The problem with Wrede's theory is that there is no evidence that a nonmessianic tradition about Jesus ever existed. Every stratum of Gospel material contains messianic implications. Thus there is no reason not to accept Mark's "messianic secret" as historical.

10 The disciples obeyed Jesus' injunction. But they were puzzled by his statement about the resurrection of the Son of Man. As Jews they were familiar with the idea of a general resurrection of the dead. But this special resurrection of the Son of Man baffled them, as their discussion of it showed.

11 Apparently the disciples did not feel free to ask Jesus what he meant by his "rising from the dead" (v.10). Instead they asked him about Elijah. No doubt the fact that three of them had seen Elijah at the Transfiguration reminded them of what the teachers of the law said about him—viz., he would come before the Messiah and restore all things (Mal 4:5–6). Restoring all things involved, among other things, leading the people to repentance. Now if Elijah comes first and does his preparatory work, how is it that when the Son of Man comes he finds people so unprepared for him that they completely reject him and, indeed, kill him? If this represents a correct reconstruction of the thinking of the disciples, behind their question lay the stumbling block of a suffering Messiah. They were still perplexed by this.

12 Jesus' answer is that the teachers of the law are right about Elijah. He will come first and restore all things. But whatever that involves it does not preclude the suffering of the Son of Man. The Scriptures, Jesus says, predict it: "It is written." This probably is a reference to the Suffering Servant passage in Isaiah 52:13–53:12.

13 Jesus' statement about Elijah goes beyond that of the teachers of the law: not only must Elijah come, he already has come in the person of John the Baptist. Though John is not named here, the reference to him is obvious. "They have done to him everything they wished" is a reference to his treatment by Herod, i.e., his imprisonment and death. "Just as it is written about him" refers to what the OT says about Elijah in his relationship to Ahab and Jezebel (cf. 1 Kings 19:1–2). Herod and Herodias were foreshadowed in Ahab and Jezebel. Although there is no prediction of suffering associated with Elijah's eschatological ministry, the main thrust of Jesus' reply in vv.12–13 makes clear to the disciples that the eschatological ministry of Elijah in no way does away with the necessity for the Son of Man to suffer and die.

E. *Healing a Boy With an Evil Spirit*

9:14–29

> [14]When they came to the other disciples, they saw a large crowd around them and the teachers of the law arguing with them. [15]As soon as all the people saw Jesus, they were overwhelmed with wonder and ran to greet him.
> [16]"What are you arguing with them about?" he asked.
> [17]A man in the crowd answered, "Teacher, I brought you my son, who is possessed by a spirit that has robbed him of speech. [18]Whenever it seizes him, it

throws him to the ground. He foams at the mouth, gnashes his teeth and becomes rigid. I asked your disciples to drive out the spirit, but they could not."

[19]"O unbelieving generation," Jesus replied, "how long shall I stay with you? How long shall I put up with you? Bring the boy to me."

[20]So they brought him. When the spirit saw Jesus, it immediately threw the boy into a convulsion. He fell to the ground and rolled around, foaming at the mouth.

[21]Jesus asked the boy's father, "How long has he been like this?"

"From childhood," he answered. [22]"It has often thrown him into fire or water to kill him. But if you can do anything, take pity on us and help us."

[23]"'If you can'?" said Jesus. "Everything is possible for him who believes."

[24]Immediately the boy's father exclaimed, "I do believe; help me overcome my unbelief!"

[25]When Jesus saw that a crowd was running to the scene, he rebuked the evil spirit. "You deaf and mute spirit," he said, "I command you, come out of him and never enter him again."

[26]The spirit shrieked, convulsed him violently and came out. The boy looked so much like a corpse that many said, "He's dead." [27]But Jesus took him by the hand and lifted him to his feet, and he stood up.

[28]After Jesus had gone indoors, his disciples asked him privately, "Why couldn't we drive it out?"

[29]He replied, "This kind can come out only by prayer."

14 Mark has a more complete account of this story than either Matthew or Luke. This, the last exorcism story in Mark's Gospel, occurs when Jesus, Peter, James, and John rejoin the other disciples after the experience of the Transfiguration. The disciples were engaged in a debate with the teachers of the law while a large crowd looked on. If the Transfiguration took place on Mount Hermon, the presence of the teachers of the law so far north in Palestine indicates their concern in monitoring the teaching and preaching of Jesus.

15 Why were the people so amazed (Mark says that "they were overwhelmed with wonder") when they saw Jesus? Was this because the afterglow of the Transfiguration lingered on his face? This is unlikely, especially in view of his instruction for the disciples to keep the event a secret. It may have been because he arrived at an opportune time for meeting a critical need. Or perhaps it was simply because Jesus' very presence provoked wonder.

16–18 Jesus' inquiry as to what the other disciples and the crowd were arguing about (v.16) brought a reply from a man who had brought his son for healing (v.17). The description the father gives of his son's illness is graphic: he is possessed by a spirit, and this has caused a speech loss. He also has seizures accompanied by foaming at the mouth, grinding of the teeth, and bodily rigidity (v.18). These symptoms suggest epilepsy (cf. SBK, 1:758), one of a group of diseases that have had particular attention because of their mysterious nature. In Jesus' absence the man had brought his possessed son to the disciples for healing. Doubtless the disciples had fully expected to be able to exorcise the demon. Had that not been a part of their commission (cf. 3:15), and had they not already been successful at it (cf. 6:13)?

19 It seems best to restrict the meaning of "unbelieving generation" to the disciples. Thus the cry of Jesus reveals his bitter disappointment with them. In the crucial moment they had failed because of their lack of faith. Van der Loos (*Miracles of Jesus*, p. 399) says, "It is not too bold to presume that during the absence of Jesus and His three intimates, a spirit of unbelief and laxity had overcome the disciples, perhaps partly as a result of conversations between them, leading to their impotence."

"How long shall I stay with you" suggests Jesus' longing, in the face of unbelief, for his heavenly Father. "How long shall I put up with you" suggests his weariness with the disciples' spiritual obtuseness. But in teaching his disciples, Jesus was never at the end of his patience. Mark seems particularly anxious to show him persisting in his instruction of them (9:30–31; 14:28; 16:7).

20–22 Here Mark describes the deadly conflict between Jesus and the demonic powers. Confronted by Jesus, the demon immediately threw the boy into a convulsion and made him fall on the ground and foam at the mouth (v.20). Mark alone tells us that Jesus asked how long the boy had had the disease (v.21)—a detail that shows Jesus' sympathetic concern. The boy had been sick since childhood and had experienced numerous attacks in which the demon had attempted to kill him by convulsing him and throwing him into fire and water (v.22). Mark uses the plural form of water (*hydata*), which in this context may mean pools or streams. Pathetically the father asked Jesus for help. When he left home to bring his son to Jesus' disciples, he apparently believed the boy would be healed. Now he is not sure and says, "If you can do anything."

23–24 Jesus immediately fixed on the father's "if" clause. The question was not whether Jesus had the power to heal the boy but whether the father had faith to believe Jesus could—"Everything is possible for him who believes." Or perhaps the reference is to the failure of the disciples. In that case the statement is not about belief as a condition necessary for receiving healing; it is about belief as an active force in the accomplishment of healing (cf. Van der Loos, *Miracles of Jesus*, p. 400). This would help explain Jesus' rebuke of his disciples in v.19. However, in view of Mark's emphasis in his Gospel of the importance of faith for healing, the first interpretation is to be preferred. Jesus' statement, which is really a promise, elicited faith from the father. "I do believe," he exclaimed; but he recognized that his faith was far from perfect (v.24). It was still mixed with unbelief. So in a beautiful display of honesty, he asked Jesus to help him overcome his unbelief. Calvin (2:325) comments: "He declares that he *believes* and yet acknowledges himself to have *unbelief*. These two statements may appear to contradict each other but there is none of us that does not experience both of them in himself" (emphasis his).

25 The mention of a crowd "running to the scene" seems strange in view of v.14, which states that a crowd was already there. No mention is made of the crowd withdrawing; so we conclude that the crowd of v.25 is in addition to the one already present. Jesus, wanting to avoid as much as possible further publicity, exorcised the demon before additional people arrived on the scene. "He did not want to perform miracles for gaping sightseers" (D.E. Hiebert, *The Gospel According to Mark* [Chicago: Moody, 1974], p. 223). The demon, referred to as "a deaf and mute spirit," i.e., one that causes deafness and muteness, was exorcised by Jesus' direct command. He was ordered to come out and stay out for good.

26–27 The demon's exorcism is accompanied by cries and convulsions (v.26). The effect on the boy was so severe that he seemed to the crowd to be dead. He was not in fact dead (*hōsei nekros*, "as one dead"), even though "many" declared him to be dead. Completely exhausted and looking like a corpse, the boy responded to the touch of Jesus (v.27). Lane (p. 334), though granting that the text does not say the boy was dead, remarks that "the accumulation of the vocabulary of death and resurrection in vv.26-27, and the parallelism with the narrative of the raising of Jairus' daughter, suggest that Mark wished to allude to a death and resurrection. The dethroning of Satan is always a reversal of death and an affirmation of life."

28-29 Why were the nine disciples powerless to act in behalf of this boy (v.28)? Here Mark gives us the answer. In private the disciples went to Jesus and asked him why they had failed. The question expressed their deep concern. They had been given authority over evil spirits (6:7) and had successfully cast out many demons before this incident (6:13). Why their failure now? Jesus answered, "This kind can come out only by prayer" (v.29). Apparently they had taken for granted the power given them or had come to believe that it was inherent in themselves. So they no longer depended prayerfully on God for it, and their failure showed their lack of prayer.

Notes

29 After ἐν προσευχῇ (*en proseuchē*, "by prayer") most MSS add καὶ νηστεία (*kai nēsteia*, "and fasting"). But among the MSS that support the omission of "and fasting" are important representatives of the Alexandrian, Western, and Caesarean types of texts. In the light of the early church's increasing stress on fasting, the words *kai nēsteia* are probably an early scribal gloss.

F. *Second Prediction of the Passion*

> 9:30-32

> ³⁰They left that place and passed through Galilee. Jesus did not want anyone to know where they were, ³¹because he was teaching his disciples. He said to them, "The Son of Man is going to be betrayed into the hands of men. They will kill him, and after three days he will rise." ³²But they did not understand what he meant and were afraid to ask him about it.

30-31 Jesus' return to Galilee (v.30) from the territory of Herod Philip was not for the purpose of pursuing another public Galilean ministry. His public ministry was finished in Galilee. Now he was on his way to Jerusalem to complete his redemptive mission. He was focusing his teaching ministry on the Twelve, and he sought seclusion to do this. The disciples needed to be away from the distractions of the crowds to concentrate on what Jesus was saying to them. Jesus continued to teach them about his passion (v.31) because they by no means had understood his first prediction of his passion. This second prediction of it included the new element of betrayal. The verb *paradidotai* ("is going to be betrayed") is a futuristic present. Although the betrayal is still in the future, it is as good as happening right now.

By translating *paradidotai* as "betrayed," NIV opts for Judas as the implied subject of the action. The word literally means "to be delivered up" or "to be handed over." As early as Origen, it was interpreted to mean "delivered up by God." Plummer (p. 222) points out that if this refers to Judas, "into the hands of men" is almost superfluous. It seems better to understand it as Origen did. God took the initiative in providing man's salvation. The delivering up of Jesus was part of God's plan for the world's redemption (cf. Rom 4:25; 8:32). If this is what the verb means, "the play on the words Son of man . . . men is no doubt deliberate; in a fallen world men had become so hostile to God that when, as the culmination of his plans for their salvation, he sent to them the Man, their Saviour and ultimate model, they regarded and treated him as their worst enemy. Men and the Son of Man stood on opposite sides in God's eschatological battle against the powers of evil" (Plummer, p. 222). (For a discusison of Son of Man, see commentary at 8:31.)

32 The disciples still did not understand. Mark does not soften this. But perhaps some light was getting through to them. Was their fear of asking Jesus about what he had said due to their fear of facing a full disclosure of the suffering that lay ahead? Or was it because before when they had asked about the coming of Elijah (9:1) they had not understood Jesus' answer? Or were they fearful of being rebuked as Peter had been (8:33)? Whatever their reasons, they were afraid to ask Jesus about it. Instead they chose to occupy themselves with arguing about who was the greatest among them (cf. vv.33–34).

G. A Question About Greatness

9:33–37

> 33They came to Capernaum. When he was in the house, he asked them, "What were you arguing about on the road?" 34But they kept quiet because on the way they had argued about who was the greatest.
> 35Sitting down, Jesus called the Twelve and said, "If anyone wants to be first, he must be the very last, and the servant of all."
> 36He took a little child and had him stand among them. Taking him in his arms, he said to them, 37"Whoever welcomes one of these little children in my name welcomes me; and whoever welcomes me does not welcome me but the one who sent me."

Ropes (pp. 23–24) states clearly the purpose of this section in Mark's Gospel:

> The series of incidents and sayings in the last part of chapter nine . . . are not accidental in their place here, mere survivals of the crude context of an earlier source, nor are they due to a biographical motive. They are deliberately brought in by the evangelist as part of Jesus' instruction regarding the inseparable connection, both for Leader and for followers, of sufferings with the career and the cause of the Messiah. In this situation the dispute as to who is greatest (v.33ff.) betrays failure to understand; again, for them to reject any friends, however uninstructed and slight in their attachment (v.38ff.), is an arrogance that reveals their inadequate comprehension; what is requisite is sacrifice and self-denial, and persistence in it (vv.43–49), and that repression of jealousy and ill-feeling (v.50) which alone befits men who are entering on a march toward a cross.

33–34 Jesus returned to Capernaum (v.33) where his great Galilean ministry had begun (1:21) and where his headquarters in Galilee had been located. This time he did not linger there long, since his public ministry in the region had ended. He instructed his disciples "in the house," i.e., privately. The house is probably the one belonging to Peter and Andrew (cf. 1:29). The instruction runs from v.33 to v.50.

The disciples must have been embarrassed and ashamed of their arguing among themselves about who was greatest (v.34) because Jesus' question about it elicited only silence. And well might they have been ashamed. Instead of contemplating Jesus' passion and the suffering it would involve for both him and them, they had been occupied with senseless argument about greatness. Since questions of this sort were common among the Jews of the day, the disciples' dispute shows how much they were influenced by the culture of their time.

35 Jesus assumed the posture of a Jewish rabbi—he sat down (Matt 5:1; 13:1; Luke 5:3; John 8:2) and called the Twelve to him. True greatness comes through service of others. "The spirit of service is the passport to eminence in the Kingdom of God, for it is the spirit of the Master Who Himself became διάκονος πάντων ['servant of all']" (Swete, p. 205). This is a complete reversal of worldly values. How important this principle is can be seen by its repetition in the tradition (cf. Mark 10:31, 43–44; Matt 23:8–11; Luke 22:24–27). The very fact that the disciples were concerned about who was greatest underscores again their failure to understand Jesus' statements about his suffering and death. The kind of service Jesus was talking about involved sacrifice.

36–37 To illustrate the principle in v.35, Jesus took a child, perhaps one from the family in whose house he was teaching, and first stood him by his side (v.36). Then Jesus took him into his arms (cf. 10:16); and while all were watching, Jesus spoke. Black makes the suggestion that since the words "child" and "servant" represent one word in Aramaic, we have here a picture parable. The Twelve are to become like little children in their discipleship; and Jesus assures them that when they do this, they are his true representatives. Those who welcome them welcome Christ (v.37), and in welcoming Christ they welcome God himself (M. Black, "The Markan Parable of the Child in the Midst," ET 59 [1947–48]: 14–16). This is an attractive suggestion. It seems simpler and more natural, however, to take the saying as meaning that true greatness entails caring about people—insignificant people like children—because Jesus himself is concerned about them. When one cares about such people, one is really "receiving" Jesus and God himself. Moule (*Gospel of Mark*, p. 75) reminds us that "Jesus was one of the first ever to see how essentially precious any person is, particularly a young child. A concern for children was not invented by the welfare state: it goes back to the teaching of Jesus."

H. Driving Out Demons in Jesus' Name

9:38–42

38"Teacher," said John, "we saw a man driving out demons in your name and we told him to stop, because he was not one of us."

39"Do not stop him," Jesus said. "No one who does a miracle in my name can in the next moment say anything bad about me, 40for whoever is not against us is for us. 41I tell you the truth, anyone who gives you a cup of water in my name because you belong to Christ will certainly not lose his reward.

42"And if anyone causes one of these little ones who believe in me to sin, it would be better for him to be thrown into the sea with a large millstone tied around his neck.

38 John's use of "we" shows that he is speaking for all the disciples. This is the only time Mark mentions John alone. The exorcist had been driving out demons in Jesus' name, i.e., with his authority. What irked the disciples was that, though he was not one of them, he was being successful at it! What made things even worse was that they doubtless remembered their own failure to exorcise the demon from the epileptic (cf. 9:14-18). The strange exorcist must have been a believer. However, he was not one of the exclusive company of the Twelve, and this apparently was the sore point so far as they were concerned. So they took it on themselves to stop him.

39-40 Jesus' reply shows that he did not have as restrictive a view of who could legitimately participate in his mission as his disciples did (v.39). The casting out of demons was done by God's power, and his power was not limited to the Twelve. So Jesus tells his disciples not to stop the strange exorcist because he is not likely soon to speak badly of Jesus if he does a miracle in his name (cf. Num 11:26-29, where Joshua tried to get Moses to stop Eldad and Medad from prophesying in the camp of the Israelites). "The idea is, that if any man be conscious of exerting . . . a great and beneficent influence through the name of Jesus, *it will take a considerable time*, to say the least of it, before his mind can become so altered that he could either speak or think depreciatingly of the 'worthy name' in which he has found a source of power and blessing" (Morison, p. 261; emphasis his).

Casting out demons definitely demonstrated that the man was not against Jesus, and "whoever is not against us is for us" (v.40). Cranfield, p. 311, sees in this statement an indication of the messianic veiledness of Jesus. Jesus did not want to force men quickly into a decision about himself. He desired to give them plenty of time to decide, during which the principle in Mark 9:40 applies. But when the critical moment for decision arrives, then the principle laid down in Matthew 12:30 takes over: "He who is not with me is against me."

41 This verse seems to go best with v.37, before John's interruption. However, it could serve as a concrete example of the principle stated in v.40. Jesus introduced it with the solemn affirmation: "I tell you the truth." The giving of a cup of water is a very small act of hospitality. Yet if it is given to one who belongs to Christ, this act will be rewarded. Here again the Jewish idea that the representative of a man is as the man himself applies. To give a cup of water to one of Christ's followers is the same as giving it to Christ. The reward here is best understood as God's approval.

42 This verse is probably better taken with what precedes it than with what follows. On this understanding the warning it contains points back to the disciples' attempt to prevent the unknown exorcist from doing his work in Jesus' name (v.38) or to prevent anyone from giving a cup of water in his name. "Little ones" here does not refer to children as such but to followers of Jesus, and "to sin" (*skandalizein*) means to prevent them from acting in Jesus' name. The offense is so serious that it would have been better for one to be drowned than to commit it. The millstone referred to is the kind turned by donkey power rather than by hand—in other words, a big one!

Notes

41 The phrase ὅτι Χριστοῦ ἔστε (*hoti Christou este,* "because you belong to Christ") presents a problem since Jesus does not use the title "Christ" without the definite article in the synoptic Gospels. א * reads ἐμόν (*emon,* "me") instead of *Christou*. The suggestion that the original reading was ἐμοί (*emoi,* "mine") goes back to T.W. Manson in a verbal communication to Taylor. It is possible that Mark originally wrote *emoi* and that *emon* is a copyist's error. If this is true, then the meaning of the phrase would be "because you are mine" (Taylor, p. 408).

I. Demanding Requirements of Discipleship

9:43–50

43If your hand causes you to sin, cut it off. It is better for you to enter life maimed than with two hands to go into hell, where the fire never goes out. 45And if your foot causes you to sin, cut it off. It is better for you to enter life crippled than to have two feet and be thrown into hell. 47And if your eye causes you to sin, pluck it out. It is better for you to enter the kingdom of God with one eye than to have two eyes and be thrown into hell, 48where

" 'their worm does not die,
and the fire is not quenched.'

49Everyone will be salted with fire.
50"Salt is good, but if it loses its saltiness, how can you make it salty again? Have salt in yourselves, and be at peace with each other."

43–48 The main point of vv.43–50 is that it is so important to enter into life—i.e., eternal life, eschatological life—that radical means must be taken to remove what can prevent it, viz., sin. Here sin is connected with the physical self—the hand (v.43), foot (v.45), and eye (v.47). Jesus is not demanding the excision of our bodily members; he is demanding the cessation of the sinful activities of these members. Radical spiritual surgery is demanded. Nothing less is at stake than life, eternal life (cf. v.47, where "kingdom of God" stands in parallel to "life" in vv.43, 45).

The word translated "hell" is *gehenna,* a Greek form of the Hebrew words *gê hinnōm* ("Valley of Hinnom"). This was the valley along the south side of the city of Jerusalem, which was used in OT times for human sacrifices to the pagan god Molech (cf. Jer 7:31; 19:5–6; 32:35). King Josiah put a stop to this dreadful practice (2 Kings 23:10); and the Valley of Hinnom came to be used as a place where human excrement and rubbish, including animal carcasses, were disposed of and burned. The fire of *gehenna* never went out, and the worms never died. So it came to be used symbolically of the place of divine punishment. Isaiah 66:24 may reveal the beginning of this use, but it becomes much clearer during the intertestamental period, e.g., in the Book of Enoch: "This accursed valley is for those who are accursed forever; here will all those be gathered who utter unseemly words against God, and here is the place of their punishment" (27:2). "A like abyss was opened in the midst of the earth, full of fire, and they were all judged and found guilty and cast into that fiery abyss, and they burned" (90:26; cf. 48:9; 4 Ezra 7:36; M *Pirke Aboth* 1.5; 5.19–20).

Verses 44 and 46 (identical with v.48) are omitted in NIV. They are lacking in important early MSS but later on were added to round out the parallelism in vv. 47–48.

49 This is admittedly one of the most difficult verses in Mark. Over a dozen different interpretations are found in the commentaries. Of these, two commend themselves; and both take their clue from the insertion by a copyist (see Notes) of the words "and every sacrifice shall be salted with salt." This is a reference to Leviticus 2:13: "Season all your grain offerings with salt. Do not leave the salt of the covenant of your God out of your grain offerings; add salt to all your offerings."

One interpretation sees in the sacrificial salt a symbol of the covenant relationship the children of Israel had with God. For every disciple of Jesus, the salt of the covenant is the Divine Fire (cf. Matt 3:11), "which purifies, preserves and consummates sacrifice—the alternative to the Fire that consumes" (Swete, p. 213). The fire is the Holy Spirit.

Another interpretation sees in the fire the trials and persecutions of the disciples of Jesus. The previous verses relate to the dedication of the various members of the body (hand, foot, eye) to God. These must be sacrificed, if need be, to enter into the kingdom of God. Here in v.49 the total self is in mind. Every true disciple is to be a total sacrifice to God (cf. Rom 12:1); and as salt always accompanied the temple sacrifices, so fire—i.e., persecution, trials, and suffering—will accompany the true disciple's sacrifices (cf. 1 Peter 1:7; 4:12).

This saying, which is preserved only by Mark, must have had special meaning for the persecuted Roman church. It helped them understand that the purifying fires of persecution were not to be thought of as foreign to their vocation as Christians because "everyone will be salted with fire."

50 In this verse salt must be understood in a domestic setting and not in a religious or ritual one as in v.49. Salt played an important role in the ancient world. The rabbis considered it necessary to life. "The world cannot survive without salt" (*Sopherim* 15.8). It was also used as a preservative to keep food from spoiling. But salt could lose its saltiness. Jesus is warning his disciples not to lose that characteristic in them that brings life to the world and prevents its decay. But what is that characteristic that, if lost, will make the disciples of Jesus worthless? It is the disciples' spirit of devotion and self-sacrifice (cf. v.49) to Jesus Christ and his gospel. It will only be possible for disciples to be at peace with one another where that kind of devotion instead of self-interest prevails (cf. v.34).

Notes

49 The first words of this verse have come down to us in essentially three forms: (1) as translated in the NIV—"Everyone will be salted with fire." This reading has the best MS evidence; (2) "Every sacrifice will be salted with salt"; and (3) "Every one will be salted with fire and every sacrifice will be salted with salt." The history of these variants is probably as follows: The original reading was (1); a copyist finding Lev 2:13 a clue to the understanding of this difficult saying noted the OT passage in the margin; subsequently his marginal gloss was either substituted for (1) or added to it.

J. Teaching on Divorce

10:1–12

[1]Jesus then left that place and went into the region of Judea and across the Jordan. Again crowds of people came to him, and as was his custom, he taught them.

[2]Some Pharisees came and tested him by asking, "Is it lawful for a man to divorce his wife?"

[3]"What did Moses command you?" he replied.

[4]They said, "Moses permitted a man to write a certificate of divorce and send her away."

[5]"It was because your hearts were hard that Moses wrote you this law," Jesus replied. [6]"But at the beginning of creation God 'made them male and female.' [7]'For this reason a man will leave his father and mother and be united to his wife, [8]and the two will become one flesh.' So they are no longer two, but one. [9]Therefore what God has joined together, let man not separate."

[10]When they were in the house again, the disciples asked Jesus about this. [11]He answered, "Anyone who divorces his wife and marries another woman commits adultery against her. [12]And if she divorces her husband and marries another man, she commits adultery."

1 Jesus had completed his ministry in Galilee. He was moving closer and closer to the ancient city of Jerusalem where the final acts of the redemptive drama were to take place. He set his face to the accomplishment of his divine mission. Although the textual tradition (cf. Notes) reveals that the copyists had problems with the sequence of his journey ("into the region of Judea and across the Jordan"), there is no compelling reason why Jesus could not have traveled south from Capernaum, over the mountains of Samaria into Judea, and then eastward across the Jordan into Perea. Since 9:30 Jesus had been directing his teaching ministry toward his disciples, but now again he is among the crowds and teaching them.

2 The question posed by the Pharisees was not a sincere one, i.e., they were not honestly seeking information from Jesus about divorce. They were testing him, trying to catch him in some statement about a subject on which they themselves had no agreement, and then to use it against him. The fact that Jesus was in Perea, Herod Antipas's territory, may be significant. Antipas had put John the Baptist to death because John had denounced Antipas's marriage to Herodias. Perhaps the Pharisees hoped that Jesus, by his statements on marriage and divorce, would get himself into trouble with Antipas and would suffer the same cruel fate as John.

On the question of the lawfulness of divorce, there was general unanimity among the Jews: divorce was allowed. The real difference of opinion centered in the grounds for divorce. The crucial text was Deuteronomy 24:1: "If a man marries a woman who becomes displeasing to him because he finds something indecent about her, and he writes her a certificate of divorce . . ." The crucial words are "something indecent." What did that include? The school of Shammai, the stricter of the schools, understood these words to mean something morally indecent, in particular, adultery. The school of Hillel interpreted the words much more freely. Just about anything in a wife that a husband did not find to his liking was suitable grounds for divorce. Even if she burned his food! So where did Jesus stand in this? That was their question.

3 Jesus, as he often did when in controversy with the Jewish religious leaders, instead of answering the question directly, countered with a question of his own. Moses was their authority—what did *he* say? Jesus knew they would appeal to Moses; so he made them make the first commitment.

Johnson (pp. 169–70) writes:

> Jewish marriage was not a contract between equals; a woman did not marry, but was "given in marriage". It is only fair, however, to add that Pharisaic rules afforded a certain protection to the more helpless party. Her husband had to give her a writ of divorce that was valid in every respect, written on durable material and with ink that did not fade, and once he had delivered the writ he could not retract it; the woman was free. While a wife could not divorce her husband, she could go before the court and force him to divorce her if he engaged in disgusting occupations such as tanning, had certain diseases, took vows to her detriment, or forced her to take such vows. Furthermore, the rabbis bitterly condemned indiscriminate divorce even if it was legal.

4–5 Jesus did not question the law. But his answer reaches back to first principles. Moses' permission to divorce (v.4) was an accommodation to human weakness (v.5). It was an attempt to bring some sort of order in a society that disregarded God's standards. But that is not what God intended in marriage. His design in creating man and woman was that marriage should be an unbroken lifelong union. Cranfield (p. 319) points out that a distinction must be made between what is the absolute will of God and what the provisions are that take into account the sinfulness of man and are intended to limit and control its effects. Moses' bill of divorcement falls into the second category. The rabbis mistook God's gracious provision in allowing divorce as his approval of it.

6–8 Jesus refers back to the original creation (v.6), when God created them male and female.

> Marriage is grounded in this male and female constitution: as to its nature it implies that the man and the woman are united in one flesh; as to its sanction, it is divine; as to its continuance it is permanent. The import of all this is that marriage from its very nature and from the divine institution by which it is constituted is ideally indissoluble. It is not a contract of temporary convenience and not a union that may be dissolved at will. (J. Murray, *Divorce* [Philadelphia: Presbyterian and Reformed, 1974], p. 29)

Since marriage is a lifelong union between a man and a woman, its claims take precedence over ties to father and mother (v.7). "The forsaking of the house of one's father was far more meaningful at that time, since a man would forsake the solidarity and protection of his own clan" (Schweizer, p. 203). In the marriage relationship, husband and wife become one; "one flesh" is a Semitic expression that simply means "one" (v.8).

9 Behind the concept of the indissolubility of marriage is the authority of God himself. "Divorce is contrary to the divine institution, and contrary to the nature of marriage, contrary to the divine action by which the union is effected. It is precisely

here that its wickedness becomes singularly apparent—it is the sundering by man of a union God has constituted. Divorce is the breaking of a seal which has been engraven by the hand of God" (Murray, *Divorce*, p. 33).

10–12 Mark records no response of the Pharisees to Jesus' teaching about divorce. Instead he moves directly to Jesus' private teaching of the Twelve. The disciples wanted a clarification of the teaching Jesus had just given (v.10). Jesus gave them a straightforward answer: divorce and remarriage by husband or wife is adultery (v.11). Jesus did what the rabbis refused to do: he recognized that a man could commit adultery against his wife. In rabbinic Judaism a woman by infidelity could commit adultery against her husband; and a man, by having sexual relations with another man's wife, could commit adultery against him. But a man could never commit adultery against his wife, no matter what he did. Jesus, by putting the husband under the same moral obligation as the wife, raised the status and dignity of women.

The phrase "and if she divorces her husband" (v.12) shows that Jesus recognized the right of a woman to divorce her husband, a right not recognized in Judaism. Matthew, writing for Jews, omits v.12; but Mark, writing for Romans, includes it.

Notes

1 The textual history of this verse reveals that the copyists had difficulty with Mark's geography. The most substantiated reading is that in NIV: "in the region of Judea and across the Jordan." KJV translates the reading of the TR: "into the coasts of Judaea by the farther side of Jordan." This is clearly an attempt by copyists to "correct" Mark's geography. A third reading omits the καὶ (*kai*, "and") before the word πέραν (*peran*, "across"). This probably represents an assimilation to the parallel in Matt 19:1.

9 Συνέζευξεν (*synezeuxen*) means literally "yoked together" (NIV, "joined together"). It graphically stresses the importance of husband and wife working together as a team of oxen yoked together. The word is often used in Greek literature of the marriage relationship.

12 Lane (p. 352) favors the reading, supported by the Western and Caesarean texts, that speaks of the woman "separating" (ἐξέλθῃ, *exelthē*) from her husband (without divorce) and marrying another man. His argument is that not only is the text tradition that supports this reading strong but it is particularly appropriate to the situation of Herodias and Herod Antipas. Taylor (pp. 420–21) also favors this reading. Cranfield (*Gospel of Mark*, p. 322), in support of the UBS text (followed by NIV), remarks: "The words in Mk may represent an adaptation of Jesus' teaching to the situation of a Gentile church (Jewish law did not allow a wife to divorce her husband), or it may be that Jesus himself was looking beyond the custom of his own people (he can hardly have been altogether unaware of Gentile practice)."

K. *Blessing the Children*

10:13–16

[13]People were bringing little children to Jesus to have him touch them, but the disciples rebuked them. [14]When Jesus saw this, he was indignant. He said to

them, "Let the little children come to me, and do not hinder them, for the kingdom of God belongs to such as these. ¹⁵I tell you the truth, anyone who will not receive the kingdom of God like a little child will never enter it." ¹⁶And he took the children in his arms, put his hands on them and blessed them.

13 Here we have a pronouncement story that has lost all details of time and place. Mark may have placed it at this point because a story about children is a fitting sequel to Jesus' teaching about marriage. Matthew also places it in this context but makes a closer connection with what precedes by the use of the word "then" (Mark uses the conjunction "and," untranslated in NIV).

Mark does not identify those who were bringing the children to Jesus. In the Greek the subject of the verb is indefinite—"they." NIV translates it "people were bringing." However, from the use of the masculine pronoun "them" (*autois*) in the last part of this verse, it may be assumed that, in addition to mothers, fathers and perhaps brothers and sisters also brought the children. Among Jews, as among other peoples, it was customary to bring children to great men to have them blessed (cf. Gen 48:13–20; SBK, 1:807–8). The word Mark uses for children (*paidia*) in this verse is the same one used of the twelve-year-old daughter of Jairus. Here, however, it denotes small children (Jesus took them into his arms). In the parallel passage in his Gospel, Luke uses the word *brephē*, which means "babies." Why the disciples wanted to prevent the children from coming to Jesus is not stated. Perhaps they wanted to protect his privacy and shield him from needless interruptions. Though their motives may have been commendable, they again show lack of spiritual sensitivity.

14 Only Mark records that Jesus was "indignant" when he realized what the disciples were doing. Mark never softens the human emotions of Jesus, nor is he less than candid about the failings of the disciples. Jesus was indignant that anyone should think children unimportant. The error of the disciples was in a smaller degree a repetition of the error of Peter (cf. 8:32). Peter wished to keep Jesus from future suffering and death; the disciples now wish to keep him from present trouble and fatigue. But Jesus wanted children to come to him and not to be hindered in their coming. His reason for this was that "the kingdom of God belongs to such as these"—i.e., children in their receptivity and dependence exemplify the characteristics of those who possess God's kingdom.

15 The solemn pronouncement "I tell you the truth" reiterates and expands the statement in v.14. The kingdom of God is to be received as a little child receives.

> The point of comparison is not so much the innocence and humility of children (for children are not invariably either innocent or humble): it is rather the fact that children are unselfconscious, receptive, and content to be dependent on others' care and bounty; it is in such a spirit that the kingdom must be "received" —it is a gift of God, and not an achievement on the part of man; it must be simply accepted, inasmuch as it can never be deserved. (Rawlinson, p. 137)

The kingdom is both a gift to be received and a realm to enter.

This saying is found in another context in Matthew 18:3. But it does not seem strange to the historical context of Mark and could be an independent saying placed here by him.

16 Jesus took the children in his arms (cf. 9:36)—a striking act showing his love for them. Apparently they were fairly small children. The verb *katalogein* means to "bless fervently," the prefix *kata* having an intensive force. This was the overflowing of Jesus' divine love for children. It was this experience that the disciples in their insensitivity were preventing the children from having and Jesus from giving! No wonder Jesus was indignant.

L. *Riches and the Kingdom of God*

10:17–31

> ¹⁷As Jesus started on his way, a man ran up to him and fell on his knees before him. "Good teacher," he asked, "what must I do to inherit eternal life?"
> ¹⁸"Why do you call me good?" Jesus answered. "No one is good—except God alone. ¹⁹You know the commandments: 'Do not murder, do not commit adultery, do not steal, do not give false testimony, do not defraud, honor your father and mother.' "
> ²⁰"Teacher," he declared, "all these I have kept since I was a boy."
> ²¹Jesus looked at him and loved him. "One thing you lack," he said. "Go, sell everything you have and give to the poor, and you will have treasure in heaven. Then come, follow me."
> ²²At this the man's face fell. He went away sad, because he had great wealth.
> ²³Jesus looked around and said to his disciples, "How hard it is for the rich to enter the kingdom of God!"
> ²⁴The disciples were amazed at his words. But Jesus said again, "Children, how hard it is to enter the kingdom of God! ²⁵It is easier for a camel to go through the eye of a needle than for a rich man to enter the kingdom of God."
> ²⁶The disciples were even more amazed, and said to each other, "Who then can be saved?"
> ²⁷Jesus looked at them and said, "With man this is impossible, but not with God; all things are possible with God.
> ²⁸Peter said to him, "We have left everything to follow you!"
> ²⁹"I tell you the truth," Jesus replied, "no one who has left home or brothers or sisters or mother or father or children or fields for me and the gospel ³⁰will fail to receive a hundred times as much in this present age (homes, brothers, sisters, mothers, children and fields—and with them, persecutions) and in the age to come, eternal life. ³¹But many who are first will be last, and the last first."

This section is made up of three parts. The most satisfactory division is (1) vv.17–22, which describe Jesus' encounter with a rich man; (2) vv.23–27, a logion on the difficulty of a rich man's entering the kingdom of God; and (3) vv.28–31, Peter's statement about leaving all to follow Jesus and Jesus' reply to it. It is possible that the three sections were historically connected. In view of the repetition of the amazement of the disciples (cf. vv.24, 26) and Jesus' statement about the difficulty of a rich man's entering the kingdom (cf. vv.23–24), it seems best to regard the three sections as separate sayings brought together by Mark because of their common theme.

The position of this section (vv.17–31) in Mark's overall outline is significant. It follows Jesus' teaching about the importance of childlikeness—viz., a recognition of the necessity of weakness and dependence for entrance into the kingdom (vv.13–16)

—and it precedes Jesus' third prediction of his passion. The impossibility of wealth as a means to gain the kingdom (v.27) looks back to the lesson from the children (v.15), and the call to commitment (vv.29–31) looks forward to the passion statement (vv.33–34).

17 This incident, unlike those in vv.2–12 and 13–17, is connected with the journey mentioned in 10:1 by the phrase "As Jesus started on his way." The man who ran up to Jesus is not identified by Mark (Luke calls him a ruler [18:18], meaning he was probably a member of some official council or court). Matthew says he was "young" (19:20). He fell on his knees before Jesus and addressed him by the revered title of "good teacher," thus expressing his high regard for Jesus. Nineham (p. 270) comments: "The stranger was altogether too obsequious and effusive in his approach." His question—"What must I do to inherit eternal life?"—indicates that he was thinking in terms of Jewish works of righteousness. He wanted to *do* something to merit eternal life, whereas Jesus taught that eternal life (the kingdom of God) is a gift to be received (cf. v.15).

18 Jesus' reply seems unnecessarily abrupt. But we must remember that he was calling attention to the man's unthinking use of language. "Jesus calls him to sober reflection. What does the epithet 'good' mean? It belongs to God who is good; and it should not be used unthinkingly or as a flippant gesture of praise" (Martin, *Mark*, p. 124). Or as Calvin (2:393) understands Jesus' reply, it is "as if he had said, 'Thou falsely calleth me a good Master, unless thou acknowledgest that I have come from God.'" In other words, Jesus is saying, "Before you address me with such a title, you had better think soberly about what the implications are, and especially what they are for you."

19–20 Jesus answered by giving the man a condensed summary of the second table of the law (v.19; cf. Exod 20:12–17). The prohibition of fraud is found only in Mark and seems to be a substitute for the commandment against coveting, fraud being a manifestation of coveting. It was a firm Jewish belief, based on OT teaching, that the man who kept the law would live (Deut 30:15–16). So Jesus began there.

The young man answered confidently. From boyhood he had kept all the commandments Jesus cited (v.20). This probably refers to the age of thirteen, when every Jewish boy became *bar miṣwāh* ("son of the commandment"; cf. Luke 2:42). At that point in a Jewish boy's life he became responsible to live by God's commands. The man spoke sincerely because to him keeping the law was a matter of external conformity. (Paul thought the same thing in his pre-Christian days [cf. Phil 3:6].) That the law required an inner obedience, which no man could comply with, apparently escaped him.

21 Recognizing the young man's sincerity, Jesus responded in love. Some commentators suggest that the words "loved him" mean that Jesus touched or hugged him. That may be, but nothing in the text indicates it.

The one thing that prevented this young man from having eternal life was the security of his wealth. Jesus put his finger on the sensitive place by commanding him to go, sell all he had, and give. These commands led up to the final and conclusive one: "Come, follow me." For this man there could be no following of

115

Jesus before he went, sold everything he had, and gave. His wealth and all it meant to him of position, status, comfort, and security prevented him from entering into eternal life. "The only way to 'life' is through the narrow gate of full surrender, and through that gate we may take, not what we want, but only what God allows. For this man his wealth was the hindrance" (Mitton, *Gospel of Mark*, p. 80). It must be emphasized, however, that there is no indication that in this incident Jesus' prescription for the young man was meant to be binding on all Christians. What Jesus does tell us is that we must not be attached to material things. Jesus' promise "you will have treasure in heaven" refers to eternal life; and since that is a gift of God and cannot be earned, no saving merit must be attached to the action of giving all to the poor.

22 Notice the intimate eyewitness details. When he heard the word of Jesus, the young man's "face fell." As Plummer (pp. 240–41) says, "He was gloomy and sullen with a double disappointment; no perilous exploit was required of him, but he was asked to part with what he valued most." To obey Jesus was too great a risk for him to take. So the security of wealth kept him out of the kingdom of God. He went away "with a heavy heart, for he was a man of great wealth" (NEB). Obedience to God brings joy; disobedience, sorrow.

23–26 The failure of the rich man to respond to the challenge led to one of Jesus' most striking pronouncements. He addressed it to the disciples, and it underscores the difficulty of a rich man's entering the kingdom of God (v.23).

The amazement of the disciples (v.24) at Jesus' words reflects their Jewish background, which placed great emphasis on the privileged position of the rich. To be wealthy was sure evidence of having the blessing of God. But with his penetrating spiritual insight, Jesus saw how wealth could hinder one from putting his trust and dependence in God.

The second half of v.24 may begin a new section, the last section ending with the amazement of the disciples. NIV considers it (along with vv.25–27) a part of the incident that begins with v.23. The fact that the disciples "were even more amazed" (v.26) looks back to their initial amazement in v.24 and supports the translators' decision.

Jesus supports his statement in v.23 by an amazing proverb. Moule paraphrases it thus: "It is easier to thread a needle with a great big camel than to get into the kingdom of God when you are bursting with riches" (*Gospel of Mark*, p. 80). Attempts have been made to play down the meaning of this proverb. A notable one identifies the "eye of the needle" with a gate leading into the city of Jerusalem before which camels had to kneel in order to get through. But the existence of any such gate is doubtful. As Rawlinson (p. 141) says, it has "no authority more trustworthy than the imaginative conjectures of modern guides to Jerusalem." Furthermore, this interpretation fails to recognize the picturesqueness of Jesus' speech or to grasp the full force of what he is saying—viz., that "for a rich man to enter the kingdom of God" is indeed "impossible." The proverb was not lost on the disciples. As their question "Who then can be saved?" shows, they completely understood it.

27 Now Jesus points to the solution. His answer makes clear that salvation is totally the work of God. Apart from the grace of God, it is impossible for any man—

especially a rich man—to enter God's kingdom. Humanly speaking, no one can be saved by his own efforts; but what we can never do for ourselves, God does for us. For he is the great Doer of the impossible. Was the rich man still within hearing and were these words meant for him, too? Mark does not say. Notice that "eternal life," "salvation," and "entrance into the kingdom" are all used synonymously here.

28 Mark makes no attempt to link vv.28–31 with vv.17–27. He does not even use a conjunction to connect the incidents. This seems to suggest that, though vv.17–22 and vv.23–27 go together historically, vv.28–31 are separate. Mark places them here because they fit the theme. Peter's response relates to what Mark had just reported: the failure of the rich man to give up what he had and to follow Jesus. By contrast they, i.e., the disciples, had given up everything to follow him. Matthew in the parallel passage reports Peter's additional words: "What then will there be for us?" (19:27). The disciples (Peter is their spokesman) were still thinking in terms of material rather than spiritual values.

29–30 Instead of rebuking Peter, Jesus makes a threefold promise introduced by the solemn "I tell you the truth" (v.29; cf. 10:15). No one who forsakes home, loved ones, or lands for Jesus' sake and the gospel's will fail (1) to receive back in his life a hundredfold what he has lost; (2) to suffer persecutions (only Mark includes this); and (3) to have eternal life in the age to come. The hundredfold return in this life (v.30) is to be understood in the context of the new community into which the believer in Jesus comes. There he finds a multiplication of relationships, often closer and more spiritually meaningful than blood ties. "God takes nothing away from a man without restoring it to him in a new and glorious form" (Lane, p. 372).

Jesus is also realistic about the Christian life. There will be persecutions. Again the relevance of this statement for the situation of the Roman church is obvious. It is through trials and persecutions that the new relationships as members of the Christian community develop and flourish. The promise is for a full, though admittedly difficult, life here and now, but not only here and now. Jesus promises eternal life in "the age to come." Everything that happens in the present is an earnest of that far richer and complete fulfillment in the future when there will no longer be any persecutions.

31 This saying of Jesus also appears in other contexts (cf. Matt 20:16; Luke 13:30). Jesus probably said it more than once; it lends itself to more than one application. Here it refers to the future when God will evaluate the lives of men and when human values will be reversed. At that time those who have rank and position now will not have them, and those who do not have them now will have them. This may be a kind of summary of Jesus' teaching in vv.17–31. In eternity the rich and the powerful will have the tables turned on them. Or perhaps it is a warning to the disciples in view of what they said, "we have left everything to follow you" (v.28). They must not conceive of their discipleship in terms of rewards. Discipleship entails suffering and service; it must be entered on in terms of love and commitment to Jesus, not because of what one hopes to get out of it either in this life or in the life to come. In his Gospel Matthew inserts the parable of the laborers in the vineyard here to illustrate the point (Matt 20:1–16).

117

Notes

19 "That man possesses the ability to fulfill the commandments of God perfectly was so firmly believed by the rabbis that they spoke in all seriousness of people who had kept the whole Law from A to Z" (SBK 1:814; quoted in Lane, p. 366).

24 The variant reading τοὺς πεποιθότας ἐπὶ [τοῖς] χρήμασιν (tous pepoithotas epi [tois] chrēmasin, "for those who trust in riches"), though found in the majority of Greek MSS, is probably a gloss intended to soften the force of the strong statement found in v.23.

M. *Third Prediction of the Passion*

10:32–34

> [32]They were on their way up to Jerusalem, with Jesus leading the way, and the disciples were astonished, while those who followed were afraid. Again he took the Twelve aside and told them what was going to happen to him. [33]"We are going up to Jerusalem," he said, "and the Son of Man will be betrayed to the chief priests and teachers of the law. They will condemn him to death and will hand him over to the Gentiles, [34]who will mock him and spit on him, flog him and kill him. Three days later he will rise."

32 The journey is resumed with Jesus taking the lead (cf. Luke 9:51). Jerusalem is mentioned for the first time as the destination of the journey southward. The astonishment of the disciples is not explained. Perhaps it was due to the determination with which Jesus proceeded to his goal (cf. Isa 50:7). He was already so preoccupied with what was to take place there that they were amazed. "Those who followed" were probably pilgrims on their way to the feast at Jerusalem. They were afraid because they sensed that something momentous was about to take place and they did not understand it. Jesus, as he so often does in Mark's Gospel, separated the Twelve from the crowd for renewed instruction about his coming passion.

33–34 This is the third major prediction of the Passion. The other two are in 8:31 and 9:31. In addition to these three, there is a brief reference to Jesus' death in the sequel to the Transfiguration narrative (cf. 9:9–12). Here the prediction is more detailed and precise than the others (for a helpful chart comparing these three predictions, see Taylor, p. 436). This prediction contains six details. Jesus is to be (1) betrayed (v.33); (2) sentenced to death; (3) handed over to the Gentiles; (4) mocked, spit on, and flogged (v.34); (5) executed; and (6) resurrected. This sounds like a brief summary of the passion narrative and so has led some scholars to consider vv.33–34 a prediction after the event—viz., that they represent postresurrection church tradition and not Jesus tradition. One's christology plays an important role in decisions like this. If Jesus was who he claimed to be—the unique Son of God—then it is not impossible that he predicted his passion in detail. If he is less than that, there are admittedly problems. That the events did not take place historically in the chronological sequence in which they are given in v.34 would tend to cast doubt on the prediction having been shaped by the passion narrative.

The word "crucify" does not occur in any of the passion predictions in Mark (cf. Matt 20:19, where it is used for the first time of Christ's death). But the statement that Jesus will be handed over to the Gentiles reveals in a veiled way his coming crucifixion. The climax of the passage is the prediction of the Resurrection. Mark does not record any response by the disciples to this startling statement. Luke (18:34), however, says, "The disciples did not understand any of this."

Notes

32 The phrase οἱ δὲ ἀκολουθοῦντες ἐφοβοῦντο (hoi de akolouthountes ephobounto, "while those who followed were afraid") created problems for the copyists because it suggests another group distinct from the disciples. The variants, none of which have strong MS support, try to eliminate this distinction. That Mark wanted to indicate two distinct groups is clearly shown by the definite article οἱ (hoi, "those") and the δὲ (de, "and," "but"; NIV, "while") used with it, which regularly indicates a change of subject. Two distinct groups are implicit in NIV's "the disciples were astonished, while those who followed were afraid."

N. The Request of James and John

10:35–45

³⁵Then James and John, the sons of Zebedee, came to him. "Teacher," they said, "we want you to do for us whatever we ask."
³⁶"What do you want me to do for you?" he asked.
³⁷They replied, "Let one of us sit at your right and the other at your left in your glory."
³⁸"You don't know what you are asking," Jesus said. "Can you drink the cup I drink or be baptized with the baptism I am baptized with?"
³⁹"We can," they answered.
Jesus said to them, "You will drink the cup I drink and be baptized with the baptism I am baptized with, ⁴⁰but to sit at my right or left is not for me to grant. These places belong to those for whom they have been prepared."
⁴¹When the ten heard about this, they became indignant with James and John. ⁴²Jesus called them together and said, "You know that those who are regarded as rulers of the Gentiles lord it over them, and their high officials exercise authority over them. ⁴³Not so with you. Instead, whoever wants to become great among you must be your servant, ⁴⁴and whoever wants to be first must be slave of all. ⁴⁵For even the Son of Man did not come to be served, but to serve, and to give his life as a ransom for many."

Mark 10:35–45 parallels 9:30–37. Both contain discussions about true greatness and both follow a prediction of Jesus' passion. And in a woeful way both reveal how spiritually dense the disciples really were. It is not likely that the church created a story that cast such disrepute on the character of two of the best-known disciples.

35–37 The request made by James and John, sons of Zebedee, seems utterly preposterous (v.35). They wanted Jesus to do for them whatever they asked—a carte blanche request! When Jesus asked what that might be (v.36), their answer was that they might have the positions of highest honor in the messianic kingdom (v.37). The request reveals clearly that before the Crucifixion the disciples believed Jesus to be the Messiah; and since it was now clear that he was going up to Jerusalem, they expected his messianic glory to be revealed there. James and John wanted to be sure of a prominent place in this about-to-be-realized messianic kingdom. Calvin (2:417) comments: "This narrative contains a bright mirror of human vanity; for it shows that proper and holy zeal is often accompanied by ambition. . . . They who are not satisfied with himself alone, but seek this or the other thing apart from him and his promises, wander egregiously from the right path."

38 Jesus' answer is sharp and penetrating. The two disciples did not really know what they were asking. The way to privileged position in the messianic kingdom is not by grabbing for power but by relinquishing it through suffering and death. Jesus explains this to them by using the analogies of the cup and baptism. The cup, symbolizing trouble and suffering, is found in the OT. "In the hand of the LORD is a cup full of foaming wine mixed with spices; he pours it out, and all the wicked of the earth drink it down to its very dregs" (Ps 75:8). "Rise up, O Jerusalem, you have drunk from the hand of the LORD the cup of his wrath, you who have drained to its dregs the goblet that makes men stagger" (Isa 51:17; cf. also Mark 14:36; Jer 49:12; Ezek 23:31–34). Baptism is a symbol of a deluge of trouble (cf. Pss 18:16; 69:1–2 and the expression "baptism of fire").

39–40 With a confident "We can," the disciples answer Jesus' question about going through the suffering of his passion (v.39). How naive! James and John failed to understand what was involved in Jesus' sufferings; yet they would indeed participate in them. But to grant them privileged positions in his kingdom was not within his authority (v.40). Jesus refused to usurp the authority of his Father. God alone will grant the places at Jesus' right and left to "those for whom they have been prepared."

41–44 Although Jesus had previously rebuked the spirit of ambition and jealousy among his disciples (cf. 9:35), it was still very much alive in them. The other ten were indignant with James and John (v.41). None of the disciples had in the least comprehended what Jesus had meant when he spoke of his passion. So Jesus had to give them another lesson in what greatness is. The Gentile rulers "lord it over them," i.e., over their subjects (v.42). But this is not the way it is among true followers of Jesus (v.43). Among them greatness is not achieved by asserting rank but by humble service (v.44). "Here is the paradox of the Kingdom of God. Instead of being lords, its great ones become servants, and its chiefs the bond-servants of all" (Gould, p. 202).

45 The climax to this section (vv.35–45) comes in this verse. In the kingdom of God humble service is the rule, and even the Son of Man is not exempt from it. He is in fact par excellence the example of it, especially in his redemptive mission. Every part of this verse is important. "Son of Man" is the veiled messianic title Jesus often uses of himself (cf. comments at 8:31). "Did not come to be served, but to serve" describes his incarnate life. He did not come as a potentate whose every personal whim was to be catered to by groveling servants, but he came as a servant himself. And his coming issued in giving "his life as a ransom for many."

The word translated "ransom" is *lytron*, which also means "the price of release" (cf. BAG, pp. 483–84). In koine Greek it is often used of money paid for the release of slaves. In the NT, however, it no longer relates to a purchase price paid someone but simply means "redemption" or "release" as a theological concept based on the experience of Israel's release from the slavery of Egypt. *Lytron* may also contain an allusion to the Suffering Servant passage of Isaiah 53 and especially to v.6b: "And the LORD has laid on him the iniquity of us all."

The prepositional phrase "for many" translates *anti pollōn*. The ordinary meaning of the preposition *anti* is "in place of" or "instead of"—a clear indication of substitution. Although it can be used to mean "in behalf of," this is not the usual meaning of *anti*. Here its use with *lytron* seems to demand the meaning "instead of." The expression "the many" is not to be understood in the sense of "some but not all" but in the general sense of "many" as contrasted with the single life that is given for their ransom (cf. Bratcher and Nida, p. 337).

The entire phrase "to give his life a ransom for many" emphasizes the substitutionary element in Jesus' death. He takes the place of the many. What should have happened to them happened to him instead. The authenticity of this saying of Jesus has often been denied, usually on the basis that it represents a Markan insertion of Pauline thought into the teaching of Jesus. But surely Richardson is right in saying that "all such contentions reflect the theological outlook of their °exponents rather than that of the NT. It would indeed be remarkable that St. Mark should have thus brilliantly summarized in a word the theology of St. Paul, in order to attribute it to Jesus, especially when we note that the word (λύτρον) is never used in the extant writings of the Apostle" (A. Richardson, *An Introduction to the Theology of the New Testament* [London: SCM, 1958], p. 220).

O. Restoring Blind Bartimaeus's Sight

10:46–52

> 46Then they came to Jericho. As Jesus and his disciples, together with a large crowd, were leaving the city, a blind man, Bartimaeus (that is, the Son of Timaeus), was sitting by the roadside begging. 47When he heard that it was Jesus of Nazareth, he began to shout, "Jesus, Son of David, have mercy on me!" 49Jesus stopped and said, "Call him."
> So they called to the blind man, "Cheer up! On your feet! He's calling you." 50Throwing his cloak aside, he jumped to his feet and came to Jesus. 51"What do you want me to do for you?" Jesus asked him.
> The blind man said, "Rabbi, I want to see." 52"Go," said Jesus, "your faith has healed you." Immediately he received his sight and followed Jesus along the road.

46 This last of the healing miracles in Mark's Gospel takes place near Jericho. Jericho is located five miles west of the Jordan and about fifteen miles northeast of Jerusalem. There was an old Jericho and a new Jericho. In Jesus' time the old Jericho was largely abandoned, but the new one extending to the south was an attractive city. It had been built by Herod the Great who had his winter palace there. Matthew speaks of two blind men. Luke says the healing occurred on the way to Jericho; Mark reports that it took place on the way out of the city. It is possible that the miracle was done somewhere between the old Israelite city and the new city of Herod. Mark is the only Evangelist who names the blind man. Bartimaeus probably means "son of Timai." In the Middle East, a blind man sitting along the road begging is a common sight.

47–48 Apparently Bartimaeus had heard of Jesus' reputation as a healer. When he discovered that Jesus was coming by, he seized the opportunity of approaching him (v.47). The title he used to address Jesus—"Son of David"—is messianic (cf. Isa 11:1, 10; Jer 23:5–6; Ezek 34:23–24). It was not an unambiguous title. In Mark's Gospel it is used only here (twice) of Jesus and in 12:35, where Jesus himself uses it in connection with the title "Christ." The crowd (they were pilgrims going up to Jerusalem for the Feast of Passover) did not appreciate Bartimaeus's loud shouting and tried to silence him, but he shouted all the more (v.49). Why they wanted him to keep quiet is not clear. Perhaps the title he gave Jesus offended them, or they did not want anyone to delay their journey to the feast.

Unlike the crowd, Jesus did not try to silence Bartimaeus. This implies that he did not reject the title "Son of David." Since Jesus was now close to the fulfillment of his messianic mission, it was no longer necessary to keep the secret. That Bartimaeus understood the significance of the title he used is doubtful. He was essentially appealing for mercy to be healed.

49–50 The loud cry stopped Jesus (v.49). Had the messianic title caught his attention? So he asked them to call the beggar to him. Only Mark gives us the graphic details of vv.49–50. The crowd's complete change of attitude toward the beggar is remarkable. Instead of trying to silence him, they encouraged him. The word translated "Cheer up!" is *tharsei*. It occurs only seven times in the NT (Matt 9:2, 22; 14:27; Mark 6:50; 10:49; John 16:33; Acts 23:11), and six of the seven are from the lips of Jesus. The exception is here. Bartimaeus's response was immediate (v.50). The cloak was his outer garment, which he had probably spread on the ground to receive the alms. The fact that he was able to get up and go to Jesus may imply that he was not completely blind.

51–52 Jesus did not immediately heal the blind beggar. Jesus first asked him a question to stimulate faith (v.51). Having done that, without any overt action or healing word on Jesus' part, he sent him away with the words "Go, . . . your faith has healed you" (v.52). The cure was immediate. Mark's statement that the blind man followed Jesus is best taken to mean, as NIV admirably brings out, that the man joined the crowd going up to the feast, not that he necessarily became a follower of Jesus in terms of discipleship.

The close of chapter 10 sets the stage for the climax of the story. The journey to Jerusalem is ended. Jesus is about to enter the Holy City where the last acts of the drama of redemption will take place. His opening the eyes of the blind man stands in sharp contrast to the blindness of the religious leaders he is about to encounter there.

VI. The Jerusalem Ministry (11:1–13:37)

At this point a new section in the Gospel of Mark begins. Jesus arrives in Jerusalem, and the rest of his ministry takes place within the confines of the city. Traditionally this period, beginning with the Triumphal Entry on Sunday and ending with the Crucifixion and Resurrection seven days later, has been designated the Passion Week. But if we had only Mark's Gospel, it would be possible to allow for a Jerusalem ministry longer than one week. Some scholars do in fact argue for an entrance into Jerusalem in the fall of the year at the time of the Feast of Tabernacles, extending Jesus' final ministry in the city to about six months. However, in view of John 12:1 and 12:12–15, which closely associate Jesus' final visit to Jerusalem with the Passover, a week-long ministry is more probable.

The section 11:1–13:37 is essentially made up of three parts: (1) the initial events of the entrance into the city and the cleansing of the temple (11:1–19); (2) instructions to his disciples (11:20–25; 12:35–44; 13:1–37); and (3) conflict with the religious leaders (11:27–33; 12:1–12, 13–17, 18–27, 28–34). The time sequence is difficult to sort out. In 11:1–25 three days are mentioned, but in 11:27–13:44 no time indicators are given. This gives rise to the possibility that some of the conflict stories could have been placed by Mark within the context of the final Jerusalem ministry of Jesus because they vividly reveal the opposition of the religious leaders that finally brought about his death. Whether or not this is true does not materially effect our understanding of the Jerusalem ministry.

A. The Triumphal Entry

11:1–11

¹As they approached Jerusalem and came to Bethphage and Bethany at the Mount of Olives, Jesus sent two of his disciples, ²saying to them, "Go to the village ahead of you, and just as you enter it, you will find a colt tied there, which no one has ever ridden. Untie it and bring it here. ³If anyone asks you, 'Why are you doing this?' tell him, 'The Lord needs it and will send it back here shortly.' "

⁴They went and found a colt outside in the street, tied at a doorway. As they untied it, ⁵some people standing there asked, "What are you doing, untying that colt?" ⁶They answered as Jesus had told them to, and the people let them go. ⁷When they brought the colt to Jesus and threw their cloaks over it, he sat on it. ⁸Many people spread their cloaks on the road, while others spread branches they had cut in the fields. ⁹Those who went ahead and those who followed shouted,

"Hosanna!"
"Blessed is he who comes in the name of the Lord!"
¹⁰"Blessed is the coming kingdom of our father David!"
"Hosanna in the highest!"

¹¹Jesus entered Jerusalem and went to the temple. He looked around at everything, but since it was already late, he went out to Bethany with the Twelve.

1–2 The approach to Jerusalem was through Bethany and Bethphage (v.1). Bethphage ("house of figs") was a village close to Jerusalem. Its precise location is not known. Bethany, located on the eastern slope of the Mount of Olives, was about two miles from Jerusalem (cf. John 11:18). The Mount of Olives is directly east of the city, rising to an elevation of about twenty-six hundred feet. Its summit commands a magnificent view of Jerusalem and especially of the temple mount.

From the vicinity of Bethphage, Jesus sent two of his disciples (they are unnamed) "to the village ahead," presumably Bethphage, to get a colt (v.2). The word translated "colt" (pōlos) can mean the young of any animal; but here, as in the LXX and papyri, it means the colt of a donkey (cf. Matt 21:2; John 12:15). Because of the prophecy of Zechariah 9:9, the donkey was considered to be the beast of the Messiah. Jesus stipulated that the colt must be an unused one ("which no one has ever ridden"). Such animals were regarded as especially suitable for sacred purposes (cf.

Num 19:2; Deut 21:3; 1 Sam 6:7). Matthew says both the colt and his mother were brought (21:7).

3 Jesus anticipated that the actions of the disciples might be questioned; so he instructed them, when asked why they were taking the colt, to answer, "The Lord needs it." By capitalizing "Lord," NIV has interpreted the passage to mean that Jesus was referring to himself. But since neither Matthew nor Mark uses *ho kyrios* ("the Lord") as a title for Jesus, and since it occurs in Luke and John only after the Resurrection, some commentators regard *ho kyrios* as a reference to the owner of the colt. Perhaps the owner was with Jesus at the time. On this understanding of *ho kyrios*, the statement of the disciples ("the owner needs it") would have been more understandable, and the last phrase of v.3—"and will send it back here shortly"—is an assurance by the owner that the animal would be returned promptly after he was through with it. However, in view of Luke 19:33, which NIV translates, "As they were untying the colt, its owners [*hoi kyrioi autou*] asked them, 'Why are you untying the colt?'" it seems more likely that *ho kyrios* in Mark 11:3 refers to our Lord. Jesus probably was well known by this time in the area around Bethany, and his authority was recognized. The fact that the Gospel writers go into such detail to explain how the colt was obtained suggests that they attached some importance to it, "and this lay in its testimony to the authority and perhaps the prescience of Jesus" (I. H. Marshall, *Commentary on Luke* [Grand Rapids: Eerdmans, 1978], p. 714).

4–6 The disciples found it as Jesus had told them (v.4) and carried out his orders to the letter. No mention is made by Mark of the owners of the colt being present, but the phrase "some people standing there" (v.5) may be equivalent to Luke's "its owners" (Luke 19:33). The people (owners?) did not object to the disciples' taking the colt (v.6) because apparently they knew Jesus and recognized His authority.

7–8 The action of the crowd was completely spontaneous. The outer garments on the back of the donkey made a kind of saddle for Jesus to ride on (v.7). When he mounted the colt (Luke 19:15 says the people put Jesus on it), others in the crowd spread their garments on the road (an act of royal homage; cf. 2 Kings 9:13) and spread branches before him (v.8; cf. 1 Macc 13:51, a description of Simon Maccabaeus entering Jerusalem to the accompaniment of green branches and antiphonal singing). The word *stibadas* (translated in NIV as "branches") means "leaves," "leafy branches" (BAG, p. 776). These could easily have been cut from the fields located nearby. Only John mentions palm branches (12:13). These probably came from Jericho; they are not native to Jerusalem, though in protected places they are known to grow there.

9–10 The crowds surrounded Jesus. Some went ahead of him, some behind (v.9). All shouted, "Hosanna." Cranfield says:

> Perhaps the foliage that was being strewn to make a path of honour for Jesus reminded someone of the *lûlabim* (bundles of palm, myrtle and willow) which were carried at the Feast of Tabernacles and shaken at the occurrence in the liturgy of the word *hosiahnna* in Ps 118:25 . . . and so called to his mind and lips the passage of the psalm, which once repeated would quite naturally be taken up by the crowd of pilgrims. (*Gospel of Mark,* p. 351)

"Hosanna" literally means "save now," but it had become simply an exclamation of praise. "Blessed is he who comes in the name of the Lord" is an accurate quotation of Psalm 118:26, one of the Hallel Psalms (Pss 113–18), which were used liturgically at the feasts of Tabernacles and Passover. This quotation was a customary religious greeting or blessing pronounced on pilgrims who had come to Jerusalem for the feast, but as Lane (p. 397) suggests, that did not exhaust its meaning, since "the formulation is ambiguous and Mark may well have intended his readers to detect a deeper, messianic significance in the phrase 'he who comes in the name of the Lord' (cf. Gen 49:10)." Verse 10 seems to support that interpretation. The kingdom blessed is the "kingdom of our father David," clearly the messianic kingdom promised to David's son. Martin (*Mark*, p. 138) reminds us that not even this statement gives away the secret of Jesus' person, "since . . . the cry of Hosanna is related to the coming kingdom and does not directly designate Jesus as Davidic King." The crowd proclaims the kingdom and not the king.

11 On entering the city Jesus went to the temple. Mark uses the word *hieron*, which means "temple area," not building. Apparently the crowd had quickly dispersed and only the disciples remained with Jesus. "He looked around at everything," not as a tourist viewing the sacred precincts for the first time (Jesus had been to Jerusalem before), but as the sovereign Lord examining the institution to see whether it was fulfilling its divinely appointed mission. The examination was in preparation for the prophetic act of cleansing. But since the hour was late, Jesus delayed his action against the temple and instead withdrew with his disciples to Bethany for the night.

As for the significance of the Triumphal Entry, Rawlinson (p. 151) writes:

> On the whole, it seems to be the most probable conclusion that the entry in this peculiar fashion into Jerusalem was deliberate on the part of our Lord, and was meant to suggest that, though He was indeed the Messiah and "Son of David," yet the Messiahship which He claimed was to be understood in a spiritual and non-political sense, in terms of the prophecy of Zechariah, rather than in terms of the "Son of David" idea as interpreted by contemporary expectation (*e.g.*, in the Psalms of Solomon). The time had in fact come for our Lord to put forward His Messianic claims, and to make His appeal to Jerusalem in a deliberately Messianic capacity. He does so, however, in a manner which is suggestive rather than explicit, and which was so calculated as to afford the minimum of pretext for a charge of quasi-political agitation.

B. *The Unfruitful Fig Tree*

11:12–14

> [12]The next day as they were leaving Bethany, Jesus was hungry. [13]Seeing in the distance a fig tree in leaf, he went to find out if it had any fruit. When he reached it, he found nothing but leaves, because it was not the season for figs. [14]Then he said to the tree, "May no one ever eat fruit from you again." And his disciples heard him say it.

12–13 This is one of the most difficult stories in the Gospels. It is not found in Luke. (Did he too have problems with it and omit it, or was it unknown to him?) Many modern commentators would just as soon it were not here at all. Rawlinson

(p. 154) says that it "approximates more closely than any other episode in Mk to the type of 'unreasonable' miracle characteristic of the non-canonical Gospel literature." Hunter (p. 110) comments: "With our knowledge of Jesus from other sources, we find it frankly incredible that he could have used his power to wither a fig tree because it did not yield figs two or three months before its natural time of fruitage." While rejecting the historicity of this account, Hunter finds the kernel of history in this story in the parable of the barren fig tree found in Luke 13:6–9. What was originally a parable has been changed into a factual story. Though admittedly difficult, the incident is not impossible. An important consideration is the position it occupies. It is one of Mark's interrupted accounts, in the middle of which stands the record of the cleansing of the temple. This is the clue to its meaning. Like the cleansing of the temple, the story of the unfruitful fig tree has to do with judgment.

The incident occurred on the way to Jerusalem from Bethany (v.12), where Jesus had spent the night. He was hungry; and, noticing a fig tree, he went to see whether it had any figs on it (v.13). Fig trees around Jerusalem usually leaf out in March or April, but they do not produce figs till June. This tree was no exception. It was in full leaf; but, as Mark tells his readers, there were no figs on it "because it was not the season for figs." It is this phrase that makes the story such a problem. Grant (p. 828) says Mark's explanation "only increases the problem, as it reflects on the good sense of Jesus." An easy solution is to consider the phrase a scribal gloss. But that will not do, because there is no textual evidence to support it. Also there is the fact that explanatory notes are a feature of Mark's style (cf. 1:16; 5:42; 7:3–4, 19; 13:14). It seems best to consider the phrase Mark's own insertion to explain to people not familiar with the characteristics of a fig tree why one fully leafed out would not have fruit on it.

14 Jesus addressed the tree directly and by his words performed a miracle of destruction. It is the only miracle of destruction attributed to Jesus in the Gospels. Manson's verdict on the action here ascribed to Jesus is well known: "It is a tale of miraculous power wasted in the service of ill temper (for the supernatural energy employed to blast the unfortunate tree might have been more usefully expended in forcing a crop of figs out of season); and as it stands it is simply incredible" (T.W. Manson, "The Cleansing of the Temple," BJRL 33 [1951]: 259).

The best explanation is to see the miracle as an acted-out parable. Jesus' hunger provides the occasion for his use of this teaching device. The fig tree represents Israel (cf. Hos 9:10; Nah 3:12; Zech 10:2). The tree is fully leafed out, and in such a state one would normally expect to find fruit. This symbolizes the hypocrisy and sham of the nation of Israel, which made her ripe for the judgment of God. "A people which honoured God with their lips but whose heart was all the time far from him (7:6) was like a tree with abundance of leaves but no fruit. The best commentary on vv.12–14 and 20f. is to be found in the narrative which these verses enframe" (Cranfield, *Gospel of Mark*, pp. 356–57).

C. *The Cleansing of the Temple*

11:15–19

> 15On reaching Jerusalem, Jesus entered the temple area and began driving out those who were buying and selling there. He overturned the tables of the money changers and the benches of those selling doves, 16and would not allow anyone

to carry merchandise through the temple courts. [17]And as he taught them, he said, "Is it not written:

> " 'My house will be called
> a house of prayer for all nations'?

But you have made it 'a den of robbers.' "
[18]The chief priests and the teachers of the law heard this and began looking for a way to kill him, for they feared him, because the whole crowd was amazed at his teaching.
[19]When evening came, they went out of the city.

All three synoptic writers have the cleansing of the temple at the end of Jesus' ministry. Only John has it at the beginning. Most commentators prefer the synoptic placement and reject the possibility of the two cleansings. But why Jesus could not have cleansed the temple twice, once at the beginning and once at the end of his public ministry, is never adequately explained.

The temple cleansing is sandwiched between the two incidents of the fig tree, an arrangement meant to link the accounts. The judgment symbolized by the cursing of the fig tree is initiated by Jesus' cleansing of the temple, and the cleansing of the temple is prophetic of the destruction of Jerusalem and the eschatological judgment (cf. Mark 13).

15–16 The cleansing of the temple, in fulfillment of Malachi 3:1–3, was Jesus' second messianic act during the Passion Week, the first having been the Triumphal Entry.

When Jesus entered the temple area (v.15), the smell of the animals entered his nostrils; and the noise from the moneychangers' tables beat on his ears. For the convenience of pilgrims, the cattlemen and the moneychangers had set up businesses in the Court of the Gentiles. The animals were sold for sacrifices. It was far easier for a pilgrim in Jerusalem to purchase one that was guaranteed kosher than to have to bring an animal with him and have it inspected for meeting the kosher requirements. The Roman money the pilgrims brought to Jerusalem had to be changed into the Tyrian currency (the closest thing to the old Hebrew shekel), since the annual temple tax had to be paid in that currency. Exorbitant prices were often charged for changing the currency. By overturning the tables of the moneychangers and the benches of those selling doves, Jesus was directly challenging the authority of the high priest, because they were there by his authorization. In John's account Jesus drove them out with a whip made from pieces of rope. Mark does not mention a whip. Nevertheless the words "driving out" and "overturned the tables" suggest that Jesus used force.

The statement of v.16 occurs only in Mark. It has been suggested that it may be Peter's own recollection of the event. Jesus not only cleansed the temple of its profanation by the merchants, but he also put a stop to its casual use by those who used it as a shortcut between the city and the Mount of Olives. Such a use of the temple area is later prohibited in the Talmud (*Berakoth* 9.5).

17 The first passage quoted by Jesus is Isaiah 56:7, a prediction that non-Jews who worship God will be allowed to worship in the temple. By allowing the Court of the Gentiles, the only place in the temple area where Gentiles were allowed to worship God, to become a noisy, smelly public market, the Jewish religious leaders were preventing Gentiles from exercising the spiritual privilege promised them. How could a Gentile pray amid all that noise and stench? And God's house was supposed to be "a house of prayer for all nations." The second quotation—"But you have made it a 'den of robbers' "—is from Jeremiah 7:11 and emphasizes that instead of allowing the temple to be what it was meant to be, a place of prayer, they had allowed it to become a robber's den. This is to be understood not so much in terms of the Jews' dishonest dealing with the pilgrims as in terms of their robbing the Gentiles by merchandising activities of their rightful claim to the worship of Israel's God.

The significance of the cleansing of the temple is that with the coming of the Messiah, "[Jesus] seeks to make available to the Gentiles the privileges which belonged to the new age and thereby he proclaims that the time of universal worship, uninhibited by Jewish restrictions, has come" (Martin, *Mark*, p. 225). This would have been particularly meaningful for Mark's predominantly Gentile readers.

18–19 The Pharisees and Herodians in Galilee had decided that Jesus must be put out of the way (cf. 3:6). Now the chief priests and teachers of the law come to the same decision (v.18). This is the first time in Mark's Gospel that they reveal active hostility to Jesus. Jesus' action had challenged their authority and no doubt cost them a good deal of money. So they went into action against him, but not openly, because they feared what the response of the people might be. Jesus' teaching was getting through to them. If he could persuade the people to follow him, the power and authority of the chief priests and teachers of the law would be broken.

Again Jesus and his disciples withdrew from Jerusalem and spent the night in Bethany (v.19). Did they do this because Jerusalem was not a safe place for Jesus at night?

D. The Withered Fig Tree and Sayings on Faith and Prayer

11:20–25(26)

> 20In the morning, as they went along, they saw the fig tree withered from the roots. 21Peter remembered and said to Jesus, "Rabbi, look! The fig tree you cursed has withered!"
>
> 22"Have faith in God," Jesus answered. 23"I tell you the truth, if anyone says to this mountain, 'Go, throw yourself into the sea,' and does not doubt in his heart but believes that what he says will happen, it will be done for him. 24Therefore I tell you, whatever you ask for in prayer, believe that you have received it, and it will be yours. 25And when you stand praying, if you hold anything against anyone, forgive him, so that your Father in heaven may forgive you your sins."

The first three verses of this section form the second part of the story of the fig tree (11:12–14) that encloses the account of the cleansing of the temple. (For the theological significance of this, see the introductory paragraph to the exposition of 11:15–19.)

20–21 The next morning, on returning to Jerusalem from Bethany, Jesus and his disciples passed the fig tree again (v.20). It was totally destroyed ("withered from the roots"). Jesus had predicted that no one would ever eat fruit from it again (v.14); and Peter, remembering what Jesus had said, called his attention to the withered tree (v.21). Jesus does not in any way interpret the event. Yet the meaning is obvious: Jesus' predicted judgment on the temple will come to pass as surely as his prediction of the withering of the fig tree.

22 The sayings found in vv.22–25 occur elsewhere in the synoptic Gospels in various contexts (Matt 6:13–14; 7:7; 17:20; 18:19; Luke 11:9; 17:6). This suggests that here they have no historical connection with what precedes. It is, however, possible to see a connection. Jesus uses the incident of the fig tree to teach incidentally (for surely the main point of the incident is the sure judgment of God on the temple) some lessons on faith and prayer. The source of the power for performing the miracle is God. He must be the object of our faith.

23 This is another of Jesus' pronouncements preceded by the solemn introductory formula "I tell you the truth"—a way of implying its importance. Since Jesus was standing on the Mount of Olives, from which the Dead Sea can be seen on a clear day, he may have been referring specifically to the Mount. Of course Jesus is speaking figuratively. (For a mountain as a symbol of a great difficulty, cf. Zech 4:7 and references to SBK, 1:759.) Jesus is saying that the greatest possible difficulties can be removed when a person has faith (cf. James 1:6).

24 There is a close connection between the kind of faith Jesus speaks of here and prayer. Stauffer clearly brings this out: "What is it that distinguishes this faith from the self-intoxication that . . . is 'beyond one's powers' and makes a man and his work end up in a fiasco? The 'faith' of Mark 11:23f. is a faith that prays. . . . Prayer is the source of its power, and the means of its strength—God's omnipotence is its sole assurance, and God's sovereignty its only restriction (E. Stauffer, *New Testament Theology* [London: SCM, 1955], p. 169).

25 Admittedly the transition between v.24 and v.25 is abrupt (v.24 speaks of faith, v.25 of forgiveness). Still there is a connection. To be effective prayer must be offered in faith—faith in the all-powerful God who works miracles. But it must be offered in the spirit of forgiveness. Faith and the willingness to forgive—these are the two conditions of efficacious prayer.

26 This verse does not occur in NIV because it is not found in the best and most ancient MSS of the NT. It represents an insertion from Matthew 6:15.

Notes

---

22 The variant reading that inserts εἰ (*ie*, "if") before ἔχετε (*echete*, "you have") has rather strong MS support. But it is probably not original because (1) the solemn "I tell you the truth" is never preceded by a conditional clause, and (2) the introductory "if" probably arose by assimilation to the saying in Luke 17:6 (cf. Matt 21:21).
23 Verses 23–25 occur in the synoptic Gospels as follows: 11:23 = Matt 17:20; Luke 17:6; with 11:24, cf. Matt 7:7; 18:19; Luke 11:9; with 11:25, cf. Matt 6:14–15.

E. *The Question About Jesus' Authority*

11:27–33

> ²⁷They arrived again in Jerusalem, and while Jesus was walking in the temple courts, the chief priests, the teachers of the law and the elders came to him. ²⁸By what authority are you doing these things?" they asked. "And who gave you authority to do this?"
>
> ²⁹Jesus replied, "I will ask you one question. Answer me, and I will tell you by what authority I am doing these things. ³⁰John's baptism—was it from heaven, or from men? Tell me!"
>
> ³¹They discussed it among themselves and said, "If we say, 'From heaven,' he will ask, 'Then why didn't you believe him?' ³²But if we say, 'From men'. . . ." (They feared the people, for everyone held that John really was a prophet.)
>
> ³³So they answered Jesus, "We don't know."
>
> Jesus said, "Neither will I tell you by what authority I am doing these things."

27–28 After the incident of the fig tree and the lesson on faith, prayer, and forgiveness, Jesus and his disciples came to Jerusalem and entered the temple area—the focal point of his ministry while in the city (v.27). On this occasion the opposition came from three elements of the Jewish religious establishment: chief priests, teachers of the law, and elders. These groups made up the Sanhedrin, the high court of the Jews. How drastic Jesus' action in cleansing the temple was is shown by their presence. They would have arrested Jesus on the spot, but his popularity among the people prevented that—at least for the time being. Instead they directed a question to him (v.28) about the source of his authority "for doing these things" (a reference to his cleansing the temple). Their hope was that by his answer Jesus would be brought into disrepute with the people and thereby clear the way for their arresting him.

29–30 Again Jesus answers a question by asking another one (v.29; cf. 10:2–3). Hunter (p. 113) paraphrases it thus: "Do you think God was behind John's mission or not?" The question was particularly appropriate for the situation. John had clearly testified to the divine source of Jesus' mission. If they recognized the divine authority of John's mission, they would be forced to recognize Jesus' also and his cleansing of the temple as the legitimate exercise of his authority. By "John's baptism" (v.30) Jesus meant John's ministry and teaching as evidenced by its outward expression. "From heaven" means "from God," since "heaven" was a common Jewish substitute for the divine name.

31–33 The question of Jesus proved too much for them. They clearly saw that either alternative—"from heaven" or "from men"—would place them in a difficult position (vv.31–32). An admission of John's divine authority would compel them to believe in Jesus; a denial would place them in an unfavorable position with the people who accepted John as a true prophet. So to save face they pleaded ignorance (v.33), which was tantamount to a refusal to answer Jesus' question. Jesus' reply was that he too would refuse to answer their question—at least directly. He had given them a veiled answer in his counterquestion (cf. v.30).

F. *The Parable of the Tenants*

12:1–12

> ¹He then began to speak to them in parables: "A man planted a vineyard. He put a wall around it, dug a pit for the winepress and built a watchtower. Then he rented the vineyard to some farmers and went away on a journey. ²At harvest time he sent a servant to the tenants to collect from them some of the fruit of the vineyard. ³But they seized him, beat him and sent him away empty-handed. ⁴Then he sent another servant to them; they struck this man on the head and treated him shamefully. ⁵He sent still another, and that one they killed. He sent many others; some of them they beat, others they killed.
>
> ⁶"He had one left to send, a son, whom he loved. He sent him last of all, saying, 'They will respect my son.'
>
> ⁷"But the tenants said to one another, 'This is the heir. Come, let's kill him, and the inheritance will be ours.' ⁸So they took him and killed him, and threw him out of the vineyard.
>
> ⁹"What then will the owner of the vineyard do? He will come and kill those tenants and give the vineyard to others. ¹⁰Haven't you read this scripture:
>
> > " 'The stone the builders rejected
> > has become the capstone;
> > ¹¹the Lord has done this,
> > and it is marvelous in our eyes'?"
>
> ¹²Then they looked for a way to arrest him because they knew he had spoken the parable against them. But they were afraid of the crowd; so they left him and went away.

Doubts have been raised about the authenticity of this parable because of its allegorical features. While it is true that most of Jesus' parables have but one point to make and the details have no separate significance, Jesus did use allegory on occasion (cf. Mark 4:13–20). There is no compelling reason to doubt the genuineness of this parable. Moule writes: "This story, so clearly directed against the irresponsible religious leaders of his own day, seems to furnish an example of a genuinely contemporary, unaltered piece of Jesus' teaching" (*Gospel of Mark*, p. 94).

Some scholars deny that the parable is an allegory. Its allegorical features, however, seem fairly obvious: the vineyard is Israel; the owner is God; the tenants are the Jewish leaders; the servants are the prophets; and the only son and heir is Jesus. Other details of the parable such as the wall, winepress, and tower have no separate significance.

1 Mark does not identify who Jesus' hearers were (he simply says "them"). Among "them" were included Jesus' opponents (the chief priests, teachers of the law, and elders; cf. 11:27), as the reaction recorded in v.12 makes clear. The description in v.1 reflects the language of Isaiah 5:1–2. The vineyard symbolizes Israel (cf. Ps 80:8–16; Isa 5:7; Jer 2:21). The details mentioned here—the wall (usually made of unmortared rocks); the pit (in which the juice of the grapes was collected); the press (usually made of solid limestone); the tower (for the protection of the vineyard and shelter for the farmer)—are all known to anyone who has traveled in Israel.

When the vineyard had been completely prepared, its owner rented it to tenants and went on a journey. This detail reflects a condition that actually prevailed in Galilee in Jesus' time, viz., much of the land was in the hands of absentee landowners who contracted with tenants on a crop-sharing basis.

2–5 When harvest time came (v.2), the absentee landlord sent one of his servants to collect what was due him from the tenants. The payment was to be made in produce of the land according to a previously agreed-on percentage. The landlord sent three servants in succession to collect the payment (vv.3–5), but the tenants repudiated the agreement. Instead they beat up the first two servants and killed the third. The detail of v.5b—"he sent many others"—Lane (p. 418) says, "was intended by Jesus to force his listeners beyond the framework of the parable to the history of Israel. In the OT the prophets are frequently designated 'the servants' of God (cf. Jer 7:25f; 25:4; Amos 3:7; Zech 1:6) and it is natural to find a reference to their rejection in the words 'beating some, and killing others.'"

6–8 The sending of the son underscores the serious view the owner of the vineyard took of the situation. He was an *agapētos* son (v.6). *Agapētos* probably means "only" here (as in the LXX of Gen 22:2, 12, 16; cf. Jer 6:26). The owner assumed that they would respect him. This statement is not to be taken as informing us as to God's expectation for the coming of Jesus into the world. He knew beforehand that Jesus would be rejected. It is simply a part of the story and should not be allegorized. The owner's expectations were thwarted. The tenants' greed led to outrageous action (v.7). They saw the coming of the son as a golden opportunity for seizing the property; they may have inferred from the son's coming that the owner had died. If they did away with his son (v.8), the property would be ownerless and therefore available to the first claimants (cf. M *Baba Bathra* 3.3 and b *Baba Bathra* 54a).

Jeremias points out that "there can be no doubt that in the sending of the son Jesus himself had his own sending in mind, but for the mass of his hearers the Messianic significance of the son could not be taken for granted, since no evidence is forthcoming for the application of the 'Son of God' to the Messiah in pre-Christian Palestinian Judaism" (*Parables of Jesus*, pp. 72–73). There was no question, however, in the minds of Jesus' hearers that he was the son in the parable; their reaction in v.12 makes this clear.

Throwing the son out of the vineyard is another detail of the story that should not be allegorized. Both Matthew and Luke have the killing of the son take place after (not before as in Mark) he is thrown out of the vineyard (v.8; cf. Matt 21:39; Luke 20:15).

9 Jesus draws out the meaning of the parable with a question and then proceeds to answer the question himself. (In Matt 21:41 the people answer the question.) Doubts have been cast on the authenticity of this verse because ordinarily Jesus does not answer his own questions (cf. Luke 17:9). But there is no inherent reason why he should not have done so in this situation. The answer underscores the seriousness of the action of the wicked tenants. Their punishment will be capital, and the vineyard will be let to other tenants who "will give him his share of the crop at the harvest time" (Matt 21:41). The allusion is to Isaiah 5:1–7. Cranfield points out that the warning "is directed specifically to the leaders of the people and not to the people at large," because "whereas in Isa 5 the vineyard was at fault, here it is only the husbandmen" (*Gospel of Mark*, pp. 367–68). The killing of the tenants may be a not-so-veiled prophecy of the destruction of Jerusalem, and the "others" to which the vineyard is given are the new Israel.

10–11 The quotation is from Psalm 118:22–23, the same psalm the joyful Hosanna cry came from (cf. 11:9). In the OT context the reference to "the stone" (v.10) is probably to the construction of Solomon's temple. One of the stones was rejected but became the *kephalē gōnias* ("capstone," NIV; "head of the corner," AV, RSV; "main cornerstone," NEB). Plummer (p.275) thinks the reference is to "a cornerstone uniting two walls; but whether at the base or at the top is not certain." Jeremias thinks it refers to a keystone that holds together and completes the building (TDNT, 1:792–93).

In the original context the rejected stone was Israel, despised by the pagan nations but, after her return from Exile, exalted to the status of nationhood. Here Jesus applies the psalm to himself. The "stoneship" of Jesus, based on this passage in Psalms, was a familiar theme in early Christianity, as shown by Acts 4:11 and 1 Peter 2:7. Although there is no specific reference to the Resurrection in the psalm, Jeremias remarks: "The early community found in Ps. 118:22 scriptural evidence for the death and resurrection of Jesus. The Crucified is the rejected stone which in the resurrection is made by God the chief corner-stone in the heavenly sanctuary (Ac. 4:11), to be manifested as such in the *parousia*" (TDNT, 1:793).

12 The application of the parable was obvious, but again the religious leaders did not dare harm Jesus because they feared the crowd (cf. 11:18, 32). It was getting close to the time of the feast, and more and more pilgrims from Galilee were arriving in Jerusalem. Many of these knew Jesus either by personal contact or by reputation. The religious leaders knew it would be unwise to make their move now; "so they left him and went away." The similarity of this verse with 11:18–19 may mark the end of Jesus' third day (Tuesday) in Jerusalem during the Passion Week.

G. *The Question About Paying Taxes to Caesar*

12:13–17

> [13]Later they sent some of the Pharisees and Herodians to Jesus to catch him in his words. [14]They came to him and said, "Teacher, we know you are a man of integrity. You aren't swayed by men, because you pay no attention to who they are; but you teach the way of God in accordance with the truth. Is it right to pay taxes to Caesar or not? [15]Should we pay or shouldn't we?"
> But Jesus knew their hypocrisy. "Why are you trying to trap me?" he asked. "Bring me a denarius and let me look at it." [16]They brought the coin, and he asked them, "Whose portrait is this? And whose inscription?"
> "Caesar's," they replied.
> [17]Then Jesus said to them, "Give to Caesar what is Caesar's and to God what is God's."
> And they were amazed at him.

13 Jesus again comes into conflict with the religious leaders. Mark does not say when or where this incident took place. It is generally agreed, however, that it was on the next day (Wednesday) and in one of the courts of the temple.

The Herodians were as obnoxious to the Pharisees on political grounds as the Sadducees were on theological grounds. Yet the two groups united in their opposition to Jesus. Collaboration in wickedness, as well as goodness, has great power. Their purpose was to trip Jesus up in his words so that he would lose the support of the people, leaving the way open for them to destroy him.

14–15a The question was prefaced with an obvious and, indeed, obnoxious piece of flattery (v. 14). Moreover it was thoroughly insincere. The Pharisees and Herodians were intending "to impale [Jesus] on the horns of a dilemma" (Hunter, p. 116). Since the time of Archelaus's banishment in A.D. 6, Jews had been required by the Romans to pay tribute money into the *fiscus*, the emperor's treasury. Some Jews (e.g., the Zealots) flatly refused to pay it, because it was for them an admission of the Roman right to rule. The Pharisees disliked paying it but did not actively oppose it, whereas the Herodians had no objections to it. The intent of this question was to force Jesus to a direct answer (v. 15a), identifying himself either with the Zealots or with the Herodians.

15b–16 Jesus was not about to fall into their trap. He recognized their question for the "hypocrisy" (*hypokrisin*) it was (v. 15b). So he asked them for a Roman denarius. There is no indication that they had to send away for the coin; one was readily available. This implies that they had already answered their own question. It was Caesar's coinage they were using (v. 16); and by using it they were tacitly acknowledging Caesar's authority and thus their obligation to pay the tax.

17 Jesus' answer avoided the trap. Caesar has a legitimate claim and so does God. Give to each his rightful claim. "So long as God's rights were safeguarded . . . there was no need to question the rights of Caesar. Civil obedience, attested by the payment of the tax, no more contradicted than it abolished the obedience due to God" (Hunter, p. 116). Jesus does not, however, say that the claims of God and those of Caesar are the same.

> Though the obligation to pay to Caesar some of his own coinage in return for the amenities his rule provided is affirmed, the idolatrous claims expressed on the coins are rejected. God's rights are to be honored. Here Jesus is not saying that there are two quite separate independent spheres, that of Caesar and that of God (for Caesar and all that is his belongs to God); but he is indicating that there are obligations to Caesar which do not infringe the rights of God but are indeed ordained by God. (Cranfield, *Gospel of Mark*, p. 372)

For a more complete doctrine of the Christian and his relationship to the state, this statement of Jesus must be taken with Romans 13:1–7; 1 Timothy 2:1–6; and 1 Peter 2:13–17.

The reply was not what they expected. It was simple yet profound, and "they were amazed at him." But because he did not give a direct yes-or-no answer, it was either misunderstood or deliberately distorted, as Luke 23:2 implies.

H. *The Question of Marriage at the Resurrection*

12:18–27

> [18]Then the Sadducees, who say there is no resurrection, came to him with a question. [29]"Teacher," they said, "Moses wrote for us that if a man's brother dies and leaves a wife but no children, the man must marry the widow and have children for his brother. [20]Now there were seven brothers. The first one married and died without leaving any children. [21]The second one married the widow, but he also died, leaving no child. It was the same with the third. [22]In fact, none of the seven left any children. Last of all, the woman died too. [23]At the resurrection whose wife will she be, since the seven were married to her?"

24Jesus replied, "Are you not in error because you do not know the Scriptures or the power of God? 25When the dead rise, they will neither marry nor be given in marriage; they will be like the angels in heaven. 26Now about the dead rising—have you not read in the book of Moses, in the account of the bush, how God said to him, 'I am the God of Abraham, the God of Isaac, and the God of Jacob'? 27He is not the God of the dead, but of the living. You are badly mistaken!"

18 Reliable information about the Sadducees (mentioned here for the first time by Mark) is difficult to obtain because no documents that are clearly Sadducean have been preserved. The word "Sadducee" probably comes from the name Zadok (*Saddouk* in Gr.) and is usually traced to the high priest of that name during the time of David. The Sadducees' relationship to the temple is not clear. Only one high priest, Hanan ben Hanan, during the 107-year period between Herod the Great's appointment to Ananel and the destruction of the temple in A.D. 70 is identified as a Sadducee by Josephus (Antiq. XX, 227 [ix.1]); and he only held the office for three months. Lane (p. 426) observes: "The disputes between Sadducean and Pharisaic scribes show a pronounced interest in the Temple but do not warrant the assertion that the Temple hierarchy was by conviction Sadducean or was inclined to follow the traditions of the Sadducees."

In the time of Jesus, the Sadducees were small numerically but exerted great influence politically and religiously. They were not, however, popular among the masses. Josephus says they were educated men and many of them held prominent positions (Antiq. XVIII, 17 [i.4]). The Sadducees represented the urban, wealthy, sophisticated class and were centered in Jerusalem. When Jerusalem was destroyed in A.D. 70, they disappeared from history.

In the NT the Sadducees are mentioned only fourteen times whereas the Pharisees are mentioned about one hundred times. Mark mentions them only in this verse and identifies them with the statement "who say there is no resurrection." The Sadducees held this position because they accepted only Scripture and rejected all beliefs and practices not found there. Since they claimed to be unable to find clear teaching about the Resurrection in the OT, they rejected the doctrine. This set them against the Pharisees, who considered the oral tradition as authoritative as the written Scriptures.

19–23 Although the Sadducees addressed Jesus with the honorific title "Teacher" (v.19), their purpose was not to learn from him. It was manifestly hostile: "the extreme case they offer for His opinion is clearly intended as a *reductio ad absurdum* of any view but their own" (Swete, p. 278). The case cited arose out of a provision in the Mosaic Law (Deut 25:5–6), which required that if a man died without children, his brother had to marry his widow. The purpose of the levirate law (from the Lat. *levir*, "brother-in-law"), as it was called, was to protect the widow and guarantee the continuance of the family line. With this law in mind, the Sadducees now presented a hypothetical case in which one woman married seven brothers in turn, all of whom died childless (vv.20–22). In the Resurrection whose wife of the seven would she be (v.23)? The case is so ludicrous it may have been a well-known Sadducean joke used for poking fun at the Pharisees' doctrine of the Resurrection.

24–25 In his answer Jesus accuses the Sadducees of ignorance of (1) the Scriptures and (2) the power of God (v.24). He then proceeds to take up the second accusation first. In the Resurrection there will be a new order of existence brought about by the power of God (v.25). "The questioners did not see that God could not only grant life in another world, but also make it very different from life in this world" (Plummer, p. 281). Marriage will not exist as it does now, but all life will be like that of the angels. This evidently means that the basic characteristics of resurrection life will be service for and fellowship with God. The mention of angels in this context is significant because it served as a correction of another theological error of the Sadducees (cf. Acts 23:8). Also, since in heaven there will be no more death, the need for marriage and the propagation of the race will not exist.

26-27 Jesus now turns to his first-mentioned cause of the Sadducees' erroneous thinking: ignorance of the teaching of the OT (cf. 2:25; 12:10). He directed them back to the story of Moses and the burning bush (v.26; Exod 3:6). His use of a text from the Pentateuch was significant because this part of the OT was considered particularly authoritative by the Sadducees. The quotation may be understood as follows: Abraham, Isaac, and Jacob had long since died when God made the statement to Moses. Nevertheless God said, "I am," not "I was," the God of Abraham, Isaac, and Jacob. Thus the patriarchs were still alive in Moses' time (v.27); and if they were alive then, we may be sure that in the Resurrection God will raise up their bodies to share in the blessedness of eternal life. The fact that the phrase "the God of Abraham, the God of Isaac, and the God of Jacob" carried with it the idea of the covenant God, the God whose promises can be relied on, underscores the basic thrust of Jesus' argument—viz., the faithfulness of God.

I. The Question Concerning the Great Commandment

12:28-34

28One of the teachers of the law came and heard them debating. Noticing that Jesus had given them a good answer, he asked him, "Of all the commandments, which is the most important?"

29"The most important one," answered Jesus, "is this: 'Hear, O Israel, the Lord our God, the Lord is one. 30Love the Lord your God with all your heart and with all your soul and with all your mind and with all your strength.' 31The second is this: 'Love your neighbor as yourself.' There is no commandment greater than these."

32"Well said, teacher," the man replied. "You are right in saying that God is one and there is no other but him. 33To love him with all your heart, with all your understanding and with all your strength, and to love your neighbor as yourself is more important than all burnt offerings and sacrifices."

34When Jesus saw that he had answered wisely, he said to him, "You are not far from the kingdom of God." And from then on no one dared ask him any more questions.

28 Mark seems to suggest that the question asked by the teacher of the law, in contrast to many that had been asked by his colleagues, was a sincere one (but cf. Matt 22:34). He had been impressed by Jesus' answer to the previous question and so ventured one of his own. The rabbis counted 613 individual statutes in the law, 365 which were negative and 248 positive. Attempts were made to differentiate between the "heavy," or "great," and the "light," or "little," commandments. The rabbis also made attempts to formulate great principles from which the rest of the law could be deduced. The most famous example comes from Hillel, who when challenged by a Gentile, "Make me a proselyte on condition that you teach me the whole law while I stand on one foot," replied, "What you hate for yourself, do not do to your neighbor: this is the whole law, the rest is commentary; go and learn" (b *Shabbath* 31a). The question arose out of a works-righteousness understanding of the law and the keeping of its commandments.

29–30 In answer to the question, Jesus quoted two passages from the OT (Deut 6:4–5; Lev 19:18). Deuteronomy 6:4 is central to the Shema, named after the first word of the verse, which means "Hear" (v.29). In Hebrew liturgy Deuteronomy 6:4–9; 11:13–21; and Numbers 13:37–41 comprise the Shema. Deuteronomy 6:4–5 is a confession of faith that is recited by pious Jews every morning and evening. It basically affirms two things: (1) the unity of God ("the Lord is one") and (2) the covenant relationship of God to the Jewish people ("the Lord our God"). In telling this story only Mark included Deuteronomy 6:4 here. Its relationship to the words that follow is important. God is to be loved completely and totally (v.30) because he, and he alone, is God and because he has made a covenant of love with his people. In the covenant God gives himself totally in love to his people; therefore he expects his people to give themselves totally ("soul," "mind," and "strength") in love to him.

31 Jesus brought Leviticus 19:18 together with Deuteronomy 6:5 to show that love of neighbor is a natural and logical outgrowth of love of God. These two commandments belong together; they cannot be separated. Thus although the teacher of the law had asked for the one most important commandment, Jesus gave him two. In Leviticus 19:18 the neighbor is identified as "one of your people," i.e., fellow Israelites. The Jews of Jesus' day interpreted "fellow Israelites" even more narrowly than the OT passage; for there (cf. Lev 19:34) it included resident aliens, whereas for Jesus' contemporaries it included only Jews and full proselytes. Jesus redefined the term to mean "anyone with whom we have dealings at all" (cf. Luke 10:25–27). Mitton, in a most practical application of this verse, remarks that "neighbor" embraces

> all within our home, those we meet at work, in our church, and in recreations. And more than that: our employer is our neighbor too; so are our work people, all who serve us in shops, the men who empty our dust bins and those who try to keep streets and parks clean. So too are the people of Jamaica, of West Africa, of Kenya, of Germany and of Russia. If we love our neighbors as we love ourselves, we shall want for them the treatment we should want for ourselves, were we in their place. (*Gospel of Mark*, p. 99)

32–33 Only Mark records the favorable response of the teacher of the law and Jesus' statement that he was "not far from the kingdom of God" (v.34). In repeating the commandment he omitted the divine name "the Lord" in keeping with the practice of pious Jews of avoiding the pronunciation of God's name (v.32). The phrase "and there is no other but him" is an interpretive addition from Deuteronomy 4:35, which underscores the uniqueness of Israel's God. The statement by the teacher of the law that love of God and neighbor are "more important than all burnt offerings and sacrifices" (v.33) is in keeping with the teachings of the OT prophets (1 Sam 15:22; Hos 6:6); but it is an advance on the teaching of Judaism in his time. In

Judaism the law and sacrifices are set side by side with love (cf. M *Pirke Aboth* 1. 2), whereas the teacher of the law was declaring the superiority of love (cf. Taylor, p. 489). In his repetition of what Jesus said, the teacher of the law substitutes *synesis* ("understanding") for *dianoia* ("mind") and omits *psychē* ("soul"). There is, however, no appreciable difference in the meaning.

34 The reply of the teacher of the law shows that what Jesus said was getting through to him and elicits the statement by our Lord that he was close to the kingdom of God—a statement no doubt meant to stimulate and challenge him to further thoughtful reflection and decisive action. Whether or not he ever entered the kingdom is not stated.

Jesus had so forcefully demonstrated his ability to answer questions meant to trap him and to turn such questions back on his accusers that from this time on "no one dared ask him any more questions." Verse 34 points forward to the next incident recorded by Mark, where Jesus, not the religious leaders, asks the question about the "son of David."

J. The Question About David's Son

12:35-37

> 35While Jesus was teaching in the temple courts, he asked, "How is it that the teachers of the law say that the Christ is the son of David? 36David himself, speaking by the Holy Spirit, declared:
>
>> " 'The Lord said to my Lord:
>> "Sit at my right hand
>> until I put your enemies
>> under your feet." '
>
> 37David himself calls him 'Lord.' How then can he be his son?"
> The large crowd listened to him with delight.

35 Jesus was still in the temple courts. Up to this point he was being asked questions. Now he takes the initiative and asks a question himself. The Messiah (cf. commentary at 8:29), the Anointed One, the King appointed by God, was expected to be from the family of David (cf. Isa 9:2-7; 11:1-9; Jer 23:5-6; 30:9; 33:15, 17, 22; Ezek 34:23-24; 37:24; Hos 3:5; Amos 9:11). The Triumphal Entry clearly shows that the restored kingdom was a popular expectation ("Blessed is the coming kingdom of our father David," 11:10). Jesus' question is "In what sense [cf. NIV's 'How is it?'] is the Messiah the son of David?"

36-37 Jesus does not wait for an answer from his listeners. He provides it himself. The quotation is from Psalm 110:1. Both the Davidic authorship is assumed and his inspiration in writing it (v.36). "Speaking by the Holy Spirit" is a typical rabbinic formula to describe inspired utterance. A messianic interpretation of Psalm 110 is unknown before the third century A.D. It may be, however, that its messianic interpretation was dropped because of Christian usage and reintroduced at a later period. The main point of Jesus' reply presupposes the psalm's messianic usage.

David calls the Messiah "my Lord." How can he at the same time be David's son and David's Lord (v.37)? The answer Jesus intended to elicit was "The Messiah is indeed to be descended from David, but he has a more exalted role than that of a successor of David; he is the Son of God." Or as Moule puts the answer intended by Jesus: "Because, although he is his son by descent and therefore his junior in age, he is also in some mysterious way, superior to David and therefore his senior in rank" (*Gospel of Mark*, p. 99).

Mark says that the crowd was delighted to listen to Jesus. Apparently they enjoyed seeing the so-called experts stumped! The remark also serves to show that, though the religious leaders opposed Jesus, the common people were for him.

Notes

36 It was once held that Ps 110, stated by Jesus to have been written by David, was actually Maccabean in date (second century B.C.). This has now been disproved as the result of the discovery at Qumran of a complete Psalter that has been dated in the third century B.C.

K. *The Warning About the Teachers of the Law*

12:38–40

> [38]As he taught, Jesus said, "Watch out for the teachers of the law. They like to walk around in flowing robes and be greeted in the marketplaces, [39]and have the most important seats in the synagogues and the places of honor at banquets. [40]They devour widows' houses and for a show make lengthy prayers. Such men will be punished most severely."

38–39 This paragraph probably is a continuing account of Jesus' teaching in the temple courts (cf. 12:35), though it is possible that Mark placed it here because, like the previous paragraph, it concerns the teachers of the law (v.38). Moule rightly says: "There is no evidence that all the theologians of Jesus' day were frauds, using their position merely as a cloak for cruelty and greed. . . . But the most influential of them seemed to have conceived a bitter hatred of Jesus, and one can only guess that this was because they were indeed using their powers selfishly and irresponsibly and detested his exposure of their real motives" (*Gospel of Mark*, p. 100).

Here Jesus condemns "their love of religious uniform ('ecclesiastical millinery') and public deference ('the raised hats of the laity'); a failing not yet wholly extinct in the clerical class" (Hunter, p. 120). Teachers of the law wore long white linen robes that were fringed and reached almost to the ground. They also were shown special respect by the majority of the people, being addressed by the honorific titles "Rabbi," "Father," and "Master." In the synagogue they occupied the bench in front of the ark that contained the sacred scrolls of the Law and the Prophets (v.39). There the teachers could be seen by all the worshipers in the synagogue. They were often invited to banquets because of their prestige and were given special places of honor. What Jesus condemns is their seeking such honor for themselves instead of for God whom they professed to serve.

139

40 Since the teachers of the law were not allowed to be paid for their services, they were dependent on the gifts of patrons for their livelihood. Such a system was vulnerable to abuses. Wealthy widows especially were preyed on by the greedy and unscrupulous among these men. Jesus particularly condemns the hypocrisy of their long prayers that were used as a mask for their greed. "For a show" is a translation of the Greek work *prophasis*. It is difficult to know whether it should be taken with what precedes and be translated "and to cover it up" (i.e., to cover up their devouring of widow's houses) or with what follows (the long prayers) and translate it, as does NIV, "and for a show." In either case there is a connection between their long prayers and their greed. "To rob the poor and the bereaved under the guise of personal piety doubles the guilt" (Hiebert, *Gospel of Mark*, pp. 310–11). Jesus promises punishment to all such—a reference to God's judgment in the Last Day.

L. *The Widow's Offering*

12:41–44

> ⁴¹Jesus sat down opposite the place where the offerings were put and watched the crowd putting their money into the temple treasury. Many rich people threw in large amounts. ⁴²But a poor widow came and put in two very small copper coins, worth only a fraction of a penny.
>
> ⁴³Calling his disciples to him, Jesus said, "I tell you the truth, this poor widow has put more into the treasury than all the others. ⁴⁴They all gave out of their wealth; but she, out of her poverty, put in everything—all she had to live on."

41–42 After this incident (the last in his public ministry), Jesus spends his time exclusively with the disciples. The placement of this story here may be to contrast the greed of the teachers of the law with the liberality of the widow. Or it may be that "with its teaching that the true gift is to give 'everything we have' (v.44) it sums up what has gone before in the Gospel and makes a superb transition to the story of how Jesus 'gave everything' for men" (Nineham, pp. 334–35). The setting is the court of the women, into which both men and women were allowed to come, and where the temple treasury was located. Jesus sat down on a bench where he could watch the people bring their offerings and put them in one of the thirteen trumpet-shaped boxes (*šôfār*) that were used for that purpose (v.41). It was not the rich with their large gifts who caught Jesus' attention but a poor widow (v.42). She placed in the box two copper coins (*lepta*), the smallest coins in circulation in Palestine (cf. Notes). Their value was, as NIV puts it, "only a fraction of a penny."

43–44 The disciples were not sitting with Jesus; so he called them to him (v.43). The lesson he wanted to teach them was important enough for them to be there to see it for themselves as well as to hear it. Again Jesus precedes his pronouncement with the solemn "I tell you the truth." The widow's offering was more (v.44) than all the others "in proportion, and also in the spirit in which she gave; it was in the latter that she was richer than all of them. . . . The means of the giver and the motive are the measure of true generosity" (Plummer, p. 290). Mark does not say how Jesus knew how much the widow gave or that what she gave constituted her entire livelihood.

Notes

---

42 A λέπτον (*lepton*, lit., "a tiny thing"; cf. the English word "mite"), the only Jewish coin mentioned in the NT, was worth one sixty-fourth of a denarius, the daily wage of a laborer (see IBD, II, 1022). Mark explains to his Roman readers, who would be unfamiliar with the value of the Palestinian coin, that a *lepton* was about equivalent to a *kodrantēs* (Gr. transliteration of the Lat. *quadrans*), which NIV translates in terms of its approximate value: "worth only a fraction of a penny." That Mark felt it necessary to explain the value of a *lepton* and that he does so by the use of a Latin coin (*quadrans*) only known in the west suggests strongly, in spite of contrary opinion, that he was writing to Romans.

M. *The Olivet Discourse* (13:1–37)

This is the longest connected discourse in Mark's Gospel. It is also the most difficult. The three major questions that present themselves in the study of Mark 13 are (1) What is the origin of the passage? (2) What is its purpose in Mark's Gospel? and (3) What is its meaning?

First, wide divergences of opinion exist as to the origin of this passage. Some scholars, concluding that Jesus teaches in Mark 13 that the end of the age will come within his own generation and being unwilling to ascribe such a serious mistake to him, have created the Little Apocalypse theory. By this means the apocalyptic element in chapter 13 is identified with a Jewish (or Jewish-Christian) apocalyptic tract that was written as a result of Pilate's placement of Roman ensigns in Jerusalem, or when Caligula, the Roman emperor, threatened to set up his image in the Jerusalem temple, or when the Roman armies surrounded the city of Jerusalem in A.D. 70. Since this apocalyptic tract was wrongly attributed to Jesus, none of the apocalyptic material in Mark 13 may be ascribed to him.

Although the Little Apocalypse theory has many adherents, it does not stand up under careful scrutiny. The chief problem with it is that the apocalyptic element in the discourse is too integrally bound up with the exhortative to posit an original apocalyptic tract. This is evident from the structure of the discourse. The apocalyptic statements are followed by exhortations that in turn are followed by clauses beginning with *gar* ("for") that state the reason for the exhortation (cf. vv.8, 11, 19, 22, 33, 35). Gaston accepts the readings that add *gar* to vv.6, 7b, and 9b and writes: "The importance of this word would have been noticed long ago were it not for the unfortunate fact that it is missing in several places from the Nestle text, even though it is required by a synoptic comparison and is well attested. . . . With the exception . . . of the longer sections 14–18 and 24–27, every apocalyptic element is attached to its context by a γάρ [*gar*]" (L. Gaston, *No Stone on Another* [Leiden: Brill, 1970], p. 52).

Other scholars opt for three kinds of material in Mark 13: (1) traditional sayings, (2) apocalyptic material, and (3) redactional comments. The difficulty of classifying the material in this way—evidenced by wide disagreement as to what falls into which category—creates skepticism as to the method. Beasley-Murray has shown that there are no compelling reasons for not accepting the discourse as substantially from Jesus. Whether he spoke its contents on a single occasion is another matter. Mark may have brought into the discourse material he felt was on the same theme (observe that Mark 13:9b–12 is not found in Matt 24 but in Matt 10:17–21 in the missionary discourse to the Twelve). Yet if Mark did this, he used the material within the bounds of its original intent and meaning in the teaching of Jesus. In summary, the discourse represents the teaching of Jesus but arranged and shaped by Mark to meet his theological purpose. This shaping and arranging was within the original intent and meaning of Jesus' words.

Second, why did Jesus speak these words and why were they included in Mark's Gospel? The discourse is patently apocalyptic in nature. This kind of literature was well known in the first century, especially to Jews. Daniel in the OT and the Revelation in the NT are examples of entire books that are apocalyptic in nature. These books, as well as the noncanonical apocalypses, are full of fantastic imagery and are highly symbolical. All of them purport to reveal information about the End. Mark's apocalypse is no exception. It has all the above characteristics, but in addition it has a distinctive exhortative character. The entire chapter is filled with exhortation and admonition. There are nineteen imperatives in vv.5–37. This makes it abundantly clear that the main purpose of the discourse is not to satisfy curiosity about the future but to give practical, ethical teaching. In this discourse Jesus combines eschatology with exhortation, with the emphasis on the latter. He is preparing his disciples—and beyond them the church—to live and to witness in a hostile world.

Mark's purpose is substantially the same. He desires "to present Jesus as Lord of history and as one in control of all events which may bring trouble to the church. Believers should in no way be startled or dispirited by what they see or have to endure. Their Lord has foretold these things. Better still, he will be with them in the Holy Spirit (v.11)" (Martin, *Mark*, p. 136).

Third, the problem of the meaning of the passage is closely tied in with the two major predictions in it: the destruction of the city of Jerusalem in A.D. 70 and the end of the age. The structure of the discourse is as follows: (1) Jesus' prophecy of the destruction of the temple and the questions of the disciples (vv.1–4—these verses form an introduction to the discourse); (2) warnings against deceivers and false signs of the End (vv.5–23); (3) the coming of the Son of Man (vv.24–27); (4) the lesson of the fig tree (vv.28–31); and (5) an exhortation to watchfulness (vv.32–37).

A simple solution to the problem of the relationship of the destruction of Jerusalem to the end of the age is to take vv.5–23 to refer to the destruction of the temple and the city, vv.24–27 to refer to the End, vv.28–31 back again to the same subject as vv.5–23, and vv.28–31 back again to the End (cf. vv.24–27). This arrangement takes the a—b a—b form. But the difficulty with this view is that the exegesis of the passage does not support it. The mention of the worldwide preaching of the gospel (v.10) and the unequaled days of distress (v.19) in vv.5–23 seem to point to something beyond A.D. 70, as does the appearance of "the abomination that causes desolation" (v.14; cf. commentary for details).

On the other hand, attempts to project the whole of vv.5–23 into the remote future with no reference to the destruction of Jerusalem are also unconvincing. The best solution is to see in vv.5–23 a shift back and forth between an immediate and a remote future. Some of the events even seem to have a dual fulfillment, one in the destruction of the city and the other in the end time. This shift from close to remote prediction may be due in part to Mark's arrangement of sayings of Jesus spoken on different occasions.

Problems of christology, i.e., whether Jesus mistakenly predicted the End within his own generation, are discussed in the commentary.

1. Prophecy of the destruction of the temple

13:1-2

> ¹As he was leaving the temple, one of his disciples said to him, "Look, Teacher! What massive stones! What magnificent buildings!"
> ²"Do you see all these great buildings?" replied Jesus. "Not one stone here will be left on another; every one will be thrown down."

1 The last reference in Mark's Gospel to Jesus entering the temple area is in 11:27. In 13:1 he comes out of the temple. This does not necessarily mean that all the events recorded in Mark between 11:27 and 13:1 occurred within the temple area. This chapter may well refer to another occasion altogether.

What prompted Jesus' prophetic words was the exclamation of one of his disciples on looking at the temple in all its grandeur.

The temple area, including the temple building itself, had been rebuilt by Herod the Great. (The second temple, built by Zerubbabel, had fallen into bad disrepair.) The courtyard had been greatly enlarged (to about four hundred by five hundred yards) in order to accommodate the large throngs of Jews who came to Jerusalem for the festivals. To accomplish this a huge platform had to be erected to compensate for the sharp falling off of the land to the southeast. An enormous retaining wall was built to hold the platform in place. The massive stones used in the construction of this wall may still be seen today, since part of the wall escaped the destruction of A.D. 70. At the southeast corner the temple platform towered two hundred feet above the Kidron Valley.

In addition to the temple building itself, on the platform stood porticoes and cloistered courts flanked by beautiful colonnades. The temple area covered approximately one-sixth of the area of the city of Jerusalem. It was an architectural wonder and its size and location dominated the ancient city.

The disciples exclaimed over the beauty of the buildings and the massiveness of the stones. Josephus says the stones were twenty-five cubits long, eight cubits high, and twelve cubits wide (Antiq. XV, 392 [xi.3]).

2 Jesus' reply was startling. Great though the temple buildings were, they would be completely destroyed. This prophecy was fulfilled in A.D. 70, when Jerusalem and the temple were destroyed by the Roman general Titus. Jesus' prophecy is very specific: "Not one stone here will be left on another." Although some of the huge stones Herod's workmen used in the great walls supporting the temple platform were not battered down by Titus's soldiers, all the buildings on the temple platform, including the temple itself to which the prophecy refers, were utterly destroyed. So completely were they destroyed that no trace of them remains today. Even their exact location on the temple mount is disputed.

Notes

---

1 For a description of Herod's temple, see Josephus, War V, 184–226 (v. 1–6) and Antiq. XV, 380–425 (xi).

2 The word translated "do you see" (βλέπεις, *blepeis*) may carry with it a slight rebuke: Are you allowing your attention to be taken up with these great and beautiful buildings when you shouldn't be? Swete (pp. 295–96) comments: "The disciples are warned that the pride which as Jews they naturally felt in this grand spectacle was doomed to complete humiliation."

2. The disciples' twofold question

13:3–4

> ³As Jesus was sitting on the Mount of Olives opposite the temple, Peter, James, John and Andrew asked him privately, ⁴"Tell us, when will these things happen? And what will be the sign that they are all about to be fulfilled?"

3–4 Between v.2 and v.3 the location shifts. Jesus is now on the Mount of Olives (v.3). With him are the four disciples who were the first to be called by him (cf. 1:16–20): Peter, James, John, and Andrew. From the top of the Mount they could clearly see the Kidron Valley running below the eastern wall of the city, and especially the temple mount. Its full grandeur was spread out below them.

The question the four disciples asked Jesus privately not only goes back to his statement made as they were leaving the temple area (cf. v.2) but actually expands it. "These things" (v.4) refers to the destruction of the temple. The disciples wanted to know when that would take place. They also wanted to know what the sign would be "that they are all about to be fulfilled?" Although from Mark's Gospel it would be possible to consider these two questions as essentially one (referring only to the destruction of the temple), Matthew's report of the questions makes this most unlikely: " 'Tell us,' they said, 'when will this happen, and what will be the sign of your coming and of the end of the age?' " (Matt 24:3). Ladd says, "There can be little doubt but that the disciples thought of the destruction of the temple as one of the events accompanying the end of the age and the coming of the eschatological Kingdom of God" (G.E. Ladd, *Theology of the New Testament* [Grand Rapids: Eerdmans, 1974], p. 196).

What the disciples wanted was a sign, some sure way by which they might know that the destruction of the temple was about to occur and that the end of the age was approaching. But Jesus refused to give them eschatological signs. Throughout the discourse he is more concerned to prepare them by exhortation and warning for the trials that lay ahead than to give them dates and signs.

3. Warnings against deceivers and false signs of the End

13:5–8

> ⁵Jesus said to them: "Watch out that no one deceives you. ⁶Many will come in my name, claiming, 'I am he,' and will deceive many. ⁷When you hear of wars and rumors of wars, do not be alarmed. Such things must happen, but the end is still to come. ⁸Nation will rise against nation, and kingdom against kingdom. There will be earthquakes in various places, and famines. These are the beginning of birth pains.

5–6 The first word of the discourse proper is *blepete* ("watch," v.5). This word reoccurs throughout the passage (cf. vv.9, 23, 33)—a clear indication that admonition is obviously one of Jesus' basic concerns. He is warning against false claimants to messiahship. This is apparently what "in my name" and "I am he" (i.e., the Messiah) refer to (v.6). That Jesus said there would be many such false messiahs suggests that his statement should be understood broadly. Speaking of the situation in Palestine before A.D. 70, Beasley-Murray writes: "Whereas the popular messianism hardly ever produced a claimant to the messianic office in the strictest sense, it both fostered and was nourished by men who asserted the possession of messianic authority or who regarded themselves as forerunners of the Kingdom" (*Mark Thirteen*, p. 31). The reference may not be limited to A.D. 70 but also look to the time preceding the End.

7–8 Wars and rumors of war are not to be a cause for alarm (v.7). These are within God's purposes. ("Such things must happen.") When they occur, they must not be mistaken as introducing the End. Jesus clearly says the "end is still to come." What "end" Jesus is talking about here is not clear. If the entire section (vv.5–23) deals only with the destruction of Jerusalem, then "the end" refers to the end of God's judgment on the Holy City. It is, however, more likely that it refers both to that event and the end of the age.

There will be other kinds of disturbances, too. In addition to international power struggles ("nation will rise against nation, and kingdom against kingdom"), there will be earthquakes and famine (v.8). These are indications of God's intervention in the historical process. Again, they are not to be taken as marking the End. They are rather the beginnings of "birth pains." The "birth pains" (*ōdin*) refer to the sufferings expected to occur in the period before the coming of the Messiah, and the word "beginning" suggests that there will be many more sufferings.

Ladd says that the last statement of v.8 is perhaps the most important of the discourse. He points out that

> the Old Testament speaks of the birth of a nation through a period of woes (Isa 66:8; Jer 22:23; Hos 13:13; Micah 4:9f.) and from these verses there arose in Judaism the idea that the messianic Kingdom must emerge from a period of suffering that was called the messianic woes or "the birth pangs of the Messiah." This does not mean the woes that the Messiah must suffer, but the woes out of which the messianic age is to be born. (*New Testament Theology*, pp. 201–2)

Notes

8 For the rabbinic expression "birth pangs of the Messiah," see SBK, 1:950. It probably was already in use in Jesus' day.

---

4. *Warnings of persecution and strife and a call to steadfastness*

13:9–13

⁹"You must be on your guard. You will be handed over to the local councils and flogged in the synagogues. On account of me you will stand before governors and kings as witnesses to them. ¹⁰And the gospel must first be preached to all nations. ¹¹Whenever you are arrested and brought to trial, do not worry beforehand

about what to say. Just say whatever is given you at the time, for it is not you speaking, but the Holy Spirit.

12"Brother will betray brother to death, and a father his child. Children will rebel against their parents and have them put to death. 13All men will hate you because of me, but he who stands firms to the end will be saved.

9 Again Jesus warns his disciples to be on their guard, because persecutions of various kinds await them. The "local councils" to which they will be handed over are the religious courts. They were made up of the elders of the synagogues assembled for the purpose of exercising their disciplinary powers. From these courts, Jesus warns, they will be taken into the synagogues and publicly flogged. They will also be brought before secular authorities ("governors and kings"), most of whom were Gentiles. But persecution, whether by Jews or Gentiles, would be an opportunity for witness. This verse clearly anticipates fulfillment in the near future.

10 The Greek impersonal verb *dei* ("must") underscores the will of God. It has been decreed by him that the gospel be preached to all the nations (or Gentiles). This is Jesus' mandate to his disciples and through them to his church. "First" (*prōton*) may mean before the destruction of the city of Jerusalem. Those who hold this view see the promise fulfilled in the proclamation of the gospel throughout the Roman world by A.D. 60. It seems best, however, to understand "first" in terms of the End. Certainly Matthew understood it that way. He immediately follows the statement of the universal preaching of the gospel with "and then the end will come" (Matt 24:14). Jesus seems to be saying here, "Instead of looking for signs of the end, get busy and spread the 'good news'! All nations must hear before the End comes."

11 The disciples will be hauled into court and crossexamined by the authorities. Jesus promises them, in that situation, strength and resources beyond their own through the Holy Spirit. The Spirit will reveal to them on the spot the appropriate words to speak (cf. Jer 1:9; Acts 6:10; 7:55). To use this verse to justify lack of careful preparation for preaching is irresponsible exegesis.

12–13 The breaking of ties of natural affection will be another trial the disciples will have to face. In Luke 12:51–53 (cf. Mic 7:2–6) Jesus warns of families being split because of the gospel:

> Do you think I came to bring peace on earth? No, I tell you, but division. From now on there will be five in one family divided against each other, three against two and two against three. They will be divided, father against son and son against father, mother against daughter and daughter against mother, mother-in-law against daughter-in-law and daughter-in-law against mother-in-law.

Only a fanatical hatred of the gospel could bring about unnatural behavior such as these verses describe. Morison (p. 359) remarks: "As there is nothing that excites such love as the gospel, when intelligently received, so there is nothing that occasions such hate as this same gospel, when passionately rejected." Moreover the hatred will not be limited to relatives (v.12), but "all men will hate you" (v.13). Temple comments, "Not all that the world hates is good Christianity; but it does hate good Christianity and always will" (*Readings in John,* pp. 271–72).

Testing will be another feature of the last times. Not all will stand the test, but he who endures to the "end" (*telos* here is a reference to the end of a person's life, not, as in v.7, the end of the age) will be saved. Jesus is not here setting forth a doctrine of salvation by works. He is rather emphasizing that genuine faith will issue in Christian living that will endure trial and persecution. A good commentary on v.13b is 2 Timothy 2:12: "If we endure, we will also reign with him." This section (vv.9–13), with its warning and encouragements, must have had special relevance for the life situation of the Roman church.

The structure of vv.9–13 is especially interesting. The section includes three separate sayings of Jesus held together by the key word (*paradidomi*, translated in NIV as "handed over" (v.9), "arrested" (v.11), and "betray" (v.12). The first speaks of being handed over to religious courts and appearing before civil authorities; the second promises the presence of the Holy Spirit when they are arrested and brought to trial; and the last deals with the family hostility and hatred that loyalty to Jesus Christ will bring about. Verse 10, which is concerned with the worldwide preaching of the gospel, is sandwiched between the first and second sayings; and for this reason some scholars consider it a gloss. Verses 9–13 are not, with the exception of v.10, found in the parallel account in Matthew 24. They occur, with the exception of v.10, in Matthew 10:17–22 in the context of the mission charge to the Twelve. Luke has them in his parallel account (21:12–17), with the exception of v.10, and in another context (12:11–12) gives a variant of v.11 as a separate logion of Jesus. All this shows that the material in Mark 13:9, 11–13 was given by Jesus on more than one occasion or that Mark has collected sayings from other contexts and put them here because of their relevance.

Notes

9 Josephus in Antiq. IV, 214–18 (viii. 14) describes the συνέδρια (*synedria*, "local courts"). The phrase εἰς μαρτύριον αὐτοῖς (*eis martyrion autois*) may be translated "for evidence against them," i.e., the authorities. If this is the meaning, the assumption is that the witness of the disciples will be rejected by the authorities and on the day of judgment will be used against them (cf. TDNT, 4:502–3). In view of Luke 21:13, it seems best to follow the NIV rendering "as witnesses to them."

10 This verse interrupts the flow of thought of the passage. Because of this and other reasons, its authenticity has been questioned. A better solution is to regard it as an independent logion inserted here by Mark to stress the missionary enterprise of the church in spite of opposition and trial.

5. The abomination that causes desolation and the necessity of flight

13:14–23

¹⁴"When you see 'the abomination that causes desolation' standing where it does not belong—let the reader understand—then let those who are in Judea flee to the mountains. ¹⁵Let no one on the roof of his house go down or enter the house to take anything out. ¹⁶Let no one in the field go back to get his cloak.

17How dreadful it will be in those days for pregnant women and nursing mothers! 18Pray that this will not take place in winter, 19because those will be days of distress unequaled from the beginning, when God created the world, until now—and never to be equaled again. 20If the Lord had not cut short those days, no one would survive. But for the sake of the elect, whom he has chosen, he has shortened them. 21At that time if anyone says to you, 'Look, here is the Christ!' or, 'Look, there he is!' do not believe it. 22For false Christs and false prophets will appear and perform signs and miracles to deceive the elect—if that were possible. 23So be on your guard; I have told you everything ahead of time.

14a This is one of the most difficult verses in Mark's Gospel if not in the entire NT. The key phrase is "abomination that causes desolation," an expression derived from the Book of Daniel (cf. Dan 9:27; 11:31; 12:11). In Matthew's Gospel (24:15) Jesus explicitly identifies it with that book. The first word of the phrase, *bdelygma* ("abomination"), suggests something repugnant to God, while the second, *erēmōsis* ("desolation"), suggests that because of the abomination the temple is left deserted, desolate. The holy and pious worshipers vacate it.

The fulfillment of Daniel's prophecy of the "abomination that causes desolation" is usually found in the profanation of the altar of burnt offering in the temple of Jerusalem by a representative of Antiochus IV, Epiphanes, in 167 B.C. (cf. 1 Macc 1:54–59; 6:7). The fact that Jesus uses the same expression here makes it clear that its fulfillment was not restricted to the events of the time of the Maccabees. What it does refer to has been hotly debated. Those who hold the view that all the events described in vv.5–23 have to do with the Fall of Jerusalem most often identify the "abomination" with either the Roman army (cf. Luke 21:20), and in particular the military standards that the Jews considered idolatrous and an abomination, or with the Zealots, or more specifically Phannias, whom they farcically made high priest (cf. Jos. War IV, 147–57 [iii.6–8]).

Others see this prophecy as being fulfilled in the end time by the Antichrist. Their evidence for this view is as follows:

1. The use of the masculine participal *hestēkota* ("standing") suggests a person (cf. NEB: "When you see the 'abomination of desolation' usurping a place that is not his").

2. Paul's statements in 2 Thessalonians 2:3–10 about the eschatological Antichrist seem to be derived from a similar tradition.

3. The person referred to must be associated with the End, because in Matthew's Gospel his appearance is immediately followed by the coming of the Son of Man (cf. 24:29–30).

A better solution, however, is to understand the abomination that causes desolation as having a multiple fulfillment in (1) the Maccabean period, (2) the events of A.D. 66–70, and (3) the end time.

The exhortation "let the reader understand" is probably Mark's editorial comment.

14b–18 It is difficult to consign the admonitions of these verses to the end time. No one will be able to flee from the judgment of God in that day. The warnings, however, make good sense in the context of the approach of the Roman army before the Fall of Jerusalem in A.D. 70. Two admonitions stress the urgency of the situation: (1) anyone on the roof of the house is not, on descending the outside staircase, to go inside to get any of his belongings (v. 15); and (2) anyone in the field is not to return to the house even to get an outer garment (v. 16).

The outer garment ("cloak") was used at night to keep one warm; in the daytime it was taken off to allow more freedom of movement in working. Though his cloak would be especially useful in case of the necessity of fleeing to the mountains (v. 14b) where the night air is cold, the situation would be too urgent to allow one even to fetch it. A hurried flight to the mountains would be very hard for pregnant women and nursing mothers (v. 17). And if the flight took place in winter (v. 18), it would be all the more difficult, since both the cold and the rain-swollen wadis would present formidable hazards. These warnings and woes seem especially appropriate to what actually occurred at the time of the destruction of Jerusalem. The Christians in the city fled to the mountains—to Pella in Perea (Eusebius *Ecclesiastical History* 3.5.3).

19–20 The primary temporal reference now shifts back to the End. The language of v. 19, though fulfilled partially in the great stress that occurred at the Fall of Jerusalem in A.D. 70, looks forward to the Great Tribulation that will precede the End. Mark uses language derived from Daniel's portrayal of the last days (Dan 12:1; cf. Jer 30:7). Nowhere else in Scripture is there a reference to the shortening of the time of tribulation (v. 20), though the pseudepigraphical 3 Baruch contains the thought (ch. 9). In the context of A.D. 70, "the elect, for whose sake the siege was shortened, are probably the faithful members of the Church of Jerusalem . . . whose intercession or whose presence secured this privilege, though it did not avail to save the city" (Swete, p. 309). In the context of the End, the elect are the people of God generally.

21–23 The section (vv. 5–23) ends as it began, with a warning against false Christs (v. 21). A crisis like that of the fall of the city would be sure to produce many false pretenders. So would the crisis of the approaching End. They will wield supernatural power great enough to perform "signs and miracles" (v. 22). Yet they will not be able to deceive God's people. This is the force of the phrase "if that were possible." But it is not possible; God will guard his elect. Beasley-Murray comments: "As in all the Scriptures, the assurance of God's care for his elect (implied in εἰ δύνατον [*ei dynaton*, 'if it were possible'], v. 22), is not regarded as ground for presumption. 'Do on your part take care. If the temptations of false prophets are strong enough to endanger the chosen of God, you will not be exempt. I have told you all these things in order that you may be fully prepared. Remain on the alert'" (*Mark Thirteen*, p. 86). Again the hortatory purpose of the discourse is evident.

6. *The coming of the Son of Man*

13:24–27

24"But in those days, following that distress,

" 'the sun will be darkened,
    and the moon will not give its light;
25the stars will fall from the sky,
    and the heavenly bodies will be shaken.'

26"At that time men will see the Son of Man coming in clouds with great power and glory. 27And he will send his angels and gather his elect from the four winds, from the ends of the earth to the ends of the heavens.

24–25 Verses 24–27 form a unit and relate to the End. They are set off from the previous verses by the strong adversative *alla* ("but"). Whereas the preceding verses (5–23) point to both the destruction of Jerusalem and the end time, vv.24–27 speak only of the end time. "In those days" (v.24) is a common OT expression having eschatological associations (cf. Jer 3:16, 18; 31:29; 33:15–16; Joel 3:1; Zech 8:23). In Mark, Jesus speaks of a period "following that distress" (the NIV translators backed off from the word "tribulation" both here and in the Matthew parallel, but see RSV). In Matthew, however, the statement is more specific—"Immediately after the distress of those days" (24:29)—making it impossible to limit the "distress" of vv.19–20 to the period preceding the destruction of the city of Jerusalem in A.D. 70, because the end time immediately follows.

The coming of the Son of Man will be associated with celestial phenomena. The imagery and language are derived from the OT descriptions of the Day of the Lord. The quotation is an echo of Isaiah 13:10, but other OT passages reveal similar language (cf. Isa 24:23; 34:4; Ezek 32:7–8; Joel 2:10, 30–31; 3:15; Amos 8:9). It is difficult to know whether the poetic language here is to be understood literally or figuratively. The repeated assertion in Scripture that the end times will be accompanied by cosmic disturbances seems to imply that there will be unprecedented celestial disturbances of some sort that are literal (cf. 2 Peter 3:10). This is not to deny that Mark may be using phenomenal language, but his language is nonetheless referring to objective events in the physical universe. These will occur when God brings history to an end by the coming of his Son. "This language does not mean necessarily the complete break-up of the universe; we know from similar language elsewhere that it designates the judgment of God upon a fallen world that has shared the fate of man's sin, that out of the ruins of judgment a new world may be born" (Ladd, *New Testament Theology*, p. 203).

26–27 The celestial drama reaches a climax when the Son of Man comes in the clouds with "great power and glory" (v.26). Jesus describes his coming in these verses almost entirely in the words of Scripture. The reference here is to Daniel 7:13, the first time our Lord definitely connects the title "Son of Man" with the Daniel prophecy (cf. Mark 14:62). (For a discussion of the title "Son of Man," see commentary at 8:31.)

The great emphasis of these verses is on disclosure and triumph. Whereas the Son of Man has been hidden or at least veiled in his first coming, now he will be revealed. Men "will see" him and see him for who he really is. Whereas he has been the lowly Suffering Servant, despised and rejected by men, the Son of Man at his parousia will come in triumph—"with great power and glory." And his chief concern at his coming will be to bring together his people (v.27) so that they may be with him. Therefore he sends forth his angels to gather the elect from all over the world. Calvin's comments (3:148) on v.27 show its continuing relevance: "For, though the Church be now tormented by the malice of men, or even broken by the violence of the billows, and miserably torn in pieces, so as to have no stability in the world, yet we ought always to cherish confident hope, because it will not be by human means, but by heavenly power, which will be far superior to every obstacle, that the Lord will *gather* his Church" (emphasis his).

7. The lesson of the fig tree

13:28–31

> 28"Now learn this lesson from the fig tree: As soon as its twigs get tender and its leaves come out, you know that summer is near. 29Even so, when you see these things happening, you know that it is near, right at the door. 30I tell you the truth, this generation will certainly not pass away until all these things have happened. 31Heaven and earth will pass away, but my words will never pass away.

28 In Palestine most trees are evergreen, but the fig tree is an exception. In the fall it loses its leaves; and when in the spring the sap rises in its branches and the tree begins to leaf out, summer cannot be far off. The parable is essentially an antidote to despair. In contrast to the sufferings and persecutions promised in the previous verses, here the prospect of the coming of the Son of Man is offered.

29 The chief problem in this verse is the identification of "these things" (*tauta*). Do they refer to the events surrounding the fall of the city of Jerusalem or the events immediately preceding the end of the age? Ladd identifies them with the signs of the end outlined in vv.5–23. Also "*tauta* in verse 29 appears to be the antecedent of the *tauta panta* that are to take place in this generation [v.30]. What Jesus appears to be saying is that the signs that presage the end are not to be confined to a remote future; his hearers would themselves experience them" (Ladd, *New Testament Theology*, p. 209). Those signs were experienced in a special way at the fall of the city of Jerusalem.

The next phrase, *engys estin*, may be translated either "it :s near" (NIV) or "he is near." Those who interpret this paragraph (vv.28–31) in its entirety to relate to the events surrounding the Fall of Jerusalem usually identify the "it" with the "abomination that causes desolation" (cf. v.14) or the fall of the city itself. If, on the other hand, vv.28–31 are descriptive of the End, then "he is near" would be a more fitting translation, though "it," referring to the Parousia, would also be suitable. Luke (21:31) has for "it" (or "he") the "kingdom of God."

30 Since Jesus' words are preceded by the solemn "I tell you the truth," they are not to be taken lightly. To suggest that Jesus was mistaken in the statement he made in this verse but that the mistake was in a matter of such small consequence that it makes no difference is to fail to take seriously the solemnity of the introductory words.

The interpretation hinges on the meaning of the expressions "this generation" (*he genea hautē*) and "all these things" (*tauta panta*). A multiplicity of interpretations have been given to "this generation"—mankind in general, the Jewish people, Christians, unbelievers. It seems best, however, to understand it to mean Jesus' own generation. Then *tauta panta* refers to the signs preceding the End found in vv.5–23. These are not confined to a remote future but "are to be experienced, though not necessarily exhausted, by the contemporary generation" (Moore, *The Parousia in the New Testament*, p. 133).

31 Jesus strongly emphasizes the certainty and reliability of his predictions in v.30. "Heaven and earth" is a reference to the whole of the universe, all creation. The certitude and absolute reliability of Jesus' words is far greater than the apparent continuance of the universe. It will some day cease to exist, but Jesus' words will always have validity (cf. Ps 102:25–27; Isa 40:6–8; 51:6).

Notes

---

30 The Greek word for "generation" is γενεά (*genea*). It "primarily denotes those descended from a single ancestor, a tribe, a race; then it comes to signify those born within the same period, a generation of contemporary men; finally a period of time occupied by a particular generation" (Beasley-Murray, *Mark Thirteen*, p. 99; cf. A-S, p. 89). Ellis, however, remarks that "in the Qumran writings the term, 'last generation' (1 Qp Hab 2.7; 7:2), apparently included several lifetimes. Their usage indicates that in the New Testament 'this (last) generation', like 'last hour' (I Jn 2.18) or 'today', means only the last phase in the history of redemption" (*Gospel of Luke*, p. 246). According to this interpretation "this generation" is the final period before the End, however long it may be.

An important problem raised by v.30, as interpreted in this commentary, is the NT insistence on the nearness of the End (cf. Rom 13:12; 1 Cor 7:29; Phil 4:5; Heb 10:25; James 5:8–9; 1 Peter 4:7; 1 John 2:18; Rev 22:20). Cranfield asks:

> Are we to say (with Dodd, Glasson, Taylor, *et al*.) that the primitive Church read into Jesus' ideas apocalyptic teachings that were alien to it? Or (with Schweitzer, Werner, T.W. Manson, Barrett, *et al*.) that Jesus was himself mistaken? Or is the solution to be found in a more theological understanding of what is meant by the nearness of the End? . . . If we realize that the Incarnation—Crucifixion—Resurrection—Ascension, on the one hand, and the Parousia, on the other, belong essentially together, and are in a real sense one Event, one divine Act, being held apart only by the Mercy of God who desires to give men opportunity for faith and repentance, then we can see that in a very real sense the latter is always imminent now that the former has happened. It was, and still is, true to say that the Parousia is at hand—and indeed this, so far from being an embarrassing mistake on the part either of Jesus or of the early Church, is an essential part of the Church's faith. Ever since the Incarnation men have been living in the last days. (*Gospel of Mark*, p. 408)

This type of thinking is difficult for contemporary man, but it seems consistent with the biblical material.

---

8. *The necessity of watchfulness*

13:32–37

32"No one knows about that day or hour, not even the angels in heaven, nor the Son, but only the Father. **33**Be on guard! Be alert! You do not know when that time will come. **34**It's like a man going away: He leaves his house and puts his servants in charge, each with his assigned task, and tells the one at the door to keep watch.

35"Therefore keep watch because you do not know when the owner of the house will come back—whether in the evening, or at midnight, or when the rooster crows, or at dawn. **36**If he comes suddenly, do not let him find you sleeping. **37**What I say to you, I say to everyone: 'Watch!' "

Jesus' call for vigilance pervades this paragraph—"Be on guard! Be alert!" (v.33); "Therefore keep watch" (v.35); "do not let him find you sleeping" (v.36); and "Watch!" (v.37).

32 Few would challenge the authenticity of this verse. The early church is unlikely to have created a logion that has resulted in such consternation and embarrassment as this one has. "That day" clearly refers to the Parousia. It is the great day, the eschatological day that will bring to an end "those days" (vv.17, 19, 24). Of "those days," i.e., the days that precede the time of the End, certain signs have been given; but of "that day" neither the angels of heaven nor Jesus himself knows the time. Only the Father knows that time. And Jesus, at his ascension, clearly says that it was not for the disciples "to know the times or dates the Father has set by his own authority" (Acts 1:7). A map of the future would be a hindrance, not a help, to faith. Their responsibility and ours is to get busy and do his work without being concerned about date setting. As Moule says:

> New Testament thought on the Last Things, at its deepest and best, always concentrates on what God has already done for men in Christ. It does not say, How long will it be before the last whistle blows full-time? Rather it says, Where ought I to be to receive the next pass? What really matters is that the kick-off has already taken place, the game is on and we have a captain to lead us on to victory. (C.F.D. Moule, *The Birth of the New Testament* [London: SCM, 1966], pp. 101–2)

Jesus' ignorance of the day or hour of his parousia must be understood in terms of the NT teaching concerning the Incarnation. A real Incarnation involved such lack of knowledge. Jesus purposely laid aside temporarily the exercise of his omniscience as part of what was involved in his becoming man.

33–36 Vigilance is the order of the day because the time of the Parousia is not known. *Blepete* ("be on guard") is the keynote of the entire discourse (v.33), and *gar* ("for"—not translated in NIV) states the reason watchfulness is necessary. "If the Master Himself does not know, the disciples must not only acquiesce in their ignorance, but regard it as a wholesome stimulus to exertion" (Swete, p. 317). The word for time here is *kairos*, meaning God's appointed time.

The parable has in it some of the features of that of the talents (Matt 25:14–30) and the pounds (Luke 19:12–27). There is a privilege (*exousia*, "charge") and a responsibility (*ergon*, "assigned task," v.34). The parable does not develop these elements but turns attention to the doorkeeper who has a special task. Then Jesus applies it to the disciples. Like a doorkeeper who must watch because he does not know when the owner will return, they too must be on guard (v.35). Evening, midnight, rooster crowing, and dawn are the names of the four watches of the night the Romans used. The Greek adverb *exaiphnēs* (NIV, "suddenly") emphasizes the suddenness of the Parousia (v.36). "The element of surprise is ineradicable from the parousia expectation. Signs, like the fig tree, are an indication of promise, not a clock" (Beasley-Murray, *Mark Thirteen*, p. 117).

37 The discourse that was addressed to four of the disciples (v.3) began with the imperative "Watch." This exhortation recurs during the discourse. Now at the end it is repeated once more, but this time it is no longer addressed only to the four disciples but to "everyone." In this way Jesus shows his concern not only for the disciples but for the whole community—all his followers for whom he was about to die—and his message is "Watch!" Beasley-Murray writes: "This word the first community took seriously. When their hour came they were ready. In crises since that day it has shone as a lamp in the gloom" (*Mark Thirteen*, p. 118).

VII. The Passion and Resurrection Narrative (14:1–16:8 [9–20])

The conflict of Jesus with the religious leaders, which in Mark's Gospel begins as early as 3:1, reaches its climax in the passion narrative and is followed by the triumph of the Resurrection on Easter morning. Since these events constitute the heart of the Christian gospel (cf. 1 Cor 15:1–4), they were the first part of the story of Jesus to be written down and circulated as a continuous whole. Mark had access to this narrative and seems to have incorporated it into his Gospel with little editorial revision. "He chose only to supplement it with parallel or complementary tradition and to orchestrate it for the development of certain themes" (Lane, p. 485).

The importance of the passion and resurrection of our Lord for the early church is evidenced by the relatively large amount of space the narrative takes in each of the Gospels and especially in Mark. Out of Mark's 661 verses, 128 are devoted to the passion and resurrection story, and a total of 242 are devoted to the last week (from the triumphal entry to the resurrection) of our Lord's life. The church obviously had more than a historical interest in Jesus' death and resurrection. These events formed the basis of the church's witness and worship—the lifeblood of early Christianity. The witnessing church proclaimed a crucified and living Savior, and the worshiping church reflected on the meaning of these events for its inner life.

This section in Mark's Gospel plays on two basic themes: suffering and triumph. The suffering of Jesus is highlighted by (1) his betrayal and denial (by Judas, Peter, and all the disciples); (2) his trial before the Sanhedrin and Pilate with its injustice and mockery; and (3) his crucifixion with its brutality and shame. The triumph of Jesus comes through his glorious resurrection on the third day after his crucifixion. This is the note on which Mark's Gospel, "the good news about Jesus Christ, the Son of God," comes to a close.

A. *The Plot to Arrest Jesus*

14:1–2

> ¹Now the Passover and the Feast of Unleavened Bread were only two days away, and the chief priests and the teachers of the law were looking for some sly way to arrest Jesus and kill him. ²"But not during the Feast," they said, "or the people may riot."

1–2 These verses serve to introduce the passion and resurrection narrative. Passover (Heb. *pesaḥ*) is the Jewish festival commemorating the occasion when the angel of the Lord passed over (*pāsaḥ*) the homes of the Hebrews on the night he killed all the firstborn sons of the Egyptians (cf. Exod 12:13, 23, 27). The lambs used in the feast were slain on the fourteenth of Nisan (March/April), and the meal was eaten that evening between sundown and midnight. According to Jewish reckoning, that would be the fifteenth of Nisan, since the Jewish day began at sundown. The Feast of Unleavened Bread followed Passover and lasted seven days (15–21 Nisan; cf. Exod 12:15–20; 23:15; 34:18; Deut 16:1–8). Since the Last Supper was probably a

Passover meal and took place on Thursday night, the incident reported here must have taken place on Wednesday of Passion Week. This is calculated from the temporal phrase *meta duo hēmeras*. If "after three days" means "on the third day" (cf. 8:31; 9:31; 10:34), then "after two days" would mean "on the second day," i.e., "tomorrow." NIV's "only two days away" (v.1) is ambiguous and must be understood in accordance with Jewish usage of the temporal phrase.

For a long time the religious authorities had been looking for a way to get rid of Jesus (cf. 3:6; 11:18; 12:12). Now they renewed and intensified their efforts. But it was necessary for them to proceed with the utmost caution. Since Passover (like Tabernacles and Pentecost) was one of the pilgrim feasts, great throngs of people invaded the Holy City to celebrate it. It is said that the population doubled (from twenty-five thousand to fifty thousand) during the week. The chief priests and teachers of the law (the two main bodies that made up the Sanhedrin, the Jewish high court) realized that it would be too risky to move in on Jesus with such a highly excitable crowd present. The possibility of a riot was too great (v.2). It would be wiser to wait for a more propitious moment—perhaps after the pilgrims had left the city to go home. God's purposes were otherwise, and this part of their plan miscarried. Perhaps the unexpected help from one of Jesus' disciples (14:10–11) changed their minds, and they decided to go through with their wicked scheme despite the presence of the Passover pilgrims.

B. *The Anointing at Bethany*

14:3–9

> [3]While he was in Bethany, reclining at the table in the home of a man known as Simon the Leper, a woman came with an alabaster jar of very expensive perfume, made of pure nard. She broke the jar and poured the perfume on his head.
> [4]Some of those present were saying indignantly to one another, "Why this waste of perfume? [5]It could have been sold for more than a year's wages and the money given to the poor." And they rebuked her harshly.
> [6]"Leave her alone," said Jesus. "Why are you bothering her? She has done a beautiful thing to me. [7]The poor you will always have with you, and you can help them any time you want. But you will not always have me. [8]She did what she could. She poured perfume on my body beforehand to prepare for my burial. [9]I tell you the truth, wherever the gospel is preached throughout the world, what she has done will also be told, in memory of her."

3 The placing of this incident in the narrative is different in John's Gospel. There it occurs before the Passion Week begins (cf. John 12:1: "six days before the Passover"). Theological emphasis is more important than chronology to Mark—at least here. His placing contrasts the hatred of the religious leaders (immediately preceding [vv.1–2]) and the betrayal of Judas (immediately following [vv.10–11]) with the love and devotion of Mary demonstrated by her anointing of Jesus with expensive perfume. Although Luke 7:36–50 is similar to John 12:1–8 and Mark 14:3–9, the differences are significant and thus it no doubt records a different incident (see Notes).

The incident takes place in the home of Simon the Leper at Bethany. The occasion for the dinner is not specified. Simon was probably a leper who had been healed. The retention of the name "the Leper" would suggest this—indeed he may

155

have been healed by Jesus. Was the dinner an expression of gratitude for this? Mark does not identify the woman who anointed Jesus, but we know from John's Gospel (12:3) that she was Mary, the sister of Martha and Lazarus. The "alabaster jar" that contained the perfume was a "vessel w. a rather long neck which was broken off when the contents were used" (BAG, p. 33). The "nard" (perfume) was made from the root of a plant found chiefly in India and was very expensive. Mary took the bottle and broke the neck so that she could pour the ointment profusely over Jesus' head.

4–5 Mark does not name those who reacted so indignantly at the "waste" of the costly perfume (v.4). Matthew, however, says it was the disciples (26:8), while John says it was Judas Iscariot (12:4–5). Judas probably expressed the most vigorous dissent because he was the treasurer of the Twelve. The chief concern of the objectors was mercenary (v.5). The perfume had a value of more than three hundred denarii (a denarius was what a man received for a day's work—thus NIV's "more than a year's wage"). The mention of the poor is natural because it was the custom for the Jews to give gifts to the poor on the evening of the Passover. The insensitivity of Jesus' disciples to this beautiful expression of love and devotion is amazing. Mark uses the word *embrimaomai* ("to be angry," "to express violent displeasure") to describe the feeling of the disciples toward Mary. This is all the more surprising since they had often enjoyed the generous hospitality of Mary, her sister, Martha, and her brother, Lazarus, while in Bethany.

6–8 Jesus rushed to Mary's defense (v.6). Instead of condemning her, they should have commended her. Her action of anointing Jesus with a bottle of expensive perfume was a beautiful expression of her love and devotion to him, and she should not be berated. In addition he would not be with them very long (v.7). Before Jesus lay Gethsemane, the trial, Golgotha, the Resurrection, and the return to glory. Time for such expression of devotion and love while he was still here was running out. In contrast, opportunities for helping the poor would continue. There is no evidence in Jesus' statement of a lack of concern for the poor. On the contrary, there is ample evidence elsewhere that their interests and needs lay close to his heart (cf. Matt 5:3; 6:2–4; 19:21; Luke 6:20, 36–38; 21:1–4; John 13:29).

In addition to being an expression of devotion, Mary's act was interpreted by Jesus as an anointing of his body beforehand in preparation for his burial (v.8). Was Mary aware of this aspect of what she was doing? Perhaps not, but it is possible that she had a greater sensitivity to what was about to happen to Jesus than the Twelve did. In Luke's Gospel she is depicted as a good listener (10:39); and perhaps by this means she wanted to do for Jesus what she knew would ordinarily not be done for one who would die the death of a criminal. Jesus' statement serves as yet another prediction of his passion.

9 This pronouncement is preceded by the solemn "I tell you the truth." In an indirect way Jesus is here predicting his resurrection, because the preaching of the gospel presupposes the Resurrection. The central message of the Good News is Jesus' defeat of sin, death, and hell by his resurrection. And anywhere in the world that Good News is preached, Mary's act of love and devotion will be remembered. Thus Jesus—in marked contrast to the disciples—assesses the significance of her act.

Notes

3 The incident in vv.3–9 should not be confused with that in Luke 7:36–50. The details, except the name Simon, are very different. "The Leper" may be added to Simon's name to differentiate him from the Simon in Luke 7:36–50, since Simon was a very common name. Plummer (p. 312) rightly comments: "The difficulty of believing in two anointings is infinitesimal. . . . Whereas the difficulty of believing that Mary of Bethany had ever been 'a sinner' is enormous. There is no evidence of a previous evil life, and what we know of her renders a previous evil life almost incredible."

C. *The Betrayal by Judas*

14:10–11

> ¹⁰Then Judas Iscariot, one of the Twelve, went to the chief priests to betray Jesus to them. ¹¹They were delighted to hear this and promised to give him money. So he watched for an opportunity to hand him over.

10–11 These verses are connected with vv.1–2. The chief priests and teachers of the law were looking for "some sly way to arrest Jesus" (v.1), and Judas "watched for an opportunity to hand him over" (v.11). Judas is identified specifically as "one of the Twelve" (v.10). He had all the advantages of being in the inner circle yet betrayed Jesus. Spiritual privilege in itself is not enough. There must be the response of faith and love.

Judas's offer to betray Jesus was readily accepted by the chief priests and teachers of the law because, being on the inside, he could choose the most opportune time to hand Jesus over to them. In that way they could avoid what they feared most, a riot of the people. It was undoubtedly the offer of Judas—he, not the religious leaders, took the initiative—that changed their minds about not arresting Jesus during the feast. It was a golden opportunity, and they were not about to lose it! Money was involved in the deal, though from Matthew's Gospel (26:15) we learn that Judas received for his treacherous act the pitiful sum of thirty silver coins.

What motivated Judas? Many guesses have been made—jealousy, greed, disappointment with Jesus' mission, to name a few. None of the Evangelists answer the question. There can be little doubt, however, that Judas was the betrayer. It is not likely that the church would have invented this story.

D. *The Lord's Supper* (14:12–26)

1. *Preparation of the meal*

14:12–16

> ¹²On the first day of the Feast of Unleavened Bread, when it was customary to sacrifice the Passover lamb, Jesus' disciples asked him, "Where do you want us to go and make preparations for you to eat the Passover?"
> ¹³So he sent two of his disciples, telling them, "Go into the city, and a man carrying a jar of water will meet you. Follow him. ¹⁴Say to the owner of the house he enters, 'The Teacher asks: Where is my guest room, where I may eat the Passover with my disciples?' ¹⁵He will show you a large upper room, furnished and ready. Make preparations for us there."

16The disciples left, went into the city and found things just as Jesus had told them. So they prepared the Passover.

12 Ordinarily "the first day of the Feast of Unleavened Bread" would mean 15 Nisan, the day following Passover. But the added description of the day—"when it was customary to sacrifice the Passover lamb"—makes it clear that 14 Nisan is meant, because Passover lambs were killed on 14 Nisan. The entire eight-day celebration, including Passover, was sometimes referred to as the Feast of Unleavened Bread (cf. Jos. Antiq. II, 315–17 [xv.1]); and there is some evidence that 14 Nisan was loosely referred to as the "first day of Unleavened Bread" (cf. SBK, 2:813–15).

The day of the week was Thursday. Jesus and his disciples were probably in Bethany. It is clear from v.13 that they were outside the city of Jerusalem. Since the Passover had to be eaten within the walls of the city (cf. M. *Pesachim* 7.9), the disciples asked Jesus where in Jerusalem they were to go to make preparation. There was no time to lose because the Passover meal had to be eaten between sundown and midnight, the first hours of 15 Nisan.

13–16 Jesus gave explicit instructions to two of his disciples (v.13). We know from Luke that the two were Peter and John (Luke 22:8). The "man carrying a jar of water" would easily be identified because customarily women, not men, carried water jars. He was to lead them to the house where the owner had a guest room (v.14). Jewish custom required that if a person had a room available, he must give it to any pilgrim who asked to stay in it, in order that he might have a place to celebrate the Passover (cf. SBK, 1:989). Mark seems to indicate that Jesus had made previous arrangements with the owner of the house. The upstairs room is described as "furnished and ready" (v.15), i.e., with what was necessary for the celebration: table, couches, cushions, etc. The disciples would have to get the food and prepare it. This would include the unleavened bread, wine, bitter herbs, sauce (*ḥārôseṯ*), and the lamb. The two disciples went into the city as instructed by Jesus, found everything as he had said, and made the necessary preparations (v.16).

Notes

12 Πάσχα (*pascha*) here means "the Passover lamb" as translated in NIV. In 14:1 it means the feast day and in 14:12b, 14, and 16 it means the Passover meal.

2. Announcement of the betrayal

14:17–21

17When evening came, Jesus arrived with the Twelve. 18While they were reclining at the table eating, he said, "I tell you the truth, one of you will betray me—one who is eating with me."
19They were saddened, and one by one they said to him, "Surely not I?"
20"It is one of the Twelve," he replied, "one who dips bread into the bowl with me. 21The Son of Man will go just as it is written about him. But woe to that man who betrays the Son of Man! It would be better for him if he had not been born."

17 Jesus and his disciples had probably spent the day in Bethany. In the evening they returned to the city. Mark says Jesus "arrived with the Twelve." This suggests that Peter and John, after making preparations, returned to Bethany, a distance of only a couple of miles, and then accompanied Jesus when he went into the city in the evening. The other possibility is that "the Twelve" was a designation of the close followers of Jesus whether all twelve were present or not. Jesus and his disciples went to the room prepared by Peter and John to celebrate the Passover. Since the Jewish day began at sundown, it was now Thursday night, 15 Nisan.

18 The Passover meal was originally eaten standing: "This is how you are to eat it: with your cloak tucked into your belt, your sandals on your feet and your staff in your hand. Eat it in haste; it is the Lord's Passover" (Exod 12:11). But in Jesus' time it had become customary to eat it in a reclining position. Jesus uses the solemn formula "I tell you the truth" to disclose the fact that one of them would betray him.

" 'One of you!' It came as a bolt from the blue. It was a stunning blow. What! Did the Master actually mean to say that one of their own number was going *to hand him over to the authorities*, for them to deal with as they pleased? Why, it was almost unbelievable—Yet, the One who never told an untruth and whose very name was 'the Truth' (John 8:46; 14:6) was saying this; so it must be true" (W. Hendriksen, *The Gospel of Matthew* [Grand Rapids: Baker, 1973], p. 905; emphasis his).

Jesus further identified the betrayer as "one who is eating with me." To betray a friend after eating a meal with him was, and still is, regarded as the worst kind of treachery in the Middle East. Jesus may have had in mind Psalm 41:9: "Even my close friend, whom I trusted, he who shared my bread, has lifted his heel against me."

19 The response of the disciples to Jesus' startling disclosure was one of sadness and self-distrust. One by one they asked Jesus, "Surely not I?" In Matthew's Gospel even Judas asks the question (Matt 26:25). It was an honest question coming from the rest of the disciples and was prompted by fear and lack of confidence in their own spiritual and moral strength. With Judas it was hypocritical and an attempt to cover his intent; for him not to have asked the question with the other disciples would have made him liable to suspicion.

20 Jesus had already given two clues as to the identity of the betrayer: he was one of the Twelve; he was eating with them at that moment. Now Jesus gives a third clue: the betrayer is the "one who dips bread in the bowl with me." The reference is to dipping a piece of unleavened bread in the sauce (*hărôset*) that was part of the Passover meal. This clue does not specifically reveal the betrayer but emphasizes again that it is one who enjoys the closest relationship with Jesus—he even dips his bread into the same bowl with him!

21 Behind Judas's action a divine purpose is being carried out. What happens to the Son of Man does not just happen. In all this the Scriptures are being fulfilled. As Hunter (p. 130) comments: "Beyond reasonable doubt Jesus is referring to Isa. 53. His words mean: 'The Son of Man travels the road marked out for the suffering Servant of the Lord, but alas for that man through whose agency he is being delivered up!' The 'delivering-up' is that predicted of the Servant: 'And he bore the sins of many and was delivered up because of their iniquities' (Isa. 53:12, LXX)."

The woe pronounced on the betrayer emphasizes the personal responsibility of Judas in his wicked deed. "The fact that God turns the wrath of man to his praise does not excuse the wrath of man" (Cranfield, *Gospel of Mark*, p. 424).

3. Institution of the Lord's Supper

14:22–26

> 22While they were eating, Jesus took bread, gave thanks and broke it, and gave it to his disciples, saying, "Take it; this is my body."
> 23Then he took the cup, gave thanks and offered it to them, and they all drank from it.
> 24"This is my blood of the covenant, which is poured out for many," he said to them. 25"I tell you the truth, I will not drink again of the fruit of the vine until that day when I drink it anew in the kingdom of God."
> 26When they had sung a hymn, they went out to the Mount of Olives.

The NT records four accounts of the Lord's Supper (Matt 26:26–30; Mark 14:22–26; Luke 22:19–20; 1 Cor 11:23–25). Matthew's account closely follows Mark's, while those of Luke and Paul have certain agreements. All four include the taking of the bread, the thanksgiving or blessing, the breaking of the bread, the saying "This is my body," and the taking of the cup. Only Paul (and Luke if the longer reading [22:19b–20] is adopted) records Jesus' command to continue to celebrate the Supper. Mark may not have included it because it was well known in the church he was writing to.

22 The bread Jesus took was the unleavened bread of the Passover meal. He first gave thanks. Two different Greek verbs are translated "give thanks" in vv.22–23. Both are equivalent to the Hebrew verb *bārak*, to "bless" or "praise" God. At Passover the blessing for the bread that immediately preceded the meal itself went thus: "Praised be Thou, O Lord, Sovereign of the World, who causes bread to come forth from the earth." After the blessing Jesus divided the bread and gave it to his disciples with the words "This is my body." Since this saying of Jesus was separated from the cup-saying by the eating of the main part of the meal, it is best to understand it as separate from that saying. The significant action of Jesus was the distribution of the bread, not its breaking. The bread represented his body, i.e., his abiding presence, promised to the disciples on the eve of his crucifixion; and the words become a pledge of the real presence of Jesus wherever and whenever his followers celebrate the Supper. Sacrificial ideas, though crucially important in the cup-saying, are not of primary importance here.

That Jesus did not mean that the bread became his body is clear. There is no indication that the bread was changed—it remained ordinary bread. Furthermore, Jesus often used symbolic language to speak of himself. He spoke of himself as the true vine, the way, the door, etc., by which he meant that certain aspects of his person or work were symbolized by these objects. In the same way the bread symbolized his body, i.e., his abiding presence; and the wine symbolized his blood about to be shed. Our Lord desired

> that by means of the supper here instituted, the church should remember his sacrifice and *love* him, should *reflect* on that sacrifice and embrace him by *faith*,

and should look forward in living *hope* to his glorious return. Surely, the proper celebration of communion is a loving remembrance. It is, however, more than that. Jesus Christ is most certainly, and through his Spirit most actively, present at this genuine feast! Cf. Matt. 18:20. His followers "take" and "eat." They appropriate Christ by means of living faith, and are strengthened in this faith. (Hendricksen, *Matthew*, p. 910; emphasis his)

23-24 The cup Jesus referred to (v.23) is the third cup of the Passover meal, which was drunk after the meal was eaten. Again Jesus gave thanks. The verb is *eucharisteō*, from which "Eucharist" is derived. The meaning of the cup, unlike that of the bread, is clearly placed in a sacrificial context. The phrase "my blood of the covenant" (v.24) echoes Exodus 24:8 LXX: "Behold the blood of the covenant that the Lord has made with you." The word *diathēkē* means "testament" or "will" in classical Greek, but here it translates the Hebrew *berît* ("covenant"). It is "that relationship of lordship and obedience which God establishes between Himself and men, and the 'blood of the covenant' is the sign of its existence and the means by which it is effected" (Taylor, p. 546). Although the reading "new" found in some MSS before the word "covenant" may be an assimilation to 1 Corinthians 11:25, it expresses an important truth. Jesus' death inaugurated a new era. Jeremiah had prophesied of just such a new day (Jer 31:31–33). The blood that establishes the covenant will be "poured out" (a clear reference to Christ's death) "for many." "Many" here means "all," as Calvin (3:214) clearly recognized: "By the word *many* he means not a part of the world only, but the whole human race" (emphasis his). The language seems to echo Isaiah 53:12.

25-26 Solemnly Jesus declared that this would be his last festal meal with them till the dawn of the messianic kingdom (v.25). "The fruit of the vine" is a liturgical formula for wine used at the feast. The drinking of the cup at the Supper anticipates the perfected fellowship of the Messianic Age. (For the idea of the messianic banquet, cf. Isa 25:6; 1 Enoch 72:14; Matt 8:11; Luke 22:29–30.) The vow of Jesus consecrated him for his sacrificial death, but it also held out the promise of victory and salvation. He will drink the festal cup anew, i.e., with a new redeemed community, in the kingdom of God (cf. Luke 14:15; Rev 3:20–21; 19:6–9).

Assuming the meal to have been a Passover meal, it ended with the singing (v.26) of the second part of the Hallel (Pss 115–118). It is significant that Jesus went to Gethsemane and its agony with such promises as follows:

> The LORD is my strength and my song;
>   he has become my salvation.

> Shouts of joy and victory
>   resound in the tents of the righteous:
> "The LORD's right hand has done mighty things!
>   The LORD's right hand is lifted high;
>   the LORD's right hand has done mighty things!"

> I will not die but live,
>   and will proclaim what the LORD has done.
>   (Ps 118:14–17)

E. *The Prediction of Peter's Denial*

14:27–31

27"You will all fall away," Jesus told them, "for it is written:

" 'I will strike the shepherd,
and the sheep will be scattered.'

28But after I have risen, I will go ahead of you into Galilee."
29Peter declared, "Even if all fall away, I will not."
30"I tell you the truth, Jesus answered, "today—yes, tonight—before the rooster'
crows twice you yourself will disown me three times."
31But Peter insisted emphatically, "Even if I have to die with you, I will never
disown you." And all the others said the same.

27–28 The predictions recorded here were probably spoken by Jesus as he walked with his disciples from the Upper Room to the Mount of Olives. The verb *skandalizō* ("fall away," NIV) is difficult (v.27). (Notice the many variant renderings in the versions.) Here it seems to be defined by the words from Zechariah that immediately follow. Thus it means, not that the disciples will lose their faith in Jesus, but that their courage will fail and they will forsake him. When the Shepherd (Jesus) is struck, the sheep (the disciples) will be scattered. The quotation is from Zechariah 13:7 and clearly indicates that the death of Jesus is the result of the action of God and that it results in the scattering of the sheep. The prediction was fulfilled. The disciples were fearful to be identified with Jesus in his trial and death, and that caused them to forsake him. This was especially true of Peter, whose actions are often representative of the rest of the disciples.

After the death of the Shepherd, however, there will be a glorious resurrection and a reunion of Shepherd and sheep in Galilee (v.28). Marxsen (pp. 86–87) sees in this verse and in the statement in Mark 16:7 a reference to the Parousia. But the obvious reference is to a postresurrection appearance.

29–31 Jesus' prediction of failure on the part of the disciples was too much for Peter to accept (v.29). For the other disciples it may come true, but certainly not for himself. But Jesus' reply emphasizes the absolute certainty of Peter's denial (v.30). Not only does Jesus use the *amēn* ("I tell you the truth") formula, but he also uses the emphatic "today—yes, tonight." The denial is not only certain, it is imminent. It was also to be a repeated denial (three times), and that in spite of warning (twice repeated) of the crowing of the rooster. The second crowing is found only in Mark and may have come from Peter himself. Cranfield rightly points out that the prediction cannot be a *vaticinium ex eventu* (postevent "prophecy"): "The early Church would hardly have created a prediction which aggravated the baseness of Peter's denial, even for the sake of showing that Jesus was not surprised" (*Gospel of Mark*, p. 429).

Jesus' explicit description of Peter's forthcoming denial was not convincing to him. He insisted on his willingness even to die with Jesus rather than deny him (v.31). But Peter did not know how weak he really was—nor did the rest of the disciples know their weakness, for they quickly chimed in with him to declare their allegiance (cf. 14:50, 71–72).

F. *The Agony of Gethsemane*

14:32-42

> [32]They went to a place called Gethsemane, and Jesus said to his disciples, "Sit here while I pray." [33]He took Peter, James and John along with him, and he began to be deeply distressed and troubled. [34]"My soul is overwhelmed with sorrow to the point of death," he said to them. "Stay here and keep watch."
>
> [35]Going a little farther, he fell to the ground and prayed that if possible the hour might pass from him. [36]"*Abba*, Father," he said, "everything is possible for you. Take this cup from me. Yet not what I will, but what you will."
>
> [37]Then he returned to his disciples and found them sleeping. "Simon," he said to Peter, "are you asleep? Could you not keep watch for one hour? [38]Watch and pray so that you will not fall into temptation. The spirit is willing, but the body is weak."
>
> [39]Once more he went away and prayed the same thing. [40]When he came back, he again found them sleeping, because their eyes were heavy. They did not know what to say to him.
>
> [41]Returning the third time, he said to them, "Are you still sleeping and resting? Enough! The hour has come. Look, the Son of Man is betrayed into the hands of sinners. [42]Rise! Let us go! Here comes my betrayer!"

Gethsemane reveals the humanity of Jesus with astonishing fidelity. He is shown to be "anything but above temptation. So far from sailing serenely through his trials like some superior being unconcerned with this world, he is almost dead with distress" (Moule, *Gospel of Mark*, p. 117). It is inconceivable that the early church could or would have created a story like this one about Jesus.

32-34 The name "Gethsemane" (v.32) is probably from the Hebrew *gat šᵉmānî* ("press of oils"). It was a garden located somewhere on the lower slopes of the Mount of Olives, in which there were olive trees and olive presses. It was one of Jesus' favorite spots (cf. Luke 22:39; John 18:2), no doubt often used by him and his disciples as a place to be alone. Here he faced one of his most crucial tests.

Leaving the rest of the disciples behind, Jesus took with him the three of the inner circle—Peter, James, and John (v.33). He must have felt his need for their presence in this time of crisis. The two verbs translated "deeply distressed and troubled" together "describe an extremely acute emotion, a compound of bewilderment, fear, uncertainty and anxiety, nowhere else portrayed in such vivid terms as here" (Bratcher and Nida, p. 446). This deep agony Jesus shared with his disciples (v.34). Why? Probably because he wanted them to know something of the depths of suffering he was about to experience for the redemption of the world. Then Jesus, having shared his feelings with Peter, James, and John, withdrew to be alone with his Father. Jesus' command to them to keep watch meant either that they were to stay awake and so share in his agony or that they were to be on the lookout for those Jesus knew were on their way to arrest him. John 18:2 says that Judas knew the place where Jesus was accustomed to pray.

35-36 Jesus did not die serenely as both Christian and Jewish martyrs have. He was no mere martyr; he was the Lamb of God bearing the penalty of the sins of all mankind. The wrath of God was turned loose on him. Only this can adequately explain what happened in Gethsemane. The burden and agony were so great he

163

could not stand up (v.35). His prayer, uttered in a prone position, was addressed to "*Abba,* Father" (v.36). The word "*Abba*" is the Aramaic intimate form for father ("Daddy")—a word the Jews did not use to address God because they thought it disrespectful. Since Jesus was the unique Son of God and on the most intimate terms with him, it was natural for him to use it. Jesus believed that with God anything was possible and therefore prayed for the cup to be removed from him. This cup is the same one Jesus referred to in 10:38–39—the cup of the wrath of God. In the OT it is regularly used as a metaphor of punishment and judgment. Here it obviously refers to Jesus' death. Jesus' desire was for the removal of the cup. But he willingly placed his will in submission to his Father's will.

37–38 Returning to his disciples, Jesus found them sleeping. They were doubtless very tired; the hour was late, probably past midnight, and they had experienced some exciting events during the long day. Nevertheless it was a critical time, and they were expected to be awake. Jesus' rebuke in v.37 is addressed to Peter whereas in v.38 it is addressed to all three disciples. Peter is probably singled out because he was the one who had boasted of his fidelity to Jesus. He who had said he was willing to die, if need be, with Christ (v.31) could not watch for one hour.

The verbs "watch" (*grēgoreite*) and "pray" (*proseuchesthe*) are both imperatives and are addressed to all three disciples, not just Peter. The conquest of temptation (to "enter into temptation" means to yield to it) can only come through these two actions. The spirit (a reference to the human spirit) might be willing to do what is right, but the human body (*sarx*) is weak. Some commentators take *sarx* to mean our poor unaided human nature. Here, however, it seems to mean the physical body and refers to the inability of the disciples to stay awake.

39–40 Again, after having left his disciples to pray (v.39), Jesus returned to find them sleeping (v.40). Because of sheer fatigue, they were unable to stay awake. When confronted by Jesus, they "did not know what to say to him"—probably because they were so embarrassed and ashamed. Even Peter had nothing to say on this occasion (cf. 9:6).

41 A third time Jesus left them to pray (cf. Matt 26:44) and on returning again found the disciples asleep. The next words may be either ironic—"Sleep then, since that's what you want; rest if you are able"—or a question—"Are you still sleeping and resting?" (NIV). The latter seems better in view of the situation. The rendering of the next word (*apechei*) is difficult, as the many translations of it indicate. NIV renders it "Enough!" apparently meaning "enough of sleep," i.e., it is time for the disciples to wake up. Some other explanations for *apechei* are (1) "he has received it," meaning that Judas has received the money for the betrayal; (2) "the account is closed," i.e., the end has come; and (3) "it is settled," i.e., it is now clear to Jesus that it is God's will for him to go to the cross; the cup will not be taken from him. It is hard to choose between (2) and (3) since both are supported by Jesus' next statement: "The hour has come," i.e., the time of his betrayal and death. The "sinners" into whose hands the Son of Man is to be betrayed are the satanic agents who bring about his death.

42 The disciples apparently were still lying on the ground; so when Jesus heard the approach of the arresting party, he told the disciples to get on their feet. "The call to 'go' ends the scene in Gethsemane, but cannot be intended to suggest flight, for the Lord had always reserved Himself for this 'hour,' and had now finally embraced the Divine Will concerning it" (Swete, p. 349). Jesus did not go to flee from Judas but to meet him.

Rawlinson (p. 211) explains the significance of the experience of the disciples in Gethsemane for the Christians at Rome to whom Mark is writing as follows:

> For the Church of Mk's day the example of Jesus in the Garden, as contrasted with the behaviour of the three disciples, must have had special value as setting forth the spirit in which the vocation of martyrdom should be approached. The Christian witness must not presume upon the fact that his spirit is willing: he must ever be mindful also of the weakness of the flesh. It is essential therefore that he should *watch and pray*, that when the hour of trial comes he may not break down (emphasis his).

Notes

33 Ἐκθαμβεῖσθαι (*ekthambeisthai*) is peculiar to Mark (1:27; 9:15; 16:5–6). It is a difficult word to translate. Swete has "terrified surprise"; Rawlinson, "shuddering awe"; Taylor, "amazement amounting to consternation."

Ἀδημονεῖν (*adēmonein*) is translated in NIV "troubled." Swete (in loc.) says it describes the "distress that follows a great shock"; NEB has "My heart is ready to break with grief"; Martin (in loc.) says "The impact of the two words is incalculable and carries its own power to stab the reader wide awake."

41 For the many interpretations of ἀπέχει (*apechei*), see Cranfield, *Gospel of Mark*, pp. 435–36, and Lane, p. 514.

42 Ἄγωμεν (*agōmen*) may be translated "Let us advance to meet them."

G. *The Betrayal and Arrest*

14:43–52

43 Just as he was speaking, Judas, one of the Twelve, appeared. With him was a crowd armed with swords and clubs, sent from the chief priests, the teachers of the law, and the elders.
44 Now the betrayer had arranged a signal with them: "The one I kiss is the man; arrest him and lead him away under guard." 45 Going at once to Jesus, Judas said, "Rabbi!" and kissed him. 46 The men seized Jesus and arrested him.
47 Then one of those standing near drew his sword and struck the servant of the high priest, cutting off his ear.
48 "Am I leading a rebellion," said Jesus, "that you have come out with swords and clubs to capture me? 49 Every day I was with you, teaching in the temple courts, and you did not arrest me. But the Scriptures must be fulfilled." 50 Then everyone deserted him and fled.
51 A young man, wearing nothing but a linen garment, was following Jesus. When they seized him, 52 he fled naked, leaving his garment behind.

43 The fact that Judas is described as "one of the Twelve," as if it were the first mention of him in the narrative, strongly suggests that at this point Mark is inserting into his account the primitive passion narrative that had no prior mention of Judas

in it. Another possibility is that "one of the Twelve" is repeated "to keep this tragic element of the situation before us" (Gould, p. 273). Judas was accompanied by a crowd sent from the three constituent groups of the Sanhedrin: chief priests, teachers of the law, and elders. This was not a motley crowd; as John's Gospel tells us, it consisted of a detachment of soldiers and some official attendants of the Sanhedrin (18:3). They came armed with swords and clubs. Apparently they thought they would meet with resistance.

44–46 The prearranged "signal" (*syssēmon*) or means of identifying Jesus was for Judas to kiss him (v.44). This suggests that the members of the arresting party did not know Jesus, or perhaps since it was dark they wanted to be sure not to arrest the wrong person (v.46). Rabbis customarily were greeted by their disciples with a kiss. Thus Judas's act would not be suspected for what it really was. Judas's instructions to the crowd were designed to assure the successful accomplishment of the arrest. They were to lead Jesus away securely—with no chance of escape. Once having become involved in the wicked affair, Judas did not want to make a fiasco of it.

47 Mark does not say who wielded the sword. But we know from John that it was Peter and that the ear belonged to Malchus, a servant of the high priest (John 18:10). Apparently Peter aimed at his head; but Malchus sidestepped, and Peter only caught his ear. Jesus' rebuke to Peter (Matt 26:52) and the restoration of the ear (Luke 22:51) are not recorded by Mark. He uses the diminutive *ōtarion* for "ear." Perhaps only the lobe was cut off. This would explain Luke's statement that Jesus healed the ear instead of replacing it (Luke 22:51).

48–50 Jesus protested against the manner of his arrest (v.48). The crowd sent from the Sanhedrin had come after him with swords and clubs, as if he were a dangerous criminal or insurrectionist of some kind. He had been teaching every day in the temple courts (v.49). They could have arrested him there. Why then had they come at night? and why had they chosen to arrest him outside the city? The obvious answer is that they feared the people's reaction to Jesus' arrest. So they carefully chose both the time and the place. Jesus' statement about his teaching daily in the temple courts may point to a period longer than two or three days and thus imply that Jesus had spent a longer period in Jerusalem before his arrest than is ordinarily supposed.

The circumstances of Jesus' arrest were a fulfillment of Scripture. Mark does not say what Scripture specifically Jesus had in mind. It may have been Isaiah 53:12: "And [he] was numbered with the transgressors." But in view of v.50—"Then everyone deserted him and fled"—he may have had Zechariah 13:7 in mind, which Jesus quoted in 14:27 and which is fulfilled here. The words of v.50 "drive home, as it were with hammer-blows, the failure of the disciples without exception . . . and the complete forsakenness of Jesus" (Cranfield, *Gospel of Mark,* p. 438).

51–52 Only Mark records this mysterious episode. The "young man" (v.51) is not identified, but the consensus is that he is Mark. Why else would he insert such a trivial detail in so solemn a story? Was this Mark's way of saying, "I was there"? Why he was there is not explained.

Ordinarily men wore an undergarment called a *chitōn*. This young man had only a *sindōn*, an outer garment. Usually this garment was made of wool. His, however, was linen, an expensive material worn only by the rich. Since he had no *chitōn*, when he fled without his *sindōn*, he was actually naked (v.51). Perhaps the main point of the story—and the reason Mark included it—was to show that the forsakenness of Jesus was total. Even this youth forsook him.

Notes

45 The verb καταφιλέω (*kataphileō*), a compounded form of φιλέω (*phileō*, "to kiss"), usually means "to kiss fervently" and here probably indicates a lingering kiss to ensure the identification of Jesus.

H. *Jesus Before the Sanhedrin*

14:53–65

> ⁵³They took Jesus to the high priest, and all the chief priests, elders and teachers of the law came together. ⁵⁴Peter followed him at a distance, right into the courtyard of the high priest. There he sat with the guards and warmed himself at the fire.
>
> ⁵⁵The chief priests and the whole Sanhedrin were looking for evidence against Jesus so that they could put him to death, but they did not find any. ⁵⁶Many testified falsely against him, but their statements did not agree.
>
> ⁵⁷Then some stood up and gave this false testimony against him: ⁵⁸"We heard him say, 'I will destroy this man-made temple and in three days will build another, not made by man.' " ⁵⁹Yet even then their testimony did not agree.
>
> ⁶⁰Then the high priest stood up before them and asked Jesus, "Are you not going to answer? What is this testimony that these men are bringing against you?" ⁶¹But Jesus remained silent and gave no answer.
>
> Again the high priest asked him, "Are you the Christ, the Son of the Blessed One?"
>
> ⁶²"I am," said Jesus. "And you will see the Son of Man sitting at the right hand of the Mighty One and coming on the clouds of heaven."
>
> ⁶³The high priest tore his clothes. "Why do we need any more witnesses?" he asked. ⁶⁴"You have heard the blasphemy. What do you think?"
>
> They all condemned him as worthy of death. ⁶⁵Then some began to spit at him; they blindfolded him, struck him with their fists, and said, "Prophesy!" And the guards took him and beat him.

The trial of Jesus took place in two stages: a religious trial followed by a civil one. Each had three episodes. The religious trial included (1) the preliminary hearing before Annas (reported only in John 18:12–14, 19–23); (2) the trial before Caiaphas and the Sanhedrin (Mark 14:53–65); and (3) the trial before the same group just after daybreak (Mark 15:1). The three episodes of the civil trial were (1) the trial before Pilate; (2) the trial before Herod Antipas (recorded only in Luke 23:6–12); and (3) the trial before Pilate continued and concluded. In Mark, since there is no account of Jesus being sent to Herod Antipas, the trial before Pilate is a continuous and unbroken narrative (15:2–15).

53 Mark makes no mention of the preliminary hearing before Annas (cf. John 18:12–14, 19–23). Annas had been high priest from A.D. 7–14 but had been deposed by

Valerius Gratus, Pilate's predecessor. Caiaphas, Annas's son-in-law, held the office; but some of the Jews probably regarded Annas as the true high priest. Caiaphas probably lived in the same palace. Jesus, according to Mark, was taken directly to Caiaphas (Mark never mentions his name), with the entire Sanhedrin present. The meeting took place in the palace of Caiaphas in an upstairs room (cf. v.66). This must have been a large room to accommodate the Sanhedrin. If all the members were present, there would have been seventy of them, though Mark's use of "all" does not necessarily mean all seventy were present. Certainly there were enough of them there to constitute a quorum, and that may be what Mark's "all" means. Since the Sanhedrin usually met in one of the market halls, the use of Caiaphas's house may have been to ensure secrecy.

54 This verse seems to interrupt the flow of the narrative. It is inserted here to prepare for the full account of Peter's denial (vv.66–72) and to indicate that the trial and the denial were concurrent. "When the first panic was over Peter's affection re-asserted itself" (Plummer, p. 335). He followed at a distance because he was afraid, but he *did* follow. Apparently he could not bring himself to desert Jesus completely. Eventually he arrived at the high priest's palace. John's Gospel informs us that there was "another disciple" with Peter; and, since this unnamed disciple knew the high priest, he spoke to the girl on duty at the gate, and Peter was let in. The palace was built around an open courtyard (*aulē*) that was entered through an archway (cf. v.68). Spring nights are cool in Jerusalem (which is at an elevation of about twenty-five hundred feet); so Peter sat with the guards and warmed himself before a charcoal fire (cf. John 18:18). From where he was sitting, he could see the upstairs room where the Sanhedrin was meeting to decide Jesus' fate.

55–56 Just how rigged the trial of Jesus was is made clear by these verses. Though it was late at night (in fact, it probably was very early Friday morning), false witnesses were available (v.56). But a problem developed—the witnesses could not agree with one another! According to the law (Num 35:30; Deut 17:6; 19:15), it was necessary in cases that required the death penalty to have two witnesses. These witnesses must, however, give consistent evidence. The smallest inconsistency was sufficient to discredit them. As is always true when witnesses testify falsely, there was no consistency in their testimony. Many came to witness against Jesus (the Sanhedrin had made careful preparation for the trial [v.55]), but the contradictory nature of the evidence frustrated the court's wicked intent.

57–59 The lack of consistent evidence did not thwart Caiaphas and the Sanhedrin for long. Although the first round of testimony proved to be of no value, soon a definite charge was made. Jesus had said he would destroy this "man-made temple" and rebuild another "not made by man" in three days (v.58). There is no statement just like this in the Gospels. The allusion is probably to Jesus' statement in John 2:19, made two years previously; but on that occasion he did not predict that he would do the destroying, and the reference is not to the Jerusalem temple but to his body. It may have been that Jesus' statement in Mark 13:2, where he predicts the destruction of the temple, was combined with John 2:19; and out of the two the charge was formulated. The charge, however, proved invalid because again the testimony of the witnesses was inconsistent (vv.57, 59).

60–61 The situation had become extremely tense. There were plenty of witnesses, but they could not pass the test of Deuteronomy 17:6. Finally in exasperation the high priest stood up in the Sanhedrin to interrogate Jesus himself (v.60). Caiaphas apparently wanted Jesus to respond to the charges made againt him in the hope of provoking an incriminating answer. But Jesus refused to give him that opportunity (v.61). "In majestic silence, Jesus refused to dignify the self-refuting testimony by any explanation of His own" (Hiebert, *Gospel of Mark*, p. 371).

The silence of Jesus to the first questions prompted the high priest to ask him another. The question "Are you the Christ, the son of the Blessed One?" indicates that by this time the religious authorities either knew or suspected that Jesus regarded himself as the Messiah. "The Blessed" is a reverential circumlocution to avoid the pronunciation of the name of God and stands in apposition to the title "Christ" or "Messiah." "Son of God" was understood by the Jews of Jesus' time solely in a messianic sense; and since the Messiah in Jewish expectations was to be a man, the question of the high priest was about Jesus' claim to messiahship and had nothing to do with deity (cf. Lane, p. 535). The question proved to be a stroke of genius. Blasphemy was a capital crime. If the religious authorities could not effect an accusation by the testimony of others, Jesus' own testimony about himself would do. Had Jesus refused to answer this question, the Sanhedrin would have had to devise some other plan.

62 Jesus' reply is a straightforward "I am." This is in sharp contrast to his deliberate avoidance of calling himself the Messiah or having others proclaim his messiahship up to this point in his ministry. It clearly was not because he had no consciousness of being the Messiah. His avoidance of the messianic claim was because of the false concepts of messiahship that were popular in his day and with which he did not want to be identified. Also, there was always the danger that an open claim to messiahship would bring about a premature crisis and abort his ministry. Now, however, the time of veiledness had passed. He was ready to unequivocally state his messiahship.

Jesus' affirmation of messiahship is followed by a Son-of-Man saying that brings together Daniel 7:13 and Psalm 110:1. The two main ideas are the enthronement of the Son of Man and his eschatological coming. Jesus is looking to the future, beyond the Crucifixion and Resurrection, to the Ascension, when he will take his place at the right hand of God—the place of authority—and to his parousia, when he will come in judgment. Now Caiaphas and the Sanhedrin are sitting in judgment on him. In that day Jesus will pass final and irrevocable judgment on them. The author of Revelation points to that day: "Look, he is coming with the clouds,/ and every eye will see him,/ even those who pierced him" (1:7). Jesus' words are a solemn warning.

63–64 The tearing of one's clothes was originally a sign of great grief (cf. Gen 37:29; 2 Kings 18:37; Jud 14:19; Ep Jer 31; 2 Macc 4:38). In the case of the high priest (v.63), it became "a formal judicial act minutely regulated by the Talmud" (Taylor, p. 569). The action of the high priest showed that he had just heard a blasphemous statement (v.64; cf. M. *Sanhedrin* 7.5). During this period the Jews defined blasphemy fairly loosely. They identified it not only with overt and definite reviling of the name of God (cf. Lev 24:10–23) but also with any affront to the majesty and authority of God (cf. Mark 2:7; 3:28–29; John 5:18; 10:33; see also SBK 1:1007ff.). Jesus' claim to be the Messiah was understood by Caiaphas in the latter sense and was therefore considered to be blasphemy. All the members of the Sanhedrin concurred with Caiaphas's judgment and condemned Jesus "as worthy of death." The death sentence had been handed down as Jesus had predicted in Mark 10:33. Leviticus 24:14 prescribes stoning as the manner of death for the sin of blasphemy.

65 The decision that Jesus deserved the death penalty was the signal for the Sanhedrin to release their pent-up hostilities against him. Although Rawlinson's suggestion (p. 223) that Mark's grammar is careless ("we are to understand a change of subject at the beginning of the verse") absolves the Sanhedrin of this barbarous display, it is almost certainly wrong. "Some" at the beginning of v.65 is in contrast to "all" in v.64, and both refer to members of the Sanhedrin. This interpretation is supported by the mention of the guards as a second and distinct group of participants in the barbarous acts.

Spitting and hitting were traditional means of expressing rejection and repudiation (cf. Num 12:14; Deut 25:9; Job 30:10; Isa 50:6). Light is shed on the significance of the covering of the face followed by blows and the demand to prophesy by the additional words in Matthew 26:88 and Luke 22:64: "Who hit you?" This was their way of trying to make a mockery of Jesus' messianic claims because a rabbinic interpretation of Isaiah 11:2–4 stated that the Messiah could judge by smell and did not need sight (cf. Lane, p. 540; b *Sanhedrin* 93b). Jesus refused to respond to their vicious jests. When the Sanhedrin had its fill of brutality and mockery, they turned Jesus over to the guards who continued the beatings.

Notes

62 The variant reading σὺ εἶπας ὅτι ἐγώ εἰμι (*sy eipas hoti egō eimi*, "You say that I am") has the support of the Caesarean text (Θ Φ pc arm geo Origen). Taylor thinks this is the original text because it is more in keeping with Jesus' reluctance in Mark's Gospel in revealing straight-out his messiahship and because it would account for Matt 26:64 and Luke 22:67–68. If this is the correct reading, Jesus' reply is affirmative, "but it registers a difference of interpretation: 'The word is yours, Yes, if you like'; as if to indicate that the Speaker has His own ideas about Messiahship" (Taylor, p. 568). Against this is the MS evidence that overwhelmingly supports the shorter reading. Also at this point Jesus was ready to reveal clearly his identity as the Messiah.

I. *Peter's Denial of Jesus*

14:66–72

> [66]While Peter was below in the courtyard, one of the servant girls of the high priest came by. [67]When she saw Peter warming himself, she looked closely at him.
>
> "You also were with that Nazarene, Jesus," she said.
>
> [68]But he denied it. "I don't know or understand what you're talking about," he said, and went out into the entryway.
>
> [69]When the servant girl saw him there, she said again to those standing around, "This fellow is one of them." [70]Again he denied it.

> After a little while, those standing near said to Peter, "Surely you are one of them, for you are a Galilean."
>
> [71]He began to call down curses on himself, and he swore to them, "I don't know this man you're talking about."
>
> [72]Immediately the rooster crowed the second time. Then Peter remembered the word Jesus had spoken to him: "Before the rooster crows twice you will disown me three times." And he broke down and wept.

66–68 The incident begun in v.54 is now developed. When Jesus was being mocked, spit upon, and beaten in the upstairs room of the high priest's palace, Peter was below in the courtyard (v.66). He was waiting to see what would happen to Jesus. The fact that Peter was there at all indicates that he loved Jesus and was concerned about him, but his love did not stand the test of fear. The servant girl (probably the "girl at the door," John 18:17) recognized Peter as he stood in the light of the fire, warming himself (v.67). Perhaps she had seen Peter with Jesus in the temple during the days immediately preceding or remembered that she had admitted him at the request of John, another one of Jesus' disciples. Her contempt for Jesus is revealed in the order of the words she used to speak about him—"that Nazarene, Jesus." Peter denied her charge (v.68) by "using the form common in rabbinical law for a formal, legal denial (*e.g.*, M. *Shebuoth* VIII. 3: 'Where is my ox?' He said to him, 'I do not know what you are saying'" Lane, p. 542). Fearful of being identified and apprehended, Peter retreated into the archway that led into the street. He was anxious for his own safety. Yet he still could not bring himself to abandon Jesus completely. So he slunk into the darkness and safety of the archway.

69–72 Peter's retreat to safety was short-lived. The servant girl saw him slip into the entryway and reiterated her contention—this time to "those standing around," presumably the guards and others in the pay of the high priest (v.69). Her words— "This fellow is one of them"—seem to show that she recognized Peter as part of a group or movement whose leader was Jesus. Peter's second denial (v.70) was not convincing. So the next time, not the servant girl, but the others, apparently having their suspicions aroused by her and detecting Peter's Galilean accent (Jesus was known to have come from Galilee), accused him. Peter was now like a cornered animal. He called down curses on himself if he was lying and swore that he didn't know "this man you're talking about" (v.71). The first two times Peter had denied being identified with Jesus. The last time he denied Jesus himself. Hendriksen comments: "How deceitful is man's heart! It is 'exceedingly corrupt. Who can know it?' (Jer. 17:9). . . . Think of it: 'Thou art the Christ, the Son of the living God.'—'I don't even know the man'" (*Matthew*, p. 937).

The third denial was followed by the second crowing of the rooster (v.72). Luke (22:61) tells us that at that very moment the Lord "turned and looked straight at Peter." The first time the rooster crowed, Peter's conscience was not awakened. This time he remembered what Jesus had said about his denial of him. The look of Jesus and the reminder of the crowing rooster proved too much for Peter. "He broke down and wept."

The importance and relevance of Peter's denial for the church to which Mark writes is obvious. To a church under severe pressure of persecution it provided a warning. If denial of Jesus Christ was possible for an apostle, and one of the leaders of the apostles at that, then they must be constantly on guard lest they too deny

171

Jesus. The story also provided assurance that if anyone did fail Jesus under the duress of persecution, there was always a way open for repentance, forgiveness, and restoration (cf. 16:7).

Notes

68 NIV omits the reading καὶ ἀλέκτωρ ἐφώνησεν (*kai alektōr ephōnēsen*, "and the rooster crowed") at the end of this verse. It is included in the UBS Greek NT but is put in brackets and given a "D" rating (very high degree of doubt). Reasons for excluding it are (1) if Peter heard the crowing of the rooster, why didn't he repent? and (2) the MS evidence favors excluding it (this was presumably the primary reason for excluding it from NIV). Reasons for including it are (1) it was omitted by copyists to make Peter's denial seem a little less shameful; (2) why do not the majority of the MSS that omit it not omit ἐκ δευτέρου (*ek deuterou*, "twice") in v.72? and (3) exclusion represents an assimilation to Matthew and Luke where only one rooster crowing is mentioned. The decision is a very difficult one. I agree with NIV.

72 The last words of this verse, καὶ ἐπιβαλὼν ἔκλαιεν (*kai epibalōn eklaien*), are very difficult to translate. Some of the renderings are as follows: "he began to cry"; "he set to and wept"; "he burst into tears"; "he thought on it and wept"; "he covered his head and wept"; "he threw himself on the ground"; "he dashed out." Plummer (p. 342) is probably right when he says that "we must be content to share the ignorance of all the ages" as to its meaning.

J. The Trial Before Pilate

15:1–15

¹Very early in the morning, the chief priests, with the elders, the teachers of the law and the whole Sanhedrin, reached a decision. They bound Jesus, led him away and handed him over to Pilate.

²"Are you the king of the Jews?" asked Pilate.

"Yes, it is as you say," Jesus replied.

³The chief priests accused him of many things. ⁴So again Pilate asked him, "Aren't you going to answer? See how many things they are accusing you of."

⁵But Jesus still made no reply, and Pilate was amazed.

⁶Now it was the custom at the Feast to release a prisoner whom the people requested. ⁷A man called Barabbas was in prison with the insurrectionists who had committed murder in the uprising. ⁸The crowd came up and asked Pilate to do for them what he usually did.

⁹"Do you want me to release to you the king of the Jews?" asked Pilate, ¹⁰knowing it was out of envy that the chief priests had handed Jesus over to him. ¹¹But the chief priests stirred up the crowd to have Pilate release Barabbas instead.

¹²"What shall I do, then, with the one you call the king of the Jews?" Pilate asked them.

¹³"Crucify him!" they shouted.

¹⁴"Why? What crime has he committed?" asked Pilate.

But they shouted all the louder, "Crucify him!"

¹⁵Wanting to satisfy the crowd, Pilate released Barabbas to them. He had Jesus flogged, and handed him over to be crucified.

1 What seems to be spoken of here is not another gathering of the Sanhedrin but the final stages of the meeting that had begun late the night before. The phrase *symboulion poiēsantes* is difficult. The best translation seems to be "reached a decision" (NIV) or "made a resolution" (cf. its use in Mark 3:6; Matt 12:14; 22:15; 27:7; 28:12). Apparently the resolution or decision made by the Sanhedrin in the final stages of its meeting was to accuse Jesus before the civil authority, not of blasphemy, but of high treason. The Roman government would not have considered blasphemy a punishable crime. It had to do with Jewish religion, and this was of little or no concern to the Roman authorities. But high treason was a crime they could not overlook. Moule points out the overpowering irony of the situation: "Jesus, who is, indeed, king of the Jews in a deeply spiritual sense, has refused to lead a political uprising. Yet now, condemned for blasphemy by the Jews because of his spiritual claims, he is accused by them also before Pilate by being precisely what he had disappointed the crowds for failing to be—a political insurgent" (*Gospel of Mark*, p. 124).

Having made their decision, the members of the Sanhedrin led Jesus away and handed him over to Pilate. Mark does not mention who Pilate is or why he was in Jerusalem at that time. Apparently he presupposes this knowledge on the part of his readers.

The official residence of the Roman governors of Judea was at Caesarea on the Mediterranean coast. Whenever they came to Jerusalem, they occupied the palace of Herod. This palatial residence, constructed by Herod the Great, was located in the northwestern section of the city. It was here that the trial of Jesus before Pilate took place. Mark uses the word "Praetorium" to indicate Herod's palace in v.16. Early in the morning Jesus was led from the palace of the high priest, located in the southwestern part of the city, through the streets of Jerusalem to Herod's palace. He was taken "early in the morning" because that is when Pilate held trials. This explains why the Sanhedrin held their session late at night and very early in the morning.

2 Pilate's first question to Jesus—"Are you the king of the Jews?"—shows that the charges against Jesus, though Mark does not mention this, had already been made known to Pilate. Mark gives us only a summary of the trial. According to Luke, the Sanhedrin brought before Pilate three charges against Jesus: (1) he is "subverting our nation"; (2) he "opposes payment of taxes to Caesar"; and (3) he "claims to be Christ, a king" (Luke 23:2). Pilate was primarily interested in the third accusation. This is clear from his question: "Are you the king of the Jews?" Jesus' answer to Pilate's question was affirmative yet somewhat qualified: "Yes, it is as you say." He seems to be saying, "Yes, I am the king of the Jews; but your concept of what that means and mine are poles apart."

3–5 The chief priests were now taking the lead in the attack against Jesus (v.3). Luke specifically mentions three accusations against Jesus (see commentary at v.2 above. But the "many" of this verse suggests there were more. Jesus, however, in his majestic serenity, refused to defend himself (v.4). His composure in the face of vicious accusations completely amazed Pilate (v.5).

6 The custom referred to here of releasing a prisoner at the Passover Feast is unknown outside the Gospels (cf. Matt 27:15; John 18:39. Luke 23:17—not included in NIV—reads: "Now he was obliged to release one man to them at the Feast"). It was, however, a Roman custom and could well have been a custom in Palestine. An example of a Roman official releasing a prisoner on the demands of the people occurs in the Papyrus Florentinus 61.59ff. There the Roman governor of Egypt, G. Septimus Vegetus, says to Phibion, the accused: "Thou hast been worthy of scourging, but I will give thee to the people" (cited in Taylor, p. 580).

7–8 According to Luke 23:19, there had been an uprising in the city, and one of the insurrectionists was a man named Barabbas (v.7). He and his fellow insurrectionists had been thrown in prison for revolution and murder. Mark speaks of the revolt as if it were well known, but there is no record of it in any of our sources. This is not surprising because the period was one of frequent insurrections. Barabbas was probably a member of the sect of the Zealots, who deeply resented the Roman occupation of Palestine.

The crowd seems to have come to Pilate's tribunal for the primary purpose of asking for Barabbas's release since it was customary for a prisoner to be released at the Passover Feast (v.8). It was Pilate who deliberately faced them with the choice between Jesus and Barabbas.

9–10 This statement (v.9) implies that the crowd had asked for the release of Jesus. If Barabbas also had the name "Jesus" (see note on v.7), it is possible that Pilate may have mistaken the crowd's request for releasing Jesus Barabbas as a request for releasing Jesus of Nazareth. Pilate, of course, used the title "king of the Jews" contemptuously, as in 15:2. He was too shrewd a politician to believe that the chief priests had handed Jesus over to him out of loyalty to Caesar! He reasoned, and rightly so, that they envied Jesus' popularity and influence with the people (v.10). Swete (p. 371) comments: "The pretense of loyalty to the Emperor was too flimsy to deceive a man of the world, and he detected under this disguise the vulgar vice of envy."

11 The original purpose of the crowd was to gain the release of the insurrectionist Barabbas. Pilate had attempted to deflect that purpose and substitute the release of Jesus instead. This was a serious threat to the murderous purposes of the chief priests. They had already condemned Jesus to death in their secret councils; now they were not about to allow Jesus to slip through their fingers through some Passover Feast clemency custom. No other alternative was open to them but to urge the crowd to force Pilate to carry out their request—the release of Jesus Barabbas, not Jesus of Nazareth. How the chief priests stirred up the crowd is not told us by Mark.

12–14 Pilate's question is surprising (v.12). Apparently he held out other options than crucifixion for Jesus. In Matthew's account Pilate had just before this received his wife's warning not to have anything to do with "that innocent man" (27:19). Perhaps his question reflects this warning. If Barabbas was to be released, what would Pilate do with Jesus? Was Pilate suggesting the possibility of releasing Jesus too? Whatever was going through his mind, it is clear that he was reluctant to carry out the murderous intent of the chief priests. His attempt to change the mind of the crowd, if it actually was that, failed. There was no dissuading them. The chief priests had stirred them up to a frenzy. "Crucify him!" they shouted (v.13). And when Pilate, in a final attempt to save Jesus, asked, "Why? What crime has he committed?" the crowd, now a mob, ignored his question (v.14). They had reached a stage where they were beyond reason. No death for Jesus but crucifixion would satisfy them. They wanted him to suffer the full ignominy of the cross. So they shouted all the louder, "Crucify him!"

15 Pilate saw that he could not change the mind of the mob. He would have to go through with Jesus' crucifixion. His previous handling of matters relating to the Jews' religion had not endeared him to the people. To risk alienating them in this crisis would be too dangerous for him politically. His wife's message had made him think more deeply about Jesus than he might otherwise had done (cf. v.12). Yet he was a Roman career politician, and a great deal was at stake for him. An official complaint to Rome by the Jewish authorities might well result in his recall. So to protect his own interests and placate the priests and the people, he released the insurrectionist and murderer Barabbas and ordered Jesus flogged.

Since flogging did not necessarily precede crucifixion, Pilate was still hoping he could dissuade the crowd from their demand for Jesus' crucifixion (cf. John 19:1–7, where after the flogging Pilate tried to persuade them against crucifixion) by administering a severe flogging instead. In any case, flogging was no light punishment. The Romans first stripped the victim and tied his hands to a post above his head. The whip (flagellum) was made of several pieces of leather with pieces of bone and lead embedded near the ends. Two men, one on each side of the victim, usually did the flogging. The Jews mercifully limited flogging to a maximum of forty stripes; the Romans had no such limitation. The following is a medical doctor's description of the physical effects of flogging.

> The heavy whip is brought down with full force again and again across Jesus' shoulders, back and legs. At first the heavy thongs cut through the skin only. Then, as the blows continue, they cut deeper into the subcutaneous tissues, producing first an oozing of blood from the capillaries and veins of the skin, and finally spurting arterial bleeding from vessels in the underlying muscles. . . . Finally the skin of the back is hanging in long ribbons and the entire area is an unrecognizable mass of torn, bleeding tissue. (C. Truman Davis, "The Crucifixion of Jesus. The Passion of Christ from a Medical Point of View," *Arizona Medicine* 22, no. 3 [March 1965]: 185)

It is not surprising that victims of Roman floggings seldom survived.

After going through this terrible ordeal, Jesus was handed over by Pilate to be crucified. The use of the phrase "handed over" may be a deliberate attempt to identify Jesus with the Suffering Servant of Isaiah 53:6, 12, since these words are used there (LXX) of the Servant.

Notes

1 The traditional site of Jesus' trial shown to most visitors to Jerusalem—the ancient pavement of the Fortress of Antonia—is almost certainly erroneous. The Antonia, located adjacent to the temple area on the northwest, served primarily as a barracks for soldiers on duty in Jerusalem. It is highly doubtful whether the Roman governors visiting Jerusalem

would prefer the spartan accommodations of the Antonia to the luxurious facilities of Herod's palace. We know from Josephus that Gessius Florus, one of the Roman procurators, resided in Herod's palace and had his tribunal set up in the square in front of it (Jos. War II, 301 [xiv.8]).

In 1961 at Caesarea on the Mediterranean coast, Italian archaeologists discovered a two-by-three foot stone that has on it the following inscription in three-inch lettering:

CAESARIENS TIBERIEVM
PONTIVS PILATVS
PRAEFECTVS IVDAEAE
DEDIT

"Pontius Pilatus, Prefect of Judea, has presented the Tiberieum to the Caesareans." What the Tiberieum was is not clear (perhaps a building or monument). What is important is that this discovery marked the first archaeological evidence for the existence of Pontius Pilate (cf. J. Vardaman, "A New Inscription which Mentions Pilate as 'Prefect,'" JBL 81 [1962]: 70–71).

2 Jesus' answer was σὺ λέγεις (sy legeis, "you say"). This appears to be intentionally qualified. Had he wanted to declare his kingship openly, he would have answered ναί (nai, "Yes!"). Martin suggests the paraphrase "You do well to ask"—"a reply which deflects the thrust of Pilate's interrogation and makes possible a continuation of the dialogue in the Trial scenario" (Mark, p. 178).

3 The variant reading at the end of v.3 that is included in KJV, αὐτὸς δὲ οὐδὲν ἀπεκρίνατο (autos de ouden apekrinato, "but he answered nothing"), is supported by predominantly Caesarean witnesses. Taylor thinks the reading may be original because the following verse (4) seems to require some such statement. The external evidence is, however, so weak that the UBS Greek text does not even list it as a variant.

6 In addition to the example of clemency cited in the commentary, there is in the Mishnah a rule that a paschal lamb may be slaughtered for one who has been promised release from prison (M Pesachim 8.6a). It is notoriously difficult to date passages in the Mishnah, but this one probably originated early enough to represent what may have been a custom as early as the first century A.D.

7 According to a variant reading of Matt 27:16–17, the full name of Barabbas is "Jesus Barabbas." This reading was known to Origen but rejected for theological reasons. Cranfield (Gospel of Mark, in loc.) thinks it may be original in Matt 27:16–17 and, since Matthew is dependent on Mark, was originally present here. Its omission is explained by the reluctance of copyists to give to Barabbas the revered name Jesus. But Jesus was actually a common name among Jews.

K. The Mocking of Jesus

15:16–20

> [16]The soldiers led Jesus away into the palace (that is, the Praetorium) and called together the whole company of soldiers. [17]They put a purple robe on him, then twisted together a crown of thorns and set it on him. [18]And they began to call out to him, "Hail, king of the Jews!" [19]Again and again they struck him on the head with a staff and spit on him. Falling on their knees, they paid homage to him. [20]And when they had mocked him, they took off the purple robe and put his own clothes on him. Then they led him out to crucify him.

16 The scourging of Jesus took place out in front of the palace of Herod and in the presence of all the people. Afterward Jesus was taken by the soldiers into the aulē

("palace," ordinarily "court," "courtyard"). NIV translates it "palace" because of Mark's explanatory clause—"that is, the Praetorium." It is used in 1 Maccabees 11:46 in this sense. Another possibility is that the courtyard (*aulē*), being the most public part of the Praetorium, "may well have been known by the Latin name of the whole" (Swete, p. 374). "Praetorium" is a Latin loan word in Greek. Used originally of a general's tent or the headquarters in a camp, here it designates the Roman governor's official residence. (For the identification of the Praetorium with Herod's palace, see commentary at 15:1.) The soldiers who led Jesus into the palace and then mocked and manhandled him were a part of the auxiliary troops Pilate had brought up to Jerusalem from Caesarea. They were non-Jews recruited from Palestine and other parts of the empire. Mark says the whole company (*speira*) took part in their perverted humor. Since a *speira* (the tenth part of a legion) consisted of two hundred to six hundred men, the word is probably used loosely here by Mark to include only the soldiers immediately at hand.

17–18 The soldiers thought it was a great joke that this gentle Jew claimed to be a king. So they took a purple robe and threw it across his shredded and bleeding back (v.17). It was probably a scarlet military cloak (cf. Matt 27:28), "a cast-off and faded rag, but with color enough left in it to suggest the royal purple" (Swete, p. 375). The crown was made of some kind of prickly plant such as abounds in Palestine. This they pressed into his scalp. Again there must have been copious bleeding because the scalp is one of the most vascular areas of the body. The royal purple and the crown were symbols of royalty. The soldiers decked him out with these for the purpose of making sport of him. "Hail, king of the Jews!" (v.18) is a parody of "Hail, Emperor Caesar!"

19 The mocking was followed by further physical violence. The blows hitting his head from the staff drove the thorns more deeply into Jesus' scalp and caused even more profuse bleeding. Matthew (27:29) says that they first forced Jesus to hold the staff as a mock scepter. They also kept spitting (Gr. imperfect tense) on him, and the climax came when they mockingly fell on their knees and paid homage to him. It is difficult to imagine a greater demonstration of insensitivity and cruelty than the soldiers' treatment of Jesus.

20 At last, tiring of their sadism, the soldiers tore the robe from Jesus' back. The fabric had probably stuck to the clots of blood and serum in the wounds. Thus when it was callously ripped off him, it caused excruciating pain, just as when a bandage is carelessly removed. Jesus' own clothes were now put back on him. The custom was for men condemned to death by crucifixion to be led naked to the place of execution and to be flogged on the way (Jos. Antiq. XIX, 269 [iv.5]). Jesus, however, had already been scourged and was too weak to have survived an additional brutal beating.

In John's account Pilate makes one final appeal to the crowd (19:4–16). He brings Jesus, badly beaten and with blood streaming down his face, before them and says, "Here is the man!" (v.5). Perhaps he wanted to appeal to their sympathy. But Satan had possessed them. The scourging was not enough. "Crucify him!" they shouted. John says that Pilate wanted to set Jesus free, but the Jews' warning that if he let Jesus go he was no friend of Caesar forced his hand. His political future was at stake. So Pilate acquiesced to their bloodthirsty cries.

L. *The Crucifixion*

15:21–32

²¹A certain man from Cyrene, Simon, the father of Alexander and Rufus, was passing by on his way in from the country, and they forced him to carry the cross. ²²They brought Jesus to the place called Golgotha (which means The Place of the Skull). ²³Then they offered him wine mixed with myrrh, but he did not take it. ²⁴And they crucified him. Dividing up his clothes, they cast lots to see what each would get.

²⁵It was the third hour when they crucified him. ²⁶The written notice of the charge against him read: THE KING OF THE JEWS. ²⁷They crucified two robbers with him, one on his right and one on his left. ²⁹Those who passed by hurled insults at him, shaking their heads and saying, "So! You who are going to destroy the temple and build it in three days, ³⁰come down from the cross and save yourself!"

³¹In the same way the chief priests and the teachers of the law mocked him among themselves. "He saved others," they said, "but he can't save himself! ³²Let this Christ, this King of Israel, come down now from the cross, that we may see and believe." Those crucified with him also heaped insults on him.

21 Men condemned to die by crucifixion were customarily required to carry the heavy wooden crosspiece (*patibulum*), on which they were to be nailed, to the place of execution. Jesus started out carrying his cross (John 19:17), but it proved too much for him. The *patibulum* usually weighed thirty or forty pounds and was usually strapped across the shoulders. One can hardly imagine the pain caused by the rough heavy beam pressing into the lacerated skin and muscles of Jesus' shoulders. The scourging and loss of blood had so weakened him that he could not go on carrying the heavy crossbeam. So apparently at random they apprehended one Simon of Cyrene and forced him into service. Since Cyrene (in North Africa) had a large Jewish population, Simon was no doubt a Jew (not an African black as some have suggested) and was on his way to the city of Jerusalem for the Passover celebration. Mark probably mentions Simon's two sons Alexander and Rufus because they were known to the Roman church (cf. Rom 16:13).

22 Both Roman and Jewish executions were customarily performed outside the city. John (19:20) says that the place where Jesus was crucified was near the city, but it was outside the city wall. In the first century A.D., as closely as it can now be determined, the northern wall of the city ran northward from Herod's palace, turned sharply to the east past Golgotha, which was just west of it, and then went on to the Fortress of Antonia.

"Golgotha" is a slightly modified transliteration of the Aramaic word for skull, whereas the name "Calvary" is derived from the Vulgate translation "*Calvariae locus,*" *calva* being the Latin word for skull. How this site was named Golgotha is not known. The common conjecture is that the place looked like a skull. The traditional site is located inside the famous Church of the Holy Sepulchre, which is within the present walls of the city.

Recent archaeological excavations tend to support the historicity of the traditional site. For example, Kathleen Kenyon's excavations in 1967 discovered a rock quarry on the south side of the church. Rock quarries were seldom found inside the walls of cities simply because the crowded conditions made it impossible to work them. Also, just west of the Church of the Holy Sepulchre, tombs have been discovered. Since burials were not allowed within the city walls, this also supports the Church of the Holy Sepulchre site. Gordon's Calvary, located on a skull-shaped knoll out-side the present northern wall of the city and between the Damascus and Herod gates, though a major tourist attraction, has no historical support as the site of the crucifixion of Jesus.

23 Jesus was offered wine mixed with myrrh when he arrived at the place of execu-tion. Mark does not identify who it was that offered Jesus the drink. Lane (p. 564) thinks it may have been the women of Jerusalem who provided a narcotic drink to condemned criminals in order to deaden the pain (cf. b *Sanhedrin* 43a). Michaelis (TDNT, 7:457–59) thinks Jesus, because he was weak and exhausted, was offered soldier's wine by the executioner. In any case it must have been meant to deaden the pain. Jesus refused the drink, choosing rather to experience the terrible suffer-ings of the Crucifixion with his senses intact.

24 Mark simply says, "And they crucified him." What incredible restraint! Espe-cially when one considers that crucifixion was, as Cicero said, "the cruelest and most hideous punishment possible" (*In Verrem* 5.64.165). What took place physically is vividly described by Davis ("Crucifixion of Jesus," pp. 186–87).

> Simon is ordered to place the patibulum on the ground and Jesus is quickly thrown backwards with His shoulders against the wood. The legionnaire feels for the depression at the front of the wrist. He drives a heavy, square, wrought-iron nail through the wrist and deep into the wood. Quickly, he moves to the other side and repeats the action, being careful not to pull the arms too tightly, but to allow some flexion and movement. The patibulum is then lifted in place at the top of the stipes [the vertical beam]. . . .
>
> The left foot is pressed backward against the right foot, and with both feet extended, toes down, a nail is driven through the arch of each, leaving the knees moderately flexed. The Victim is now crucified. As He slowly sags down with more weight on the nails in the wrists, excruciating, fiery pain shoots along the fingers and up the arms to explode in the brain—the nails in the wrists are putting pressure on the median nerves. As He pushes Himself upward to avoid this stretching torment, He places His full weight on the nail through His feet. Again there is the searing agony of the nail tearing through the nerves between the metatarsal bones of the feet.
>
> At this point, another phenomenon occurs. As the arms fatigue, great waves of cramps sweep over the muscles, knotting them in deep, relentless, throbbing pain. With these cramps comes the inability to push Himself upward. . . . Air can be drawn into the lungs, but cannot be exhaled. Jesus fights to raise Himself in order to get even one small breath. Finally carbon dioxide builds up in the lungs and in the blood stream and the cramps partially subside. Spasmodically He is able to push Himself upward to exhale and bring in the life-giving oxygen. . . .
>
> Hours of this limitless pain, cycles of twisting, joint-rending cramps, intermit-tent partial asphyxiation, searing pain as tissue is torn from His lacerated back as He moves up and down against the rough timber: Then another agony begins. A deep crushing pain deep in the chest as the pericardium slowly fills with serum and begins to compress the heart. . . .
>
> It is now almost over—the loss of tissue fluids has reached a critical level—the compressed heart is struggling to pump heavy, thick, sluggish blood into the tissues—the tortured lungs are making a frantic effort to gasp in small gulps of air. . . .

The body of Jesus is now in extremis, and He can feel the chill of death creeping through His tissues. . . .

His mission of atonement has been completed. Finally he can allow His body to die.

All this Mark describes with the words "And they crucified him"!

Death by crucifixion could come very slowly, especially if the victim was tied (as sometimes happened) instead of nailed to the cross. Nailing caused loss of blood and this hastened death. The physical condition of the victim and the severity of the scourging also affected the length of survival. If the victim was slow in dying, his legs would be broken by a club. Jesus had been so brutally beaten that when the soldiers came to him to see whether they would have to break his legs, he was dead already (cf. John 19:31–33).

Jesus' clothes had been removed when he was nailed to the cross. They were now in the hands of the soldiers who proceeded to while away their time by casting lots for them (cf. Ps 22:18).

25 Mark says that Jesus was crucified the third hour, i.e., 9:00 A.M. This conflicts with John's account, which says that the trial before Pilate was not quite over by the sixth hour, i.e., 12:00 noon, therefore implying that the Crucifixion took place later still. Several solutions to this difficult problem have been suggested.

1. John was using Roman time. Thus the sixth hour was 6:00 A.M., not 12:00 noon; and the three-hour interval was taken up with the scourging, mocking, and preparations for the Crucifixion.

2. An early copyist has confused a Greek Γ—the letter that stands for three—with a ϝ—the letter that stands for six.

3. Verse 25 is a gloss; i.e., it was added by an early copyist. Of these the first seems to be a desperate attempt at harmonization since there is no evidence whatever for it; the third is a possibility since both Matthew and Luke do not include this verse, and they ordinarily follow Mark's indications of time in the passion narrative; the second seems most likely since such a copyist error could very easily have occurred.

26 A wooden board stating the specific charge against the condemned man was commonly fastened on the cross above his head. Over Jesus' head was placed the inscription "THE KING OF THE JEWS." None of the Gospels agree on the precise wording of the inscription, but they all assert that Jesus was crucified on the charge of claiming to be the King of the Jews. For the Romans, this was high treason.

27 The two criminals crucified on either side of Jesus are called *lēstas*, a word normally meaning "robbers." Here, however, it means "insurrectionists" (cf. 14:48, where the NIV has "Am I leading a rebellion"). They had probably been a part of the same insurrection Barabbas was involved in (cf. 15:7) and had been sentenced at the same time as Jesus. They seemed to know that the charges against him were false (cf. Luke 23:41). His placement in the middle, between the two criminals, was probably to mock him as the insurrectionist par excellence. Rengstorf points out that the crucifixion of Jesus by the Jews was a decision "against His Messianism and in favour of that of the Zealots, and which thus elected war against Rome and its own crucifixion instead of the peace which the Messiah of God brings. . . . How far this decision affected the judgment of Judaism on Him is nowhere more clearly seen than when Celsus calls Jesus a λῃστής [lēstēs, 'insurrectionist'] and thus seeks to dismiss Him as a false Messiah" (TDNT, 4:262).

28 This verse (NIV mg.) does not appear in the most ancient MSS of the NT. Most textual critics consider it an interpolation from Luke 22:37 (quoting Isa 53:12), where it is authentic. Mark does not usually point out OT fulfillment.

29–30 It is evident from these verses that the Crucifixion took place in a public area, perhaps beside a thoroughfare where people were coming and going. As they passed by, they took the opportunity to vent their hostility on Jesus (v.29). Their words echo the OT (cf. Lam 2:15 and esp. Ps 22:7). They particularly remembered the charge made against him of destroying and rebuilding the temple (cf. 14:58), and they throw that into his teeth. Surely if he could destroy and rebuild the temple, he could save himself now (v.30)! Swete (p. 383) comments: "The jest was the harder to endure since it appealed to a consciousness of power held back only by the self-restraint of a sacrificed will." Here, obviously, "save" means physical deliverance.

31–32 The chief priests and teachers of the law were also there to add their mockery to that of the passersby (v.31). This must have been especially difficult for Jesus to bear. As the spiritual leaders of the people, they should have championed Jesus' cause; instead, they had condemned him and demanded his crucifixion. One would have thought that would have satisfied them. But their shriveled souls demanded more: they "mocked him among themselves," no doubt within the hearing of Jesus. Yet as they did, they unconsciously bore witness to his miraculous powers: "He saved others"—a reference to his healing miracles and perhaps the raising of Lazarus. Their statement "he can't save himself" is both false and true. In the sense they meant it—he does not have the power—it is false. But in a profound sense, if Jesus was to fulfill his messianic mission, he could not save himself. His death was necessary for man's redemption.

The epithet "This Christ, this King of Israel" is full of derision (v.32). Pilate had placed over Jesus the title "King of the Jews." But the religious leaders referred to him as "King of Israel," mocking his claim to be the King of the people of God. And they tauntingly demanded a demonstration of his power—"come down from the cross, that we may see and believe." Gould (p. 293) paraphrases as follows: "A crucified Messiah, forsooth! Let us hear no more of it. If he is really the Messianic King, let him use his Messianic power, and deliver himself from his ridiculous position by coming down from the cross. He wants us to believe in him and here is an easy way to bring that about."

Jesus also had to bear the insults of the criminals who were crucified on either side of him.

M. The Death of Jesus

15:33–41

33At the sixth hour darkness came over the whole land until the ninth hour. 34And at the ninth hour Jesus cried out in a loud voice, *"Eloi, Eloi, lama sabachthani?"*—which means, "My God, my God, why have you forsaken me?"

35When some of those standing near heard this, they said, "Listen, he's calling Elijah."

36One man ran, filled a sponge with wine vinegar, put it on a stick, and offered it to Jesus to drink. "Now leave him alone. Let's see if Elijah comes to take him down," he said.

37With a loud cry, Jesus breathed his last.

38The curtain of the temple was torn in two from top to bottom. 39And when the centurion, who stood there in front of Jesus, heard his cry and saw how he died, he said, "Surely this man was the Son of God!"

40Some women were watching from a distance. Among them were Mary Magdalene, Mary the mother of James the younger and of Joses, and Salome. 41In Galilee these women had followed him and cared for his needs. Many other women who had come up with him to Jerusalem were also there.

33 All three synoptic Gospels report the darkness; none say what caused it. It hardly could have been an eclipse of the sun at the time of the Passover full moon. Perhaps it was dark clouds obscuring the sun or a black sirocco—a wind that comes in from the desert, not uncommon in Jerusalem in the month of April. Whatever its cause, it lasted for three hours (12:00 M. to 3:00 P.M.) and was "over the whole land," i.e. Judah, not the whole earth. There can be little doubt that Mark understood the darkness as God's supernatural act and associated it with his judgment.

34 This is the only one of Jesus' seven words from the cross Mark records. The meaning of the cry of agony "My God, my God, why have you forsaken me?" lies beyond human comprehension. Taylor (p. 549) remarks: "The depths of the saying are too deep to be plumbed, but the least inadequate interpretations are those which find in it a sense of desolation in which Jesus felt the horror of sin so deeply that for a time the closeness of His communion with the Father was obscured."

Some have felt that Jesus' cry of dereliction shows his utter agony in tasting for us the very essence of hell, which is separation from God. Elizabeth Barrett Browning in her poem "Cowper's Grave" has powerfully expressed the meaning of that cry:

Deserted! God could separate from his own essence rather;
And Adam's sins have swept between the righteous Son and Father.
Yea, once, Immanuel's orphan'd cry his universe hath shaken—
It went up single, echoless, "My God, I am forsaken!"

"The orphan'd cry" of Jesus reflects something of the depth of meaning of Paul's statement in 2 Corinthians 5:21: "God made him who had no sin to be sin for us."

Interpretations that suggest that Jesus began to recite Psalm 22 with the intent of reciting the entire psalm, which ends on a note of triumph, but died before getting past v.1 are desperate attempts to dodge the reality of Jesus' forsakenness.

Matthew's version of Jesus' cry is a mixture of Hebrew and Greek with the important words in Hebrew. Jesus probably spoke the words in Hebrew, and they were in Hebrew in the earlier stage of the tradition; but, according to Nineham (p. 429), this was "changed by someone who knew that Aramaic was the language normally spoken in Jesus' time."

35 The ignorant and heartless bystanders mistook the first words of Jesus' cry "Eloi, Eloi" ("My God, my God") to be a cry for Elijah. (Or, instead of mistaking "Eloi" for "Elijah," were they indulging in a cruel joke?) Elijah was regarded as the forerunner and helper of the Messiah and was also regarded as a deliverer of those in trouble. So tauntingly they said, "Listen, he's calling Elijah."

36 Mark does not identify the person who went to get the wine vinegar. If the drink referred to is the *posca*, the sour wine drunk by laborers and soldiers, then it was probably one of the soldiers who got it. A sponge was filled with this wine vinegar and placed around the tip of a stick (*hyssōp* [John 19:29]) and held up to Jesus' lips so that he could suck the liquid from it. NIV translates *aphete* "Now leave him alone." But the equally valid rendering "Let me alone" seems more in keeping with the context. Apparently some of the bystanders wanted to prevent the soldier from giving the wine vinegar to Jesus. He insisted on doing it, however, and then added his own taunt: "Let's see if Elijah comes to take him down." Gould's paraphrase (p. 295) of the last part of this verse catches its meaning: "Let me give him this, and so prolong his life, and then we shall get an opportunity to see whether Elijah comes to help him or not."

37 After six hours of torture, Jesus cried out and died. Usually those who were crucified took long to die (cf. 15:44, where Pilate expresses surprise on hearing that Jesus had already died). The loud cry of Jesus is unusual because victims of crucifixion usually had no strength left, especially when near death. But Jesus' death was no ordinary one, nor was his shout the last gasp of a dying man. It was a shout of victory that anticipated the triumph of the Resurrection.

38 All the synoptic writers record this event. The curtain referred to was the one that separated the Holy Place from the Most Holy Place in the temple. It was torn from the top to the bottom. Mark must have regarded this as a supernatural act. Although he does not assign theological significance to it, later Christian writers so interpreted it (cf. Heb 9:1–14; 10:19–22). This information was known originally only to the priests who alone were permitted entrance into the Holy Place, but it probably became part of the tradition through the report of priests who were subsequently converted to Christianity (cf. Acts 6:7). Perhaps the experience of witnessing the tearing of the curtain in the temple prepared their hearts for receiving Jesus Christ as their Savior.

39 The Roman centurion in command of the detachment of soldiers at the cross had witnessed the scourging, mocking, spitting, crucifixion, wagging of heads, and now heard Jesus' last cry and watched him die. The soldier was deeply impressed. He had never seen anything like this before! Although it is unlikely that his statement "Surely this man was the Son of God" is to be taken in its full theological sense, yet it is the word of a man deeply moved and drawn to the person of the Righteous Sufferer on the cross (cf. Luke 23:47, where the centurion says, "Surely this was a righteous man"). In view of Mark's opening words—"The beginning of the gospel about Jesus Christ, the Son of God" (1:1)—the confession of the centurion at the climax of Jesus' passion takes on added significance. Whether or not the centurion realized the full import of his words, they were for Mark a profoundly true statement of the identity of the Man on the cross.

40–41 Women too were present at the Crucifixion, but they kept their distance (v.40). Out of the many who had come up to Jerusalem with Jesus from Galilee, Mark identifies three of the group of women who were "watching from a distance"— Mary Magdalene; Mary the mother of James the younger and Joses; and Salome, the wife of Zebedee and mother of James and John. Mary Magdalene (i.e., Mary of

Magdala, a fishing village on the west shore of the Sea of Galilee), is mentioned only here in Mark. From Luke 8:2, however, we learn that Jesus had cast seven demons out of her. The second Mary is designated as the "mother of James the younger and Joses." Although little is known about her, her sons were apparently well known in the early church. She is referred to as the "mother of Joses" in 15:47 and the "mother of James" in 16:1. In the NIV James is described as "the younger." The Greek adjective *mikros* can also mean "the less," i.e., "the smaller," "less important," or "less known." It is difficult to decide which meaning applies here. The third woman Mark mentions here is Salome, Zebedee's wife and the mother of James and John (cf. Matt 27:56). These three women had been with Jesus in Galilee (v.41) and had served him there. They had come up to Jerusalem, along with many other women also, especially to be with him and to serve him.

Notes

---

39 Although there is no definite article ὁ (*ho*, "the") before υἱὸς (*huios*, "son") in the centurion's confession, NIV translates it "Surely this man was *the* Son of God" (emphasis mine) because a definite predicate noun that precedes the verb usually does not have the article (cf. John 1:1).

N. *The Burial of Jesus*

· 15:42–47·

> [42] It was Preparation Day (that is, the day before the Sabbath). So as evening approached, [43] Joseph of Arimathea, a prominent member of the Council, who was himself waiting for the kingdom of God, went boldly to Pilate and asked for Jesus' body. [44] Pilate was surprised to hear that he was already dead. Summoning the centurion, he asked him if Jesus had already died. [45] When he learned from the centurion that it was so, he gave the body to Joseph. [46] So Joseph bought some linen cloth, took down the body, wrapped it in the linen, and placed it in a tomb cut out of rock. Then he rolled a stone against the entrance of the tomb. [47] Mary Magdalene and Mary the mother of Joses saw where he was laid.

42–43 Preparation Day was the name given to the day before a festival or a Sabbath (v.42). Here it refers to the day before the Sabbath, as Mark explains for the benefit of his Gentile readers. Since the Jewish Sabbath began at sundown, and it was now late in the afternoon (probably around 4:00 P.M.), there was not much time to take Jesus' body down from the cross. This is apparently what spurred Joseph of Arimathea into action. (Arimathea is probably to be identified with Ramathaim-Zophim, a village in the hill country of Ephraim about twenty miles north of Jerusalem. It was the birthplace of Samuel [1 Sam 1:1].)

Joseph's request for the body of Jesus (v.43) is described by Mark as a bold act, as indeed it was, because it would inevitably have identified him with Jesus and his followers. For a man in Joseph's position ("a prominent member of the Council," i.e., Sanhedrin), such an act could have serious consequences. But he was a pious

184

man who, according to Luke, had not consented in the decision and action of the council (Luke 23:51); and he "was himself waiting for the kingdom of God."

Ordinarily a relative or close friend would have requested the body, but apparently the mother of Jesus was so distraught that she was incapacitated; and all of Jesus' disciples but John had fled. There is no evidence that Jesus' brothers and sisters were in Jerusalem at the time of the Crucifixion.

44–45 Pilate was surprised to hear that Jesus had already died (v.44) because death usually came much more slowly to crucified victims than it had to Jesus. Only after he received confirmation of Jesus' death from the centurion was Pilate willing to turn Jesus' body over to Joseph (v.45). Had it not been for this loving act of Joseph, Jesus' body would have been buried in a common criminal's grave. For Pilate to release the body of a condemned criminal—especially one condemned of high treason—to someone other than a relative was highly unusual. It suggests that Pilate did not take seriously the charge of high treason against Jesus and had only pronounced sentence against him because of political expediency. This action of Pilate is consistent with Mark's account (15:1–15) of Jesus' trial before Pilate.

46 Mark does not mention anyone assisting Joseph in the actions described here. He must, however, have had help in removing the body from the cross, preparing it for burial, and carrying it to the place of burial. Matthew 27:57 describes Joseph as being rich (cf. Isa 53:9); so he doubtless had servants to help him. Moreover John says that Nicodemus, who had previously come to Jesus at night, helped Joseph and supplied some of the spices used in the preparation of the body for burial (John 19:39). Although no specific mention is made of washing the blood-soaked body, this important Jewish rite must have been performed before the body was wrapped for burial in the linen cloths. After being properly prepared for burial (cf. John 19:40), it was placed in "a tomb cut out of rock." Matthew tells us that the tomb belonged to Joseph and that it was new; i.e., it had not been used before (Matt 27:60; cf. John 19:41).

The location of the tomb was in a garden very near the site of the Crucifixion (John 19:41). Archaeological excavation has shown that the traditional site of the burial of Jesus (Church of the Holy Sepulchre in Jerusalem) was a cemetery during the first century A.D. Tombs cut out of the rock were closed by rolling a stone against the entrance. This could be either a flat stone disc that rolled in a sloped channel or simply a large rock that could be rolled in front of the opening. (For an interesting discussion of what kind of stone is meant, see Dalman, *Sacred Sites*, pp. 374ff.)

47 The two Marys mentioned in 15:40 as being witnesses of the Crucifixion were also present at Jesus' burial. Mark mentions this in anticipation of 16:1 and particularly 16:5. The two women could identify the tomb on Sunday morning because they had been present at the burial.

O. *The Resurrection*

16:1–8

[1]When the Sabbath was over, Mary Magdalene, Mary the mother of James, and Salome bought spices so that they might go to anoint Jesus' body. [2]Very

early on the first day of the week, just after sunrise, they were on their way to the tomb ³and they asked each other, "Who will roll the stone away from the entrance of the tomb?"

⁴But when they looked up, they saw that the stone, which was very large, had been rolled away. ⁵As they entered the tomb, they saw a young man dressed in a white robe sitting on the right side, and they were alarmed.

⁶"Don't be alarmed," he said. "You are looking for Jesus the Nazarene, who was crucified. He has risen! He is not here. See the place where they laid him. ⁷But go, tell his disciples and Peter, 'He is going ahead of you into Galilee. There you will see him, just as he told you.'"

⁸Trembling and bewildered, the women went out and fled from the tomb. They said nothing to anyone, because they were afraid.

The climax to Mark's Gospel is the Resurrection. Without it the life and death of Jesus, though noble and admirable, are nonetheless overwhelmingly tragic events. With it Jesus is declared to be the Son of God with power (Rom 1:4), and the disciples are transformed from lethargic and defeated followers into the flaming witnesses of the Book of Acts. The Good News about Jesus Christ is that God, by the resurrection of Jesus, defeated sin, death, and hell. It was this message that lay at the heart of the apostolic preaching.

All four Gospels tell the story of the Resurrection and do so with the same dignity and restraint they use in telling the story of the Crucifixion. As the Crucifixion was a historical event—viz., something that actually happened at a specific time and place—so the tomb in which Jesus had been placed on Friday afternoon was actually found to be empty on the following Sunday morning. To this fact all four Evangelists bear witness. The explanation of the historical event, unavailable to men apart from divine revelation, is given by the young man (his white robe identifies him as an angelic being): "He has risen!" This word of revelation, the truth of the resurrection of Jesus, is the focal point in all four gospel accounts. Any claim that the Resurrection was a fabrication (cf. Matt 27:62–65) or a delusion is implicitly denied.

1 When the Sabbath was over (about 6:00 P.M. Saturday evening), the three women mentioned at the Crucifixion (15:40), two of whom were also present at Jesus' burial (15:47), bought aromatic oils to anoint the body of Jesus. These were apparently in addition to the spices and perfumes that were prepared before the Sabbath began (cf. Luke 23:56). The anointing was not for the purpose of preserving the body (embalming was not practiced by the Jews) but was a single act of love and devotion probably meant to reduce the stench of the decomposing body. Palestine's hot climate causes corpses to decay rapidly. Thus the action of the women seems strange. Perhaps they thought that the coolness of the tomb would prevent the decomposition process from taking place as rapidly as it otherwise would. In any case, as Cranfield (*Gospel of Mark*, p. 464) says, their action "is not incredible, since love often prompts people to do what from a practical point of view is useless."

2 Since it would have been too dark Saturday night after the end of the Sabbath to go to the tomb, the women waited till Sunday morning. The expressions *lian prōi* ("very early") and *anateilantos tou hēliou* ("just after sunrise") present a problem, evidenced by the variation of readings that appear in the MS tradition. Ordinarily, "very early" would refer to the period before 6:00 A.M., when it would still be dark (cf. John 20:1); but used here with the expression "just after sunrise," it must mean the period of time immediately after the sun rose on Sunday morning.

3 As the women walked to the tomb, their chief concern was with the heavy stone they knew had been rolled in front of the opening of the tomb (cf. 15:46–47). Of the sealing of the tomb or the posting of the Roman guard, they knew nothing (cf. Matt 27:62–66). Their concern with moving the stone was a real one because, no matter what kind of stone it was, it would have been difficult to move. A circular stone, though relatively easy to put in place since usually it was set in a sloped track, once established in place was very difficult to remove. It would either have to be rolled back up the incline or lifted out of the groove and then removed. Any other kind of stone placed in front of the tomb's entrance would be as difficult or even more difficult to remove.

4–5 Mark makes no attempt to explain how the stone was removed. He does, however, say that it was very large and leaves the matter there (v.4). Once inside the tomb, the women saw a young man (*neaniskos*) dressed in a white robe (v.5). His dress suggests an angel, and though Mark does not explicitly identify him as such, Matthew 28:2 does. Cranfield's note on angels is worth repeating:

> A protest must be made against the widespread tendency to dismiss the angels as mere pious fancy. . . . It may be suggested that the purpose of the angel's presence at the tomb was to be the link between the actual event of the Resurrection and the women. Human eyes were not permitted to see the event of the Resurrection itself. But the angels as the constant witnesses of God's action saw it. So the angel's word to the women, "He is risen", is, as it were, the mirror in which men were allowed to see the reflection of this eschatological event. (*Gospel of Mark*, pp. 465–66)

The reaction of the women to the angel was what one would expect: "They were dumbfounded" (NEB)—*exethambēthēsan*, a strong verb used only by Mark in the NT.

6 The women's fright was calmed by words of reassurance: "Don't be alarmed." The angel knew whom they were seeking. These were Galilean women, and the mention of Jesus of Nazareth struck a familiar note in their memories. The angel then spoke the revelatory word "He has risen!" and invited them to see the evidence of the empty tomb. An empty tomb, however, only invites the question What happened to the body of Jesus? There needed to be a word from God to interpret the meaning of the empty tomb, and the angel was God's gracious provision. The explanation is Resurrection! Across the centuries many other explanations have been proposed: the body of Jesus was stolen; the women came to the wrong tomb; Jesus did not actually die on the cross but walked out of the tomb; etc. Some of them have had success with skeptics. But the only adequate explanation is still what the angel said to the women who were at the tomb on the first Easter morning: "He has risen!"

7 "Go, tell his disciples and Peter" reveals how gracious was the provision God made for Peter's special need through the word of the angel. Peter is singled out because he had denied Jesus (14:66–72) and now needed reassurance that he was not excluded from the company of the disciples. Jesus had forgiven and restored him. Not only had Jesus predicted the scattering of the sheep (14:27) but also their regathering in Galilee (14:28). What was the purpose of the meeting in Galilee? Jesus had done a large part of his work in Galilee. Perhaps he wanted to meet not only with the disciples but with the community of believers there to give them his last instructions before his ascension.

Galilee was a fitting place for the launching of a Gentile mission. The contention of some scholars (e.g., Lohmeyer, Marxsen) that the reference to Galilee in 14:28 and here is to the Parousia (the Second Coming) and not to a postresurrection appearance of Jesus has little to support it and has been largely rejected. Meye (*Jesus and the Twelve*, pp. 80–87) suggests that the purpose of the reunion in Galilee was to fulfill Jesus' promise in 1:17 to make the disciples fishers of men.

8 The confrontation with the angel proved to be too much for the women. They fled "trembling and bewildered." It was a natural and to-be-expected reaction. Only Mark tells us, "They said nothing to anyone," which probably means that they were so frightened and confused that they were at first silent. After they had collected their wits, they did a lot of talking (cf. Matt 28:8; Luke 24:9).

If the Gospel of Mark ends with 16:8, as some believe, Mark intentionally emphasizes the mystery and awesomeness of the Resurrection. The women were afraid because God's eschatological action in the resurrection of his Son had been revealed to them, an event Mark understood to be the climax of all God's saving acts and the inauguration of the time of the End.

Notes

2 In D ἀνατέλλοντος (*anatellontos*, "while [the sun] was rising") in place of ἀνατείλαντος (*anateilantos*, "after [the sun] rose") solves the temporal problem but is obviously a copyist's emendation.

3 k (Codex Bobiensis) has a gloss to this verse that is an attempt to describe how the Resurrection actually took place: "Suddenly at the third hour of the day there was darkness over the whole earth, and angels descended from heaven, and rising in the splendor of the living God they ascended together with him, and immediately it was light." Another early attempt to describe the Resurrection is found in the pseudepigraphical Gospel of Peter (35–44).

P. The Longer Ending—The Appearances and Ascension of Jesus

16:9–20

> [9]When Jesus rose early on the first day of the week, he appeared first to Mary Magdalene, out of whom he had driven seven demons. [10]She went and told those who had been with him and who were mourning and weeping. [11]When they heard that Jesus was alive and that she had seen him, they did not believe it.
>
> [12]Afterward Jesus appeared in a different form to two of them while they were walking in the country. [13]These returned and reported it to the rest; but they did not believe them either.

¹⁴Later Jesus appeared to the Eleven as they were eating; he rebuked them for their lack of faith and their stubborn refusal to believe those who had seen him after he had risen.

¹⁵He said to them, "Go into all the world and preach the good news to all creation. ¹⁶Whoever believes and is baptized will be saved, but whoever does not believe will be condemned. ¹⁷And these signs will accompany those who believe: In my name they will drive out demons; they will speak in new tongues; ¹⁸they will pick up snakes with their hands; and when they drink deadly poison, it will not hurt them at all; they will place their hands on sick people, and they will get well."

¹⁹After the Lord Jesus had spoken to them, he was taken up into heaven and he sat at the right hand of God. ²⁰Then the disciples went out and preached everywhere, and the Lord worked with them and confirmed his word by the signs that accompanied it.

There are four sections of the Longer Ending: (1) the appearance to Mary Magdalene (vv.9–11); (2) the appearance to the two men (vv.12–13); (3) the appearance to the Eleven and the Great Commission (vv.14–18); and (4) the Ascension, session, and the disciples' response (vv.19–20). A discussion of the problem of the authenticity of this ending follows the commentary on vv.9–20.

9 The break in the continuity of the narrative seems to indicate that vv.9–20 were not originally a part of Mark's Gospel but are rather a summary of postresurrection appearances of Jesus composed independently. The Greek text of this verse has no subject (it is supplied for clarification by NIV), as if Jesus, not Mary, had just been mentioned. Also, Mary Magdalene is mentioned for the fourth time (cf. 15:40, 47; 16:1). It is strange, assuming 16:9 to be part of Mark's original Gospel, that the detail "out of whom he had driven seven demons" is for the first time mentioned here.

10–11 Mary carried out the command of the angel given in 16:7. She found the disciples in a state of mourning (v.10). While the people of Jerusalem were celebrating the Passover and the Feast of Unleavened Bread, the disciples were weeping, but not for long. Her witness to them was that Jesus was alive, and she knew it to be so because she had seen him. The reluctance of the disciples to believe her is certainly understandable (v.11; cf. Matt 28:17; Luke 24:11). A resurrection is no ordinary event!

12–13 These verses are obviously a shortened account of the story of the two men on the way to Emmaus (cf. Luke 24:13–35). It adds nothing to Luke's account except the statement "but they did not believe them either" (v.13). The element of unbelief on the part of the disciples on hearing the report of the two men may represent a different tradition. It certainly is not dependent on Luke. Plummer (p. 372) comments: "The Apostles may have been allowed to hear of the Resurrection before seeing the risen Christ in order that they might know from personal experience what it was to have to depend upon the testimony of others, as would be the case with their converts."

14 Again the account in Luke (24:36–44) is briefly summarized. The rebuke Jesus gave his disciples is particularly severe—more severe, in fact, than any other rebuke

he gives them elsewhere in the Gospels. Neither of the words used here, *apistia* ("without faith") and *sklērokardia* ("stubborn refusal to believe," "obtuseness") is ever used by Jesus of his disciples. Taylor (pp. 611–12) concludes that the rebuke "can be understood only by the supreme importance attached to the Resurrection by the writer, who has in mind the conditions of his day."

At this point in W (the Gr. MS Washingtonianus, also called Freer), the following interpolation occurs:

> And they excused themselves, saying, "This age of lawlessness and unbelief is under Satan, who does not allow the truth and power of God to prevail over the unclean things of the spirits. Therefore, reveal thy righteousness now"—thus they spoke to Christ. And Christ replied to them, "The term of years of Satan's power has been fulfilled, but other terrible things draw near. And for those who have sinned I was delivered over to death, that they may return to the truth and sin no more, in order that they may inherit the spiritual and incorruptible glory of righteousness which is in heaven."

This, of course, is clearly not a part of Mark's Gospel but was probably inserted at this point to tone down the severe condemnation of the disciples in v.14 and to provide a smoother transition to v.15.

15–16 The Great Commission given here seems to be an independent version of Matthew 28:18–20. The unusual scope of the preaching of the gospel is not new to Mark's Gospel. It is clearly anticipated in 14:9. Belief and baptism are so closely associated that they are conceived of as virtually a single act. The inward reception (belief) is immediately followed by the external act or witness to that faith (baptism). The result is salvation. Here the word has its eschatological sense. Refusal to believe results in judgment. One of the primary themes of this entire section (vv.9–20) is the importance of belief and the sinfulness of unbelief.

17–18 The promise of signs (v.17) is not limited to the apostles. They will accompany "those who believe." These include the converts of the apostles. The apostles had already been given power to exorcise demons; now this power was to be shared by other believers. Speaking in tongues is not mentioned elsewhere in the Gospels and seems to reflect a post-Pentecost situation. Luke 10:19 speaks of trampling on snakes but not of picking them up with one's hands (v.18; cf. Acts 28:3–6). The drinking of poison without harm is unknown in the NT. Anointing the sick with oil is mentioned in 6:13, but no laying on of hands by the apostles occurs in the Gospels. Paul, however, lays hands on Publius's sick father (cf. Acts 28:8). Superstitious use of this verse has given rise to the snake-handling and poison-drinking sects of Appalachia.

19–20 "After the Lord Jesus had spoken to them" (v.19) may refer to vv.15–18 or to some other occasion. Mark gives us no geographical or time references. The ascension and session of Jesus are stated in the simplest terms: "he was taken up into heaven and he sat at the right hand of God." The Ascension was predicted by Jesus (cf. 14:7) and witnessed by the apostles (cf. Acts 1:9); the session was a matter of faith but firmly believed and preached in the early church (cf. Acts 2:33–35; 7:56).

There is nothing like v.20 in any of the Gospels. It sounds more like a summary statement from the Book of Acts of the activities of the apostles.

Notes

9 In addition to the Longer Ending (vv. 9–20), a Shorter Ending has come down to us in the MS tradition. It reads as follows: "But they reported briefly to Peter and those with him all that they had been told. And after this Jesus himself sent out by means of them, from east to west, the sacred and imperishable proclamation of eternal salvation." The witnesses to this ending are four uncial MSS of the seventh, eighth, and ninth centuries (L Ψ 099 0112), Old Latin k, the margin of the Harclean Syriac, several Sahidic and Bohairic MSS, and a good number of Ethiopic MSS. All of them, except k, continue with vv. 9–20. Both the external and internal evidence are clearly against the authenticity of this ending.

The Ending of the Gospel of Mark

The Gospel of Mark has four different endings in the MS tradition. The Freer or Washingtonianus addition, which occurs after v. 14 in the Longer Ending, is clearly an interpolation intended to soften the severe condemnation of the disciples in v. 14. It has extremely limited external attestation (only one MS—W). The Shorter Ending, cited above in the note to v. 9, also has weak external evidence and seems to be either an attempt to provide an ending in itself (in only one MS, however, does it appear without vv. 9–20 following it) or to provide a smoother transition between v. 8 and v. 9. This leaves only two endings that have any significant claim to authenticity: (1) the ending that concludes the gospel with v. 8 and (2) the so-called Longer Ending (vv. 9–20).

1. *External Evidence*

(The material cited here is mainly from Metzger, *Textual Commentary*, pp. 122–26). Evidence for (1) above (i.e., the absence of vv. 9–20) is as follows: ℵ and B (the two oldest Gr. uncial MSS of the NT), the Old Latin codex Bobiensis, the Sinaitic Syriac MS, about one hundred Armenian MSS, and the two oldest Georgian MSS (A.D. 897 and A.D. 913). Neither Clement of Alexandria nor Origen show any knowledge of the existence of vv. 9–20. Almost all the Greek copies of Mark known to Eusebius and Jerome did not contain these verses. The original form of the Eusebian sections makes no provision for numbering sections beyond 16:8. Some MSS that include the verses have scribal notes stating that they are absent in older Greek copies, and in other Greek MSS the verses are marked with obeli or asterisks to indicate they are spurious.

In addition there is the evidence provided by those MSS and versions in which the Shorter Ending (followed by the Longer Ending) is found. Warfield rightly says: "The existence of the shorter conclusion . . . is *a fortiori* evidence against the longer one. For no one doubts that this shorter conclusion is a spurious invention of the scribes; but it would not have been invented, save to fill the blank." (B.B. Warfield, *An Introduction to the Textual Criticism of the New Testament* [New York: Whittaker, 1890], p. 200).

The Longer Ending is contained in the great majority of the MSS. This includes A C D K X W Δ Θ Π Ψ 099 0112 f¹³ 28 33 et al. Irenaeus and Tatian's Diatessaron are the earliest patristic witnesses for the inclusion. Justin Martyr is uncertain. The external evidence seems to indicate that the Longer Ending was in circulation by the middle of the second century and was probably composed in the first half of the same century.

2. Internal Evidence

(The evidence cited here is from Bratcher and Nida, pp. 519ff.)

a. *Vocabulary*. In the Nestle Greek text there are 101 different words in vv.9–16 (167 words totally). After disregarding unimportant words such as the definite article, connectives, proper names, etc., there remain 75 different significant words. Of these, 15 do not appear in Mark and 11 others are used in a sense different from Markan usage. This means that slightly over one-third of the words are "non-Markan." After due allowance is made for different subject matter requiring different vocabulary, it would seem that the marked difference in vocabulary between 16:9–20 and the rest of Mark's Gospel makes it difficult to believe that they both came from the same author.

b. *Style*. Here the argument against Markan authorship of vv.9–20 is even stronger. The connection between v.8 and and vv.9–20 is abrupt and awkward. Verse 9 begins with the masculine nominative participle *anastas*, which demands for its antecedent "he," i.e., Jesus; but the subject of the last sentence of v.8 is the women, not Jesus. Mary Magdalene is referred to as if she had never been mentioned before; yet she appears three times in the crucifixion, burial, and resurrection narratives that immediately precede. Also, the women who were commissioned in v.7 to go tell Peter and the disciples of Jesus' resurrection are not mentioned at all (except Mary Magdalene, and she in another capacity) in the Longer Ending. The angel at the tomb spoke of a postresurrection appearance in Galilee to the disciples, but Jesus' appearances are confined to Jerusalem and its immediate vicinity. All these factors weigh heavily against the Longer Ending. To this evidence should be added the words of Bratcher and Nida (p. 520): "The narrative is concise and barren, lacking the vivid and lifelike details so characteristic of Markan historical narrative."

3. Content

It is in the area of content that the most serious objections are found. The first has to do with the severe rebuke by Jesus of his disciples. Nothing like this is found in the rest of Mark's Gospel (see commentary at v.14). The second relates to the "signs" of vv.17–18.

> The bizarre promise of immunity from snakes and poisonous drinks is completely out of character with the person of Christ as revealed in the Gospel of Mark, the other Gospels and in the whole of the New Testament. Nowhere did Jesus exempt himself or his followers from the natural laws which govern this life, nor did he ever intimate that such exemptions would be given those who believe in him. That such miracles have in fact occasionally taken place is a matter of record; what is to be doubted is that the Lord should have promised them indiscriminately to all believers as part of the blessings which would have been bestowed upon them. (Bratcher and Nida, pp. 520–21)

External and especially internal evidence make it difficult to escape the conclusion that vv.9–20 were originally not a part of the Gospel of Mark.

One further question arises: Did Mark actually intend to end his Gospel at 16:8? If he did not, then either (1) the Gospel was never completed, or (2) the last page was lost before it was multiplied by copyists.

Although there are staunch supporters of the view that it was Mark's intention to end his Gospel with 16:8, this view does not adequately explain (1) why the early church felt so strongly its lack of completion, witnessed by the insertion of both the Shorter and Longer endings; (2) why a book that purports to be the "good news about Jesus Christ" should end with the women being afraid (even allowing for Mark's emphasis on the awesomeness and mystery of Christ's person); and (3) why there is no recorded fulfillment of Jesus' promised postresurrection appearance in Galilee to Peter and the other disciples (cf. 16:7).

Thus the best solution seems to be that Mark did write an ending to his Gospel but that it was lost in the early transmission of the text. The endings we now possess represent attempts by the church to supply what was obviously lacking.